NYSTCE
003
CST
English
Teacher Certification Exam

By: Sharon Wynne, M.S
Southern Connecticut State University

"And, while there's no reason yet to panic, I think it's only prudent that we make preparations to panic."

XAMonline, INC.
Boston

To obtain permission(s) to use the material from this work for any purpose including workshops or seminars, please submit a written request to:

XAMonline, Inc.
21 Orient Ave.
Melrose, MA 02176
Toll Free 1-800-301-4647
Email: info@xamonline.com
Web www.xamonline.com
Fax: 1-781-662-9268

Library of Congress Cataloging-in-Publication Data

Wynne, Sharon A.
    CST English 003: Teacher Certification / Sharon A. Wynne. -2nd ed.
    ISBN 978-1-58197-851-3
    1. CST English 003.   2. Study Guides.   3. NYSTCE
    4. Teachers' Certification & Licensure.   5. Careers

Disclaimer:

The opinions expressed in this publication are the sole works of XAMonline and were created independently from the National Education Association, Educational Testing Service, or any State Department of Education, National Evaluation Systems or other testing affiliates.

Between the time of publication and printing, state specific standards as well as testing formats and website information may change that is not included in part or in whole within this product. Sample test questions are developed by XAMonline and reflect similar content as on real tests; however, they are not former tests. XAMonline assembles content that aligns with state standards but makes no claims nor guarantees teacher candidates a passing score. Numerical scores are determined by testing companies such as NES or ETS and then are compared with individual state standards. A passing score varies from state to state.

Printed in the United States of America

NYSTCE: CST English 003
ISBN: 978-1-58197-851-3

Requirements for English Certification in New York

- Hold a Valid Provisional Certificate - English 7-12
- Completion of a NYS Registered Program - English 7-12
- Institutional Recommendation - English 7-12
- New York State Teacher Certification Exam - Liberal Arts & Science Test (LAST)
- New York State Teacher Certification Exam - Secondary Assessment of Teaching Skills (ATS-W)
- New York State Teacher Certification Exam - Assessment of Teaching Skills - Performance/Video (ATS-P)
- Content Specialty Test (CST) - English
- Paid, full-time Classroom Teaching experience - 2 Yrs
- Fingerprint Clearance
- Citizenship Status - INS Permanent Residence or U.S. Citizenship

About the CST English Exam

The CST English Exam is given on all test dates. It is held during the afternoon session, from 1:00 pm to 5:45pm. It is criterion-referenced and objective-based, designed to determine a candidate's knowledge and skills in relation to an established standard rather than in relation to the performance of other candidates.

The total test score is reported in a range from 100 to 300 and is based on performance on all sections of the test. An examinee's multiple-choice score and scores on constructed-responses are combined to obtain the total test score. The minimum passing score for each test is 220. Candidates who do not pass may retake the exam as long as they re-register for the test.

The CST English Exam contains approximately 90 multiple-choice test questions and one constructed-response (written) assignment. There are six domain areas covered in the exam:

- **Listening and Speaking**
- **Writing**
- **Reading**
- **Fundamentals of Literature**
- **Language and Literature**
- **Fundamentals of Literature: Constructed-Response Assignment**

Great Study and Testing Tips!

What to study in order to prepare for the subject assessments is the focus of this study guide but equally important is *how* you study.

You can increase your chances of truly mastering the information by taking some simple, but effective steps.

Study Tips:

1. <u>Some foods aid the learning process.</u> Foods such as milk, nuts, seeds, rice, and oats help your study efforts by releasing natural memory enhancers called CCKs (*cholecystokinin*) composed of *tryptophan*, *choline*, and *phenylalanine*. All of these chemicals enhance the neurotransmitters associated with memory. Before studying, try a light, protein-rich meal of eggs, turkey, and fish. All of these foods release the memory enhancing chemicals. The better the connections, the more you comprehend.

Likewise, before you take a test, stick to a light snack of energy boosting and relaxing foods. A glass of milk, a piece of fruit, or some peanuts all release various memory-boosting chemicals and help you to relax and focus on the subject at hand.

2. <u>Learn to take great notes.</u> A by-product of our modern culture is that we have grown accustomed to getting our information in short doses (i.e. TV news sound bites or USA Today style newspaper articles.)

Consequently, we've subconsciously trained ourselves to assimilate information better in <u>neat little packages</u>. If your notes are scrawled all over the paper, it fragments the flow of the information. Strive for clarity. Newspapers use a standard format to achieve clarity. Your notes can be much clearer through use of proper formatting. A very effective format is called the <u>*"Cornell Method."*</u>

Take a sheet of loose-leaf lined notebook paper and draw a line all the way down the paper about 1-2" from the left-hand edge.

Draw another line across the width of the paper about 1-2" up from the bottom. Repeat this process on the reverse side of the page.

Look at the highly effective result. You have ample room for notes, a left hand margin for special emphasis items or inserting supplementary data from the textbook, a large area at the bottom for a brief summary, and a little rectangular space for just about anything you want.

3. <u>Get the concept then the details.</u> Too often we focus on the details and don't gather an understanding of the concept. However, if you simply memorize only dates, places, or names, you may well miss the whole point of the subject.

A key way to understand things is to put them in your own words. If you are working from a textbook, automatically summarize each paragraph in your mind. If you are outlining text, don't simply copy the author's words.

Rephrase them in your own words. You remember your own thoughts and words much better than someone else's, and subconsciously tend to associate the important details to the core concepts.

4. Ask Why? Pull apart written material paragraph by paragraph and don't forget the captions under the illustrations.

Example: If the heading is "Stream Erosion", flip it around to read "Why do streams erode?" Then answer the questions.

If you train your mind to think in a series of questions and answers, not only will you learn more, but it also helps to lessen the test anxiety because you are used to answering questions.

5. Read for reinforcement and future needs. Even if you only have 10 minutes, put your notes or a book in your hand. Your mind is similar to a computer; you have to input data in order to have it processed. *By reading, you are creating the neural connections for future retrieval.* The more times you read something, the more you reinforce the learning of ideas.

Even if you don't fully understand something on the first pass, *your mind stores much of the material for later recall.*

6. Relax to learn so go into exile. Our bodies respond to an inner clock called biorhythms. Burning the midnight oil works well for some people, but not everyone.

If possible, set aside a particular place to study that is free of distractions. Shut off the television, cell phone, pager and exile your friends and family during your study period.

If you really are bothered by silence, try background music. Light classical music at a low volume has been shown to aid in concentration over other types.

Music that evokes pleasant emotions without lyrics are highly suggested. Try just about anything by Mozart. It relaxes you.

7. Use arrows not highlighters. At best, it's difficult to read a page full of yellow, pink, blue, and green streaks.

Try staring at a neon sign for a while and you'll soon see my point, the horde of colors obscure the message.

A quick note, a brief dash of color, an underline, and an arrow pointing to a particular passage is much clearer than a horde of highlighted words.

8. Budget your study time. Although you shouldn't ignore any of the material, *allocate your available study time in the same ratio that topics may appear on the test.*

Testing Tips:

1. Get smart, play dumb. Don't read anything into the question. Don't make an assumption that the test writer is looking for something else than what is asked. Stick to the question as written and don't read extra things into it.

2. Read the question and all the choices *twice* before answering the question. You may miss something by not carefully reading, and then re-reading both the question and the answers.

If you really don't have a clue as to the right answer, leave it blank on the first time through. Go on to the other questions, as they may provide a clue as to how to answer the skipped questions.

If later on, you still can't answer the skipped ones . . . ***Guess.***
The only penalty for guessing is that you *might* get it wrong. Only one thing is certain; if you don't put anything down, you will get it wrong!

3. Turn the question into a statement. Look at the way the questions are worded. The syntax of the question usually provides a clue. Does it seem more familiar as a statement rather than as a question? Does it sound strange?

By turning a question into a statement, you may be able to spot if an answer sounds right, and it may also trigger memories of material you have read.

4. Look for hidden clues. It's actually very difficult to compose multiple-foil (choice) questions without giving away part of the answer in the options presented.

In most multiple-choice questions you can often readily eliminate one or two of the potential answers. This leaves you with only two real possibilities and automatically your odds go to Fifty-Fifty for very little work.

5. Trust your instincts. For every fact that you have read, you subconsciously retain something of that knowledge. On questions that you aren't really certain about, go with your basic instincts. **Your first impression on how to answer a question is usually correct.**

6. Mark your answers directly on the test booklet. Don't bother trying to fill in the optical scan sheet on the first pass through the test.

Just be very careful not to miss-mark your answers when you eventually transcribe them to the scan sheet.
7. Watch the clock! You have a set amount of time to answer the questions. Don't get bogged down trying to answer a single question at the expense of 10 questions you can more readily answer.

TABLE OF CONTENTS
DOMAIN/COMPETENCY/SKILL #   **PG #**

DOMAIN 1. LISTENING AND SPEAKING

COMPETENCY 1.0 UNDERSTAND LISTENING AND SPEAKING FOR INFORMATION AND UNDERSTANDING

Skill 1.1 Analyzing techniques for selecting and organizing information for oral presentations.

Preparing to speak on a topic should be seen as a process that has stages: **Discovery**, **Organization**, and **Editing**.

Discovery: There are many possible sources for the information that will be used to create an oral presentation. The first step in the discovery process is to settle on a topic or subject. Answer the question, What is the speech going to be about? For example, the topic or subject could be immigration. In the discovery stage, one's own knowledge, experience, and beliefs should be the first source, and notes should be taken as the speaker probes this source. The second source can very well be interviews with friends and possibly experts. The third source will be research: what has been written or said publicly on this topic. This stage can get out of hand very quickly, so a plan for the collecting of source information should be well-organized with time limits set for each part.

Organization: At this point, several decisions need to be made. The first is what the *purpose* of the speech is. Does the speaker want to persuade the audience to believe something or to act on something, or does the speaker simply want to present information that the audience might not have? Once that decision is made, a thesis should be developed. What point does the speaker want to make? And what are the points that will support that point? And in what order will those points be arranged? Introductions and conclusions should be written last. The purpose of the introduction is to draw the audience into the topic. The purpose of the conclusion is to polish off the speech, making sure the thesis is clear, reinforcing the thesis, or summarizing the points that have been made.

Editing: This is the most important stage in preparing a speech. Once decisions have been made in the discovery and organization stages, it's good to allow time to let the speech rest for awhile and to go back to it with "fresh eyes." Objectivity is extremely important, and the speaker should be willing to make drastic changes if they are needed. It's difficult to turn loose of one's own composition, but good speech-makers are able to do that. On the other hand, this can also get out of hand, and it should be limited. The speaker must recognize that at some point, the decisions must be made, the die must be cast, commitment to the speech as it stands must be made if the speaker is to deliver the message with conviction.

The concept of recursiveness is very useful to one who writes speeches.

That is, everything must be written at the outset with full knowledge that it can be changed, and the willingness to go backward, even to the discovery stage, is what makes a good speech-writer.

Skill 1.2 Recognizing factors affecting a listener's ability to understand spoken language in different contexts.

The more information a speaker has about an audience, the more likely he/she is to communicate effectively with them. Several factors figure into the speaker/audience equation: age, ethnic background, educational level, knowledge of the subject, and interest in the subject.

Speaking about computers to senior citizens who have, at best, rudimentary knowledge about the way computers work must take that into account. Perhaps handing out a glossary would be useful for this audience. Speaking to first-graders about computers presents its own challenges. On the other hand, the average high-school student has more experience with computers than most adults and that should be taken into account. Speaking to a room full of computer systems engineers requires a rather thorough understanding of the jargon related to the field.

In considering the age of the audience, it's best not to make assumptions. The gathering of senior citizens might include retired systems engineers or people who have made their livings using computers, so research about the audience is important. It might not be wise to assume that high-school students have a certain level of understanding, either.

With an audience that is primarily Hispanic with varying levels of competence in English, the speaker is obligated to adjust the presentation to fit that audience. The same would be true when the audience is composed of people who may have been in the country for a long time but whose families speak their first language at home. Black English presents its own peculiarities, and if the audience is composed primarily of African-Americans whose contacts in the larger community are not great, some efforts need to be made to acquaint oneself with the specific peculiarities of the community those listeners come from.

It's unwise to "speak down" to an audience; they will almost certainly be insulted. On the other hand, speaking to an audience of college graduates will require different skills than speaking to an audience of people who have never attended college.

Finally, has the audience come because of an interest in the topic or because they have been influenced or forced to come to the presentation? If the audience comes with an interest in the subject already, efforts to motivate or draw them into the discussion might not be needed.

On the other hand, if the speaker knows the audience does not have a high level of interest in the topic, it would be wise to use devices to draw them into it, to motivate them to listen.

Skill 1.3 Distinguishing styles of language and levels of usage (slang, informal and formal language, jargon, technical language, regionalisms).

Slang comes about for many reasons: Amelioration is an important one that results often in euphemisms. Examples are "passed away" for dying; "senior citizens" for old people. Some usages have become so embedded in the language that their sources are long-forgotten. For example, "fame" originally meant rumor. Some words that were originally intended as euphemisms such as "mentally retarded" and "moron" to avoid using "idiot" have themselves become pejorative.

Slang is lower in prestige than Standard English; tends to first appear in the language of groups with low status; is often taboo and unlikely to be used by people of high status; tends to displace conventional terms, either as a shorthand or as a defense against perceptions associated with the conventional term.

Informal and formal language is a distinction made on the basis of the occasion as well as the audience. At a "formal" occasion, for example, a meeting of executives or of government officials, even conversational exchanges are likely to be more formal. A cocktail party or a golf game are examples where the language is likely to be informal. Formal language uses fewer or no contractions, less slang, longer sentences, and more organization in longer segments.

Speeches delivered to executives, college professors, government officials, etc., is likely to be formal. Speeches made to fellow employees are likely to be informal. Sermons tend to be formal; Bible lessons will tend to be informal.

Jargon is a specialized vocabulary. It may be the vocabulary peculiar to a particular industry such as computers or of a field such as religion. It may also be the vocabulary of a social group. Black English is a good example. A Hardee's ad has two young men on the streets of Philadelphia discussing the merits of one of their sandwiches, and bylines are required so others may understand what they're saying. A whole vocabulary that has even developed its own dictionaries is the jargon of bloggers. The speaker must be knowledgeable about and sensitive to the jargon peculiar to the particular audience. That may require some research and some vocabulary development on the speaker's part.

Technical language is a form of jargon. It is usually specific to an industry, profession, or field of study. Sensitivity to the language familiar to the particular audience is important.

Regionalisms are those usages that are peculiar to a particular part of the country. A good example is the second person plural pronoun: you. Because the plural is the same as the singular, various parts of the country have developed their own solutions to be sure that they are understood when they are speaking to more than one "you." In the South, "you-all" or "y'all" is common. In the Northeast, one often hears "youse." In some areas of the Middlewest, "you'ns" can be heard.

Vocabulary also varies from region to region. A small stream is a "creek" in some regions but "crick" in some. In Boston, soft drinks are generically called "tonic," but it becomes "soda" in other parts of the northeast. It is "liqueur" in Canada, and "pop" when you get very far west of New York.

Skill 1.4 Determining styles of language appropriate to diverse purposes, content, audiences, and occasions.

Oral use of communication forms

Different from the basic writing forms of discourse is the art of debating, discussion, and conversation. The ability to use language and logic to convince the audience to accept your reasoning and to side with you is an art. This form of writing/speaking is extremely confined/structured, logically sequenced, with supporting reasons and evidence. At its best, it is the highest form of propaganda. A position statement, evidence, reason, evaluation and refutation are integral parts of this writing schema.

Interviewing provides opportunities for students to apply expository and informative communication. It teaches them how to structure questions to evoke fact-filled responses. Compiling the information from an interview into a biographical essay or speech helps students to list, sort, and arrange details in an orderly fashion.

Speeches that encourage them to describe persons, places, or events in their own lives or oral interpretations of literature help them sense the creativity and effort used by professional writers.

Useful resources

Price, Brent - *Basic Composition Activities Kit* - provides practical suggestions and student guide sheets for use in the development of student writing.

Simmons, John S., R.E. Shafer, and Gail B. West. (1976). *Decisions About The Teaching of English - "Advertising, or Buy It, You'll Like It."* Allyn & Bacon.

Additional resources may be found in the library, social studies, economic, debate and journalism textbooks and locally published newspapers.

Skill 1.5 Recognizing that information may be communicated through the rate and volume of speech.

Voice: Many people fall into one of two traps when speaking: using a monotone, or talking too fast. These are both caused by anxiety. A monotone restricts your natural inflection, but can be remedied by releasing tension in upper and lower body muscles. Subtle movement will keep you loose and natural. Talking too fast on the other hand, is not necessarily a bad thing if the speaker is exceptionally articulate. If not though, or if the speaker is talking about very technical things, it becomes far too easy for the audience to become lost. When you talk too fast and begin tripping over your words, consciously pause after every sentence you say. Don't be afraid of brief silences. The audience needs time to absorb what you are saying.

Volume: Problems with volume, whether too soft or too loud, can usually be combated with practice. If you tend to speak too softly, have someone stand in the back of the room and give you a signal when your volume is strong enough. If possible, have someone in the front of the room as well to make sure you're not overcompensating with excessive volume. Conversely, if you have a problem with speaking too loud, have the person in the front of the room signal you when your voice is soft enough and check with the person in the back to make sure it is still loud enough to be heard. In both cases, note your volume level for future reference. Don't be shy about asking your audience, "Can you hear me in the back?" Suitable volume is beneficial for both you and the audience.

Pitch: Pitch refers to the length, tension and thickness of a person's vocal bands. As your voice gets higher, the pitch gets higher. In oral performance, pitch reflects upon the emotional arousal level. More variation in pitch typically corresponds to more emotional arousal, but can also be used to convey sarcasm or highlight specific words.

Skill 1.6 Evaluating visual aids and technologies for use in an oral presentation.

Tips for using print media and visual aids
- Use pictures over words whenever possible.
- Present one key point per visual.
- Use no more than 3-4 colors per visual to avoid clutter and confusion.
- Use contrasting colors such as dark blue and bright yellow.
- Use a maximum of 25-35 numbers per visual aid.
- Use bullets instead of paragraphs when possible.
- Make sure it is student-centered, not media-centered. Delivery is just as important as the media presented.

Tips for using film and television
- Study programs in advance.
- Obtain supplementary materials such as printed transcripts of the narrative or study guides.
- Provide you students with background information, explain unfamiliar concepts, and anticipate outcomes.
- Assign outside readings based on their viewing.
- Ask cuing questions.
- Watch along with students.
- Observe students' reactions.
- Follow up viewing with discussions and related activities.

Skill 1.7 Interpreting and analyzing information presented in films, news broadcasts, lectures, and live performances.

More money is spent each year on advertising towards children than educating them. Thus, the media's strategies are considerably well thought out and effective. They employ large, clear letters, bold colors, simple line drawings, and popular symbols to announce upcoming events, push ideas and advertise products. By using attractive photographs, brightly colored cartoon characters or instructive messages, they increase sales, win votes or stimulate learning. The graphics are designed to communicate messages clearly, precisely, and efficiently. Some even target subconscious yearnings for sex and status.

Because so much effort is being spent on influencing students through media tactics, just as much effort should be devoted to educating those students about media awareness. A teacher should explain that artists and the aspect they choose to portray, as well as the ways in which they portray them, reflect their attitude and understanding of those aspects. The artistic choices they make are not entirely based on creative license—they also reflect an imbedded meaning the artist wants to represent. Colors, shapes, and positions are meant to arouse basic instincts for food, sex, and status, and are often used to sell cars, clothing, or liquor.

To stimulate analysis of media strategies, ask students such questions as:
- Where/when do you think this picture was taken/film was shot/piece was written?
- Would you like to have lived at this time in history, or in this place?
- What objects are present?
- What do the people presented look like? Are they happy or sad?
- Who is being targeted?
- What can you learn from this piece of media?
- Is it telling you something is good or bad?
- What message is being broadcasted?

COMPETENCY 2.0 UNDERSTAND LISTENING AND SPEAKING FOR LITERARY RESPONSE AND EXPRESSION, PERSONAL APPRECIATION, AND ENTERTAINMENT

Skill 2.1 Recognizing how oral presentations for the purpose of literary response make reference both to elements in the text and to the student's prior knowledge and personal experience.

When preparing to present a book analysis orally, the analyst should become acquainted with the elements of the story such as setting, characterization, style (language, both technically with regard to dialect but also structurally with regard to use of description, length of sentences, phrases, etc.), plot (particularly conflicts and pattern), tone (what is the *attitude* of the writer toward characters, theme, etc.) and particularly theme (the message or point the story conveys). It's not essential to know the writer's biography, but it is often helpful, especially in responding from the analyst's point of view.

Literature is written to evoke a personal response in readers. This is why so many books are sold. Once the analyst has a grip on the story—a thorough understanding of the story—then an analysis of one's own response to it is in order.

The following questions are useful:

1. Do you respond emotionally to one of the characters? Why? Is a character similar to someone you know or have known?
2. Is the setting evocative for you because of a place, situation, or milieu that you have experienced and that had meaning for you? Why?
3. Did the vocabulary, descriptions, or short or long sentences have impact on you? Why? For example, short, simple sentence after short, simple sentence may be used deliberately, but do you find it annoying?
4. Do you agree with the author's attitude toward the characters, setting, story, etc.? For example, has a character been written unsympathetically that you felt deserved more consideration? Does the author demonstrate a distaste for the setting he has chosen, and do you feel he is being unjust? Or do you experience the same distaste? Etc.

Reading is personal. Responding to it personally adds important dimensions to an analysis for others.

Skill 2.2 Analyzing the uses of oral presentations to offer literary interpretations that explicate multiple layers of meaning.

In order to discover multiple layers of meaning in a literary work, the first step is a thorough analysis, examining such things as setting, characters and characterization, plot (focusing particularly on conflicts and pattern of action), theme, tone, figures of speech, and symbolism. It's useful in looking for underlying themes to consider the author's biography, particularly with regard to setting and theme, and the date and time of the writing, paying particular attention to literary undercurrents at the time as well as political and social milieu.

Once the analysis is complete and data accumulated on the historical background, determine the overt meaning. What does the story say about the characters and their conflicts, where does the climax occur, and is there a denouement? Once the forthright, overt meaning is determined, then begin to look for undercurrents, subthemes that are related to the author's life and to what is going on in the literary, political, and social background at the time of writing.

In organization of the presentation, it's usually best to begin with an explication of the overt level of meaning and then follow up with the other messages that emerge from the text.

Skill 2.3 Recognizing the different roles of voice, intonation patterns, pacing, and emphasis in oral presentations of stories, poetry and drama.

Shifting into a new character calls for an analysis of that character's ways of talking, moving, and relating to others in the world. Everything a student does to give themselves the appearance—both physically and emotionally—of a character, involves an interpretation of that character's motivations, intentions and passions. Characterization is the basic decisions a student makes regarding the why and how of his or her character. They may justify their decisions based on details they notice in illustration or word, on understanding they have about similar characters in real life, and on their own motivations and intentions.

Basic frame sentence for character analysis:
"Since my character is _____, then he/she would act like _____."

This may result in a student employing a goofy, clumsy shuffle when acting in their role, or addressing everyone as "baby." The student must evolve from a child into an actor, and finally, into a specific character. It is your job to facilitate this transformation.

Child > Actor > Character

To further the immersion in their role, encourage students to call each other by their characters' names.

Emphasize the "as if" nature of a play, in which the students treat characters as if they were real, with real emotions and motivations driving them to act the way they do. Do not give students your own interpretation of a character's personality. Let them create their own interpretation, and follow along with their reading of the character.

Vocal Techniques

Voice is perhaps the most important tool of interpretation in classroom theater. It can portray anger, sadness, jealousy, happiness, fear and excitement. Vocal techniques integrate word choice, emphasis, and attitude, accentuating or deemphasizing them as the student sees fit. The voice puts life into the words of the play, with intonation, pitch, loudness or softness and even accent reflecting or obscuring the intent of the speaker.

Just look at the phrase, "It's all right," as an example of the impact of voice and tone. Said with a soothing voice, it implies patience and understanding. Said with a sarcastic, cynical voice, it gives off a dismissive feeling. A host of a patry might say the same phrase with suppressed frustration to a guest who has broken a favorite vase. In each case, the vocal choices made either highlight or shadow the inner thoughts of the speaker.

Encourage students to try on different vocal roles. Explain to students that while you must use the words in the script, *how* you say them is up to individual interpretation. A simple explanation is to simply tell them to "read something and then say it in your own way." Have students decide on words they want to stress by highlighting or underlining them in their scripts. Circle words that should be spoken louder and draw a line lightly through words that should be whispered. Allow students to transform vocal inflection to match with their vision of their character. They will soon combine their own attitudes and analyses with attitudinal hints the text supplies to create an effective emotional portrayal.

Storytelling Techniques

- It's important to try to have complete silence before you begin, so that the students are concentrating and focused on the story and the person reading it. Turn off any background music.
- Make eye contact with everyone. At least you should be able to see all the students from where you are sitting or standing. Move them around if necessary.
- Make sure that there are no distractions behind you – stand in front of a wall, not an interesting bookshelf or a window.
- Think about yourself telling a favorite anecdote to your friends. "Did I tell you about the time when I…" How do you tell it? What gestures and effects do you use? At what points are you sure of getting a laugh? What are you doing with your body language and how are you telling the story?

Is there a particular pause before the punch-line that works wonders? Apply your style to the story you're telling.

Skill 2.4 Judging the effectiveness of given details or examples for making a presentation of a performance more interesting or appealing.

Posture: Maintain a straight, but not stiff posture. Instead of shifting weight from hip to hip, point your feet directly at the audience and distribute your weight evenly. Keep shoulders orientated towards the audience. If you have to turn your body to use a visual aid, turn 45 degrees and continue speaking towards the audience.

Movement: Instead of staying glued to one spot or pacing back and forth, stay within four to eight feet of the front row of your audience, and take maybe a step or half-step to the side every once in a while. If you are using a lectern, feel free to move to the front or side of it to engage your audience more. Avoid distancing yourself from the audience, you want them to feel involved and connected.

Gestures: Gestures are a great way to keep a natural atmosphere when speaking publicly. Use them just as you would when speaking to a friend. They shouldn't be exaggerated, but they should be utilized for added emphasis. Avoid keeping your hands in your pockets or locked behind your back, wringing your hands and fidgeting nervously, or keeping your arms crossed.

Eye Contact: Many people are intimidated by using eye contact when speaking to large groups. Interestingly, eye contact usually *helps* the speaker overcome speech anxiety by connecting with their attentive audience and easing feelings of isolation. Instead of looking at a spot on the back wall or at your notes, scan the room and make eye contact for one to three seconds per person.

Tips for creating visual media
- Limit your graph to just one idea or concept
- Keep the content simple and concise (avoid too many lines, words, or pictures)
- Balance substance and visual appeal
- Make sure the text is large enough for the class to read
- Match the information to the format that will fit it best

Skill 2.5 Selecting appropriate technological applications and tools for oral presentations related to literature.

See Skill 3.5.

COMPETENCY 3.0 UNDERSTAND LISTENING AND SPEAKING FOR CRITICAL ANALYSIS, EVALUATION, AND PERSUASION

Skill 3.1 Evaluating strategies of organization and delivery in relation to given content, audience, purpose, and occasion.

The content in material to be presented orally plays a big role in how it is organized and delivered. For example, a literary analysis or a book report will be organized inductively, laying out the details and then presenting a conclusion, which will usually be what the author's purpose, message, and intent are. If the analysis is focusing on multiple layers in a story, that will probably follow the preliminary conclusion. On the other hand, keeping in mind that the speaker will want to keep the audience's attention, if the content has to do with difficult-to-follow facts and statistics, slides (or PowerPoint) may be used as a guide to the presentation, and the speaker will intersperse interesting anecdotes, jokes, or humor from time to time so the listeners don't fall asleep.

It's also important to take the consistency of the audience into account when organizing a presentation. If the audience can be counted on to have a high level of interest in what is being presented, little would need to be done in the way of organizing and presenting to hold interest. On the other hand, if many of those in the audience are there because they have to be, or if the level of interest can be counted on not to be very high, something like a PowerPoint presentation can be very helpful. Also the lead-in and introduction need to be structured not only to be entertaining and interest-grabbing, it should create an interest in the topic. If the audience is senior citizens, it's important to keep the presentation lively and to be careful not to "speak down" to them. Carefully written introductions aimed specifically at this audience will go a long way to attract their interest in the topic.

No speaker should stand up to make a presentation if the purpose has not been carefully determined ahead of time. If the speaker is not focused on the purpose, the audience will quickly lose interest. As to organizing for a particular purpose, some of the decisions to be made are where it will occur in the presentation—beginning, middle, or end—and whether displaying the purpose on a chart, PowerPoint, or banner will enhance the presentation. The purpose might be the lead-in for a presentation if it can be counted on to grab the interest of the listeners, in which case, the organization will be deductive. If it seems better to save the purpose until the end, the organization, of course, will be inductive.

The occasion, of course, plays an important role in the development and delivery of a presentation. A celebration speech when the company has achieved an important accomplishment will be organized around congratulating those who were most responsible for the accomplishment and giving some details about how it was achieved and probably something about the competition for the achievement.

The presentation will be upbeat and not too long. On the other hand, if bad news is being presented, it will probably be the CEO who is making the presentation and the bad-news announcement will come first followed with details about the news itself and how it came about, and probably end with a pep talk and encouragement to do better the next time.

Skill 3.2 Recognizing fallacies in logic.

A fallacy is, essentially, an error in reasoning. In persuasive speech, logical fallacies are instances of reasoning flaws that make an argument invalid. For example, a premature generalization occurs when you form a general rule based on only one or a few specific cases, which do not represent all possible cases. An illustration of this is the statement, "Bob Marley was a Rastafarian singer. Therefore, all Rastafarians sing."

Skill 3.3 Analyzing the role of critical-thinking skills (selecting and evaluating supporting data, evaluating a speaker's point of view, distinguishing fact from opinion, recognizing bias) in effective listening and speaking.

See Skills 1.1, 1.4, 2.4, 3.1, 3.2, 4.5.

Skill 3.4 Recognizing the role of body language, gestures, and visual aids in communicating a point of view in various cultures.

Physicality in a classroom calls for the performer to embody the emotion of the words into the motion of the character. This can drastically alter the perception of the character's personality, dilemma or situation.

Take a look at the phrase, "No, I don't mind waiting." Said while leaning back in a chair with a casual wave of the hand, the speaker comes off as easy going and calm. On the other hand, if the speaker is tapping their foot and constantly checking their watch, the message is very different. Simple gestures, from the raise of an eyebrow to a jump in the air, indicate the speaker's state of mind, supplementing vocal tone and inflection.

Physical techniques can be especially helpful for students that have trouble getting into their character. For young people who naturally gravitate towards physical activity, getting into the physical quality of a character can lead to the emotional quality as well. Ask students to draw on their own experiences to determine what the most natural physical expression would be. Generally, boys are more physically active than girls. They are willing to fall down, hunch over, jump on top of desks and dramatically exaggerate their movements to enhance the performance (or often just to be comical).

Skill 3.5 Identifying and assessing options for using technology in oral presentations involving critical analysis, evaluation, and persuasion.

Media's impact on today's society is immense and ever-increasing. As children, we watch programs on television that are amazingly fast-paced and visually rich. Parent's roles as verbal and moral teachers are diminishing in response to the much more stimulating guidance of the television set. Adolescence, which used to be the time for going out and exploring the world first hand, is now consumed by the allure of MTV, popular music, and video games. Young adults are exposed to uncensored sex and violence.

But media's affect on society is beneficial and progressive at the same time. Its affect on education in particular provides special challenges and opportunities for teachers and students.

Thanks to satellite technology, instructional radio and television programs can be received by urban classrooms and rural villages. CD-roms can allow students to learn information through a virtual reality experience. The internet allows instant access to unlimited data and connects people across all cultures through shared interests. Educational media, when used in a productive way, enriches instruction and makes it more individualized, accessible, and economical.

COMPETENCY 4.0 UNDERSTAND LISTENING AND SPEAKING FOR SOCIAL INTERACTION IN A VARIETY OF FORMAL AND INFORMAL SITUATIONS

Skill 4.1 Recognizing language conventions for different social situations (informal conversations, job interviews, workplace interactions).

The content in material to be presented orally plays a big role in how it is organized and delivered. For example, a literary analysis or a book report will be organized inductively, laying out the details and then presenting a conclusion, which will usually be what the author's purpose, message, and intent are. If the analysis is focusing on multiple layers in a story, that will probably follow the preliminary conclusion. On the other hand, keeping in mind that the speaker will want to keep the audience's attention, if the content has to do with difficult-to-follow facts and statistics, slides (or PowerPoint) may be used as a guide to the presentation, and the speaker will intersperse interesting anecdotes, jokes, or humor from time to time so the listeners don't fall asleep.

It's also important to take the consistency of the audience into account when organizing a presentation. If the audience can be counted on to have a high level of interest in what is being presented, little would need to be done in the way of organizing and presenting to hold interest.

On the other hand, if many of those in the audience are there because they have to be, or if the level of interest can be counted on not to be very high, something like a PowerPoint presentation can be very helpful. Also the lead-in and introduction need to be structured not only to be entertaining and interest-grabbing, it should create an interest in the topic. If the audience is senior citizens, it's important to keep the presentation lively and to be careful not to "speak down" to them. Carefully written introductions aimed specifically at this audience will go a long way to attract their interest in the topic.

No speaker should stand up to make a presentation if the purpose has not been carefully determined ahead of time. If the speaker is not focused on the purpose, the audience will quickly lose interest. As to organizing for a particular purpose, some of the decisions to be made are where it will occur in the presentation—beginning, middle, or end—and whether displaying the purpose on a chart, PowerPoint, or banner will enhance the presentation. The purpose might be the lead-in for a presentation if it can be counted on to grab the interest of the listeners, in which case, the organization will be deductive. If it seems better to save the purpose until the end, the organization, of course, will be inductive.

The occasion, of course, plays an important role in the development and delivery of a presentation.

A celebration speech when the company has achieved an important accomplishment will be organized around congratulating those who were most responsible for the accomplishment and giving some details about how it was achieved and probably something about the competition for the achievement. The presentation will be upbeat and not too long. On the other hand, if bad news is being presented, it will probably be the CEO who is making the presentation and the bad-news announcement will come first followed with details about the news itself and how it came about, and probably end with a pep talk and encouragement to do better the next time.

Skill 4.2 Analyzing elements of effective listening and speaking in conversation (using appropriate language, providing verbal and nonverbal responses to the speaker, allowing "wait time" for questions.

Communication skills are crucial in a collaborative society. In particular, a person can not be a successful communicator without being an active listener. Focus on what others say, rather than planning on what to say next. By listening to everything another person is saying, you may pick up on natural cues that lead to the next conversation move without so much added effort.

Skill 4.3 Analyzing techniques of effective listening and speaking in small- and large-group situations (paraphrasing to clarify, monitoring reactions by interpreting nonverbal cues).

Facilitating
It is quite acceptable to use standard opening lines to facilitate a conversation. Don't agonize over trying to come up with witty "one-liners," as the main obstacle in initiating conversation is just getting the first statement over with. After that, the real substance begins. A useful technique may be to make a comment or ask a question about a shared situation. This may be anything from the weather, to the food you are eating, to a new policy at work. Use an opener you are comfortable with, because most likely, your partner in conversation will be comfortable with it as well.

Stimulating Higher Level Critical Thinking Through Inquiry
Many people rely on questions to communicate with others. However, most fall back on simple clarifying questions rather than open-ended inquiries. Try to ask open-ended, deeper-level questions, since those tend to have the greatest reward and lead to a greater understanding. In answering those questions, more complex connections are made and more significant realizations are achieved.

Skill 4.4 Applying knowledge of techniques for engaging in conversations and discussions on academic, technical, and community and social issues and concerns.

The successful conversationalist is a person who keeps up with what's going on in the world both far and near and ponders the meanings of events and developments. That person also usually reads about the topics that are of the most interest to him, both in printed materials and online. In addition, the effective conversationalist has certain areas that are of particular interest that have been probed in some depth. An interest in human behavior is usually one of this person's most particular interests. Why do people behave as they do? Why do some succeed and some fail? This person will also be interested in and concerned about social issues, particularly in the immediate community but also on a wider scale and will have ideas for solving some of those problems.

With all of this, the most important thing a good conversationalist can do is to *listen*, not just wait until the other person quits speaking so he or she can take the floor again but actually listening to learn what the other person has to say and also to learn more about that other person. Following a gathering, the best thing a person can think about another is that a person was interested enough to listen to the other's ideas and opinions, and that is the person who will be remembered the longest and with the most regard.

It's acceptable to be passionate about one's convictions in polite conversation; it is not acceptable to be overbearing or unwilling to hear and consider another's point of view. It's important to keep one's emotions under control in these circumstances even if the other person does not.

Skill 4.5 Applying knowledge of listening and speaking in debates and panel discussions.

Debates and panel discussions fall under the umbrella of formal speaking, and the rules for formal speaking should apply here although lapsing into conversation language is acceptable. Swear words should be avoided in these situations.

A debate presents two sides of a debatable thesis—pro and con. Each side will posit a hypothesis, prove it, and defend it. A formal debate is a sort of formal dance with each side following a strictly defined format. However, within those guidelines, debaters are free to develop their arguments and rebuttals as they choose. The successful debater prepares by developing very thoroughly both sides of the thesis: "Mexico's border with the United States must be closed" and "Mexico's border with the United States must remain open." Debaters must be thoroughly prepared to argue their own side, but they must also have a strategy for rebutting the opposing side's arguments.

All aspects of critical thinking and logical argument are employed, and the successful debaters will use ethical appeal (their own credibility) and emotional appeal to persuade the judges who will determine who wins—that is, the side that best establishes its thesis, proves it logically, but also *persuades* the audience to come over to its position.

A panel is typically composed of *experts* who explain and defend a particular topic. Often, panels will include representatives from more than one field of study and more than one position on the topic. Typically, each will have a limited amount of time to make an opening statement either presenting explanatory material or arguing a point of view. Then the meeting will be opened up to the audience for questions. A moderator will keep order and will control the time limits on the opening statements and responses and will sometimes intervene and ask a panel member that was not the target of a particular question from the audience to elaborate or rebut the answer of the panel member who was questioned. Panel are usually limited to four or five people although in special cases, they may be much larger.

Skill 4.6 Recognizing elements of effective listening and speaking in situations involving people of different ages, genders, cultures, and other personal characteristics.

See Skills 1.4 and 4.1.

Skill 4.7 Applying knowledge of listening and speaking to communicate and model regard for the individual and respect for cultural differences.

"Political correctness" is a new concept tossed around frequently in the 21st century. It has always existed, of course. The successful speaker of the 19th century understood and was sensitive to audiences. However, that person was typically a man, of course, and the only audience that was important was a male audience, and more often than not, the only important audience was a white one.

Many things have changed in discourse since the 19th century just as the society the speaker lives in and addresses has changed, and the speaker who disregards the existing conventions for "political correctness" usually finds himself/herself in trouble. Rap music makes a point of ignoring those conventions, particularly with regard to gender, and is often the target of very hostile attacks. On the other hand, rap performers often intend to be revolutionary and have developed their own audiences and have become outrageously wealthy by exploiting those newly-developed audiences based primarily on thumbing their noses at establishment conventions.

Even so, the successful speaker must understand and be sensitive to what is current in "political correctness." The "n word" is a case in point.

There was a time when that term was thrown about at will by politicians and other public speakers, but no more. Nothing could spell the end of a politician's career more certainly than using that term in his campaign or public addresses.

These terms are called "pejorative"—A word or phrase that expresses contempt or disapproval. Such terms as *redneck*, *queer*, or *cripple* may only be considered pejorative if used by a non-member of the group they apply to. For example, the "n word," which became very inflammatory in the 1960s, is now being used sometimes by African-American artists to refer to themselves, especially in their music, with the intention of underscoring their protest of the establishment.

References to gender have became particularly sensitive in the 20th century as a result of the women's rights movement, and the speaker who disregards these sensitivities does so at his/her peril. The generic "he" is no longer acceptable, and this requires a strategy to deal with pronominal references without repetitive he/she, his/her, etc. Several ways to approach this: switch to a passive construction that does not require a subject; switch back and forth, using the male pronoun in one reference and the female pronoun in another one, being sure to sprinkle them reasonably evenly; or switch to the plural. The last alternative is the one most often chosen. This requires some care, and the speaker should spend time developing these skills before stepping in front of an audience.

DOMAIN 2. WRITING

COMPETENCY 5.0 UNDERSTAND PROCESSES FOR GENERATING AND DEVELOPING WRITTEN TEXTS

Skill 5.1 Applying strategies for generating ideas before writing (brainstorming, clustering, and other graphic organizers).

Prior to writing, you will need to prewrite for ideas and details as well as decide how the essay will be organized. In the hour you have to write you should spend no more than 5-10 minutes prewriting and organizing your ideas. As you prewrite, it might be helpful to remember you should have at least three main points and at least two to three details to support your main ideas. There are several types of graphic organizers that you should practice using as you prepare for the essay portion of the test.

PRACTICE - Choose one topic from the chart on page and complete the cluster.

PREWRITE TO EXPLAIN HOW OR WHY

Reread a question from the chart on the previous page that asks you to explain how a poet creates tone and mood use imagery and word choice. Then fill out the organizer on the following page that identifies how the poet effectively creates tone and mood. Support with examples from the poem.

VISUAL ORGANIZER: GIVING REASONS

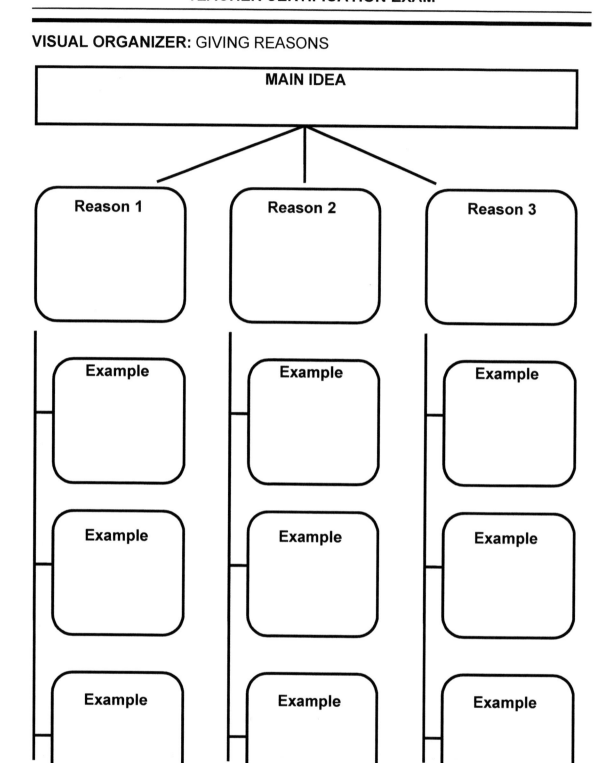

STEP 3: PREWRITE TO ORGANIZE IDEAS

After you have completed a graphic organizer, you need to decide how you will organize your essay. To organize your essay, you might consider one of the following patterns to structure your essay.

1. Examine individual elements such as **plot**, **setting**, **theme**, **character**, **point of view**, **tone**, **mood**, or **style**.

   SINGLE ELEMENT OUTLINE
   Intro - main idea statement
   Main point 1 with at least two supporting details
   Main point 2 with at least two supporting details
   Main point 3 with at least two supporting details
   Conclusion (restates main ideas and summary of main pts)

2. **Compare and contrast two elements**.

POINT-BY-POINT	BLOCK
Introduction Statement of main idea about A and B	Introduction Statement of main idea about A and B
Main Point 1 Discussion of A Discussion of B	Discussion of A Main Point 1 Main Point 2 Main point 3
Main Point 2 Discussion of A Discussion of B	Discussion of B Main Point 1 Main Point 2 Main Point 3
Main Point 3 Discussion of A Discussion of B	Conclusion Restate main idea
Conclusion Restatement or summary of main idea	

PRACTICE:
Using the cluster on the next page, choose an organizing chart and complete for your topic.

VISUAL ORGANIZER: GIVING INFORMATION

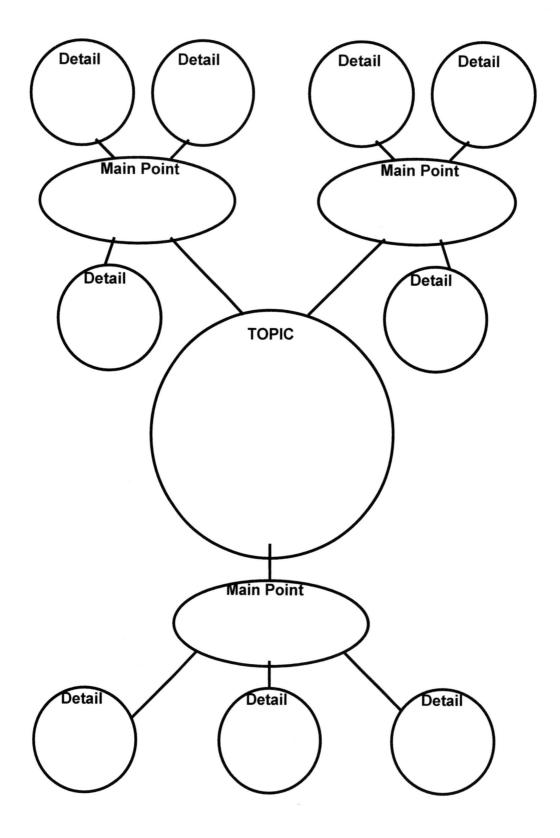

Skill 5.2 Identifying techniques for taking notes and developing drafts.

Seeing writing as a process is very helpful in saving preparation time, particularly in the taking of notes and the development of drafts. Once a decision is made about the topic to be developed, some preliminary review of literature is helpful in thinking about the next step, which is to determine what the purpose of the written document will be. For example, if the topic is immigration, a cursory review of the various points of view in the debate going on in the country will help the writer decide what this particular written piece will try to accomplish. The purpose could just be a review of the various points of view, which would be an informative purpose. On the other hand, the writer might want to take a point of view and provide proof and support with the purpose of changing the reader's mind. The writer might even want the reader to take some action as the result of reading. Another possible purpose might be simply to write a description of a family of immigrants.

Once that cursory review has been completed, it's time to begin research in earnest and to prepare to take notes. If the thesis has been clearly defined, and some thought has been given to what will be used to prove or support it, a tentative outline can be developed. A thesis plus three points is typical. Decisions about introduction and conclusion should be deferred until the body of the paper is written. Note-taking is much more effective if the notes are being taken to provide information for an outline. There is much less danger that the writer will go off on time-consuming tangents.

Formal outlines inhibit effective writing. However, a loosely constructed outline can be an effective device for note-taking that will yield the information for a worthwhile statement about a topic. Sentence outlines are better than topic outlines because they require the writer to do some thinking about the direction a subtopic will take.

Once this preliminary note-taking phase is over, the first draft can be developed. The writing at this stage is likely to be highly individualistic. However, successful writers tend to just write, keeping in mind the purpose of the paper, the point that is going to be made in it, and the information that has been turned up in the research. Student writers need to understand that this first draft is just that—the first one. It takes more than one draft to write a worthwhile statement about a topic. This is what successful writers do. It's sometimes helpful to have students read the various drafts of a story by a well-known writer.

Once the draft is on paper, a stage that is sometimes called editing occurs. With word processors, this is much more easily achieved than in the past. Sections can be deleted, words can be changed, and additions can be made without doing the entire project over a second time.

What to look for: mechanics, of course, spelling, punctuation, etc., but it's important that student writers not mistake that for editing. Editing is rereading objectively, testing the effectiveness on a reader of the arrangement and the line of reasoning. The kinds of changes that will need to be made are: rearranging the parts, adding information that is missing and needed, and deleting information that doesn't fit or contribute to the accomplishment of the purpose.

Once the body of the paper has been shaped to the writer's satisfaction, the introduction and conclusion should be fashioned. An introduction should grab the reader's interest and, perhaps, announce the purpose and thesis of the paper unless the reasoning is inductive, in which case, purpose and thesis may come later in the paper. The conclusion is to reaffirm the purpose in some way.

Skill 5.3 Evaluating the appropriateness of given details for supporting the development of a main point.

The best place to start research is usually at your local library. Not only does it have numerous books, videos, and periodicals to use for references, the librarian is always a valuable resource for information, or where to get that information.

"Those who declared librarians obsolete when the internet rage first appeared are now red-faced. We need them more than ever. The internet is full of 'stuff' but its value and readability is often questionable. 'Stuff' doesn't give you a competitive edge, high-quality related information does."
      -Patricia Schroeder, President of the Association of American Publishers

The internet is a multi-faceted goldmine of information, but you must be careful to discriminate between reliable and unreliable sources. Stick to sites that are associated with an academic institution, whether it be a college or university or a scholarly organization.

Keep **content** and **context** in mind when researching. Don't be so wrapped up how you are going to apply your resource to your project that you miss the author's entire purpose or message. Remember that there are multiple ways to get the information you need. Read an encyclopedia article about your topic to get a general overview, and then focus in from there. Note important names of people associated with your subject, time periods, and geographic areas. Make a list of key words and their synonyms to use while searching for information. And finally, don't forget about articles in magazines and newspapers, or even personal interviews with experts related to your field of interest!

Skill 5.4 Eliminating distracting details that interfere with the development of a main point.

Techniques to Maintain Focus:

- **Focus on a main point.** The point should be clear to readers, and all sentences in the paragraph should relate to it.
- **Start the paragraph with a topic sentence.** This should be a general, one-sentence summary of the paragraph's main point, relating both back towards the thesis and toward the content of the paragraph. (A topic sentence is sometimes unnecessary if the paragraph continues a developing idea clearly introduced in a preceding paragraph, or if the paragraph appears in a narrative of events where generalizations might interrupt the flow of the story.)
- **Stick to the point.** Eliminate sentences that do not support the topic sentence.

Be flexible. If there is not enough evidence to support the claim your topic sentence is making, do not fall into the trap of wandering or introducing new ideas within the paragraph. Either find more evidence, or adjust the topic sentence to collaborate with the evidence that is available.

Skill 5.5 Solving problems related to introductions, conclusions, and text organization.

Introductions:

It's important to remember that in the writing process, the introduction should be written last. Until the body of the paper has been determined—thesis, development—it's difficult to make strategic decisions regarding the introduction. The Greek rhetoricians called this part of a discourse *exordium*, a "leading into." The basic purpose of the introduction, then, is to lead the audience into the discourse. It can let the reader know what the purpose of the discourse is and it can condition the audience to be receptive to what the writer wants to say. It can be very brief or it can take up a large percentage of the total word count. Aristotle said that the introduction could be compared to the flourishes that flute players make before their performance—an overture in which the musicians display what they can play best in order to gain the favor and attention of the audience for the main performance.

In order to do this, we must first of all know what we are going to say; who the readership is likely to be; what the social, political, economic, etc., climate is; what preconceived notions the audience is likely to have regarding the subject; and how long the discourse is going to be.

There are many ways to do this:
- Show that the subject is important.
- Show that although the points we are presenting may seem improbable, they are true.
- Show that the subject has been neglected, misunderstood, or misrepresented.
- Explain an unusual mode of development.

- Forestall any misconception of the purpose.
- Apologize for a deficiency.
- Arouse interest in the subject with an anecdotal lead-in.
- Ingratiate oneself with the readership.
- Establish one's own credibility.

The introduction often ends with the thesis, the point or purpose of the paper. However, this is not set in stone. The thesis may open the body of the discussion, or it may conclude the discourse. The most important thing to remember is that the purpose and structure of the introduction should be deliberate if it is to serve the purpose of "leading the reader into the discussion."

Conclusions:

It's easier to write a conclusion after the decisions regarding the introduction have been made. Aristotle taught that the conclusion should strive to do five things:

1. Inspire the reader with a favorable opinion of the writer.
2. Amplify the force of the points made in the body of the paper.
3. Reinforce the points made in the body.
4. Rouse appropriate emotions in the reader.
5. Restate in a summary way what has been said.

The conclusion may be short or it may be long depending on its purpose in the paper. Recapitulation, a brief restatement of the main points or certainly of the thesis is the most common form of effective conclusions. A good example is the closing argument in a court trial.

Text Organization:

In studies of professional writers and how they produce their successful works, it has been revealed that writing is a process that can be clearly defined although in practice it must have enough flexibility to allow for creativity. The teacher must be able to define the various stages that a successful writer goes through in order to make a statement that has value. There must be a discovery stage when ideas, materials, supporting details, etc., are deliberately collected. These may come from many possible sources: the writer's own experience and observations, deliberate research of written sources, interviews of live persons, television presentations, or the internet.

The next stage is organization where the purpose, thesis, and supporting points are determined. Most writers will put forth more than one possible thesis and in the next stage, the writing of the paper, settle on one as the result of trial and error. Once the paper is written, the editing stage is necessary and is probably the most important stage. This is not just the polishing stage.

At this point, decisions must be made regarding whether the reasoning is cohesive—does it hold together? Is the arrangement the best possible one or should the points be rearranged? Are there holes that need to be filled in? What form will the introduction take? Does the conclusion lead the reader out of the discourse or is it inadequate or too abrupt, etc.

It's important to remember that the best writers engage in all of these stages recursively. They may go back to discovery at any point in the process. They may go back and rethink the organization, etc. To help students become effective writers, the teacher needs to give them adequate practice in the various stages and encourage them to engage deliberately in the creative thinking that makes writers successful.

Skill 5.6 Applying knowledge of the uses of technology to produce written texts and multimedia works.

Multimedia refers to a technology for presenting material in both visual and verbal forms. This format is especially conducive to the classroom, since it reaches both visual and auditory learners.

Knowing how to select effective teaching software is the first step in efficient multi-media education. First, decide what you need the software for (creating spreadsheets, making diagrams, creating slideshows, etc.) Consult magazines such as *Popular Computing, PC World, MacWorld,* and *Multimedia World* to learn about the newest programs available. Go to a local computer store and ask a customer service representative to help you find the exact equipment you need. If possible, test the programs you are interested in. Check reviews in magazines such as *Consumer Reports, PCWorld, Electronic Learning* or *MultiMedia Schools* to ensure the software's quality.

Software programs useful for producing teaching material
- Adobe
- Aldus Freehand
- CorelDRAW!
- DrawPerfect
- Claris Works
- PC Paintbrush
- Harvard Graphics
- Visio
- Microsoft Word
- Microsoft Power Point

Skill 5.7 Demonstrating awareness of personal bias when developing written texts.

When evaluating sources, first go through this checklist to make sure the source is even worth reading:
- Title (How relevant is it to your topic?)
- Date (How current is the source?)
- Organization (What institution is this source coming from?)
- Length (How in depth does it go?)

Check for signs of bias:
- Does the author or publisher have political ties or religious views that could affect their objectivity?
- Is the author or publisher associated with any special-interest groups that might only see one side of an issue, such as Greenpeace or the National Rifle Association?
- How fairly does the author treat opposing views?
- Does the language of the piece show signs of bias?

Keep an open mind while reading, and don't let opposing viewpoints prevent you from absorbing the text. Remember that you are not judging the author's work, you are examining its assumptions, assessing its evidence and weighing its conclusions.

COMPETENCY 6.0 UNDERSTAND HOW TO REVISE AND EDIT WRITTEN TEXTS TO ACHIEVE CLARITY AND ECONOMY OF EXPRESSION AND CONFORMITY TO CONVENTIONS OF STANDARD ENGLISH USAGE

Skill 6.1 Revising sentences to eliminate wordiness, lack of clarity, redundancy, clichés, and run-on sentences.

Enhancing Interest:

- Start out with an attention-grabbing introduction. This sets an engaging tone for the entire piece and will be more likely to pull the reader in.
- Use dynamic vocabulary and varied sentence beginnings. Keep the reader on their toes. If they can predict what you are going to say next, switch it up.
- Avoid using clichés (as cold as ice, the best thing since sliced bread, nip it in the bud). These are easy shortcuts, but they are not interesting, memorable, or convincing.

Ensuring Understanding:

- Avoid using the words, "clearly," "obviously," and "undoubtedly." Often, things that are clear or obvious to the author are not as apparent to the reader. Instead of using these words, make your point so strongly that it is clear on its own.
- Use the word that best fits the meaning you intend for, even if they are longer or a little less common. Try to find a balance, a go with a familiar yet precise word.
- When in doubt, explain further.

Skill 6.2 Revising sentences and passages to subordinate ideas, maintain parallel form, and keep related ideas together.

Sentence completeness

Avoid fragments and run-on sentences. Recognition of sentence elements necessary to make a complete thought, proper use of independent and dependent clauses (see *Use correct coordination and subordination*), and proper punctuation will correct such errors.

Sentence structure

Recognize simple, compound, complex, and compound-complex sentences. Use dependent (subordinate) and independent clauses correctly to create these sentence structures.

Simple	Joyce wrote a letter.
Compound	Joyce wrote a letter, and Dot drew a picture.

| Complex | While Joyce wrote a letter, Dot drew a picture. |
| Compound/Complex | When Mother asked the girls to demonstrate their new-found skills, Joyce wrote a letter, and Dot drew a picture. |

Note: Do **not** confuse compound sentence elements with compound sentences.

Simple sentence with compound subject
<u>Joyce</u> and <u>Dot</u> wrote letters.
The <u>girl</u> in row three and the <u>boy</u> next to her were passing notes across the aisle.

Simple sentence with compound predicate
Joyce <u>wrote letters</u> and <u>drew pictures</u>.
The captain of the high school debate team <u>graduated with honors</u> and <u>studied broadcast journalism in college</u>.

Simple sentence with compound object of preposition
Coleen graded the students' essays for <u>style</u> and <u>mechanical accuracy</u>.

Parallelism

Recognize parallel structures using phrases (prepositional, gerund, participial, and infinitive) and omissions from sentences that create the lack of parallelism.

Prepositional phrase/single modifier

Incorrect: Coleen ate the ice cream with enthusiasm and hurriedly.
Correct: Coleen ate the ice cream with enthusiasm and in a hurry.
Correct: Coleen ate the ice cream enthusiastically and hurriedly.

Participial phrase/infinitive phrase

Incorrect: After hiking for hours and to sweat profusely, Joe sat down to rest and drinking water.
Correct: After hiking for hours and sweating profusely, Joe sat down to rest and drink water.

Recognition of dangling modifiers

Dangling phrases are attached to sentence parts in such a way they create ambiguity and incorrectness of meaning.

Participial phrase

Incorrect: Hanging from her skirt, Dot tugged at a loose thread.
Correct: Dot tugged at a loose thread hanging from her skirt.

Incorrect: Relaxing in the bathtub, the telephone rang.
Correct: While I was relaxing in the bathtub, the telephone rang.

Infinitive phrase

Incorrect: To improve his behavior, the dean warned Fred.
Correct: The dean warned Fred to improve his behavior.

Prepositional phrase

Incorrect: On the floor, Father saw the dog eating table scraps.
Correct: Father saw the dog eating table scraps on the floor.

Recognition of syntactical redundancy or omission

These errors occur when superfluous words have been added to a sentence or key words have been omitted from a sentence.

Redundancy

Incorrect: Joyce made sure that when her plane arrived that she retrieved all of her luggage.
Correct: Joyce made sure that when her plane arrived she retrieved all of her luggage.

Incorrect: He was a mere skeleton of his former self.
Correct: He was a skeleton of his former self.

Omission

Incorrect: Dot opened her book, recited her textbook, and answered the teacher's subsequent question.
Correct: Dot opened her book, recited from the textbook, and answered the teacher's subsequent question.

Avoidance of double negatives

This error occurs from positioning two negatives that, in fact, cancel each other in meaning.

Incorrect: Harold couldn't care less whether he passes this class.

Correct: Harold could care less whether he passes this class.

Incorrect: Dot didn't have no double negatives in her paper.
Correct: Dot didn't have any double negatives in her paper.

Skill 6.3 Revising sentences to eliminate misplaced or dangling modifiers, eliminate sentence fragments, and correct misspellings, including the spelling of common homonyms (its/it's, their/there/they're).

Types of Clauses

Clauses are connected word groups that are composed of *at least* one subject and one verb. (A subject is the doer of an action or the element that is being joined. A verb conveys either the action or the link.)

Students are waiting for the start of the assembly.
Subject   Verb

At the end of the play, students wait for the curtain to come down.
                         Subject   Verb

Clauses can be independent or dependent.

Independent clauses can stand alone or can be joined to other clauses.

Independent clause	for and nor	
Independent clause,	but or yet so	Independent clause
Independent clause	;	Independent clause
Dependent clause	,	Independent clause
Independent clause		Dependent clause

Dependent clauses, by definition, contain at least one subject and one verb. However, they cannot stand alone as a complete sentence. They are structurally dependent on the main clause.

There are two types of dependent clauses: (1) those with a subordinating conjunction, and (2) those with a relative pronoun.

English   32

Sample coordinating conjunctions:
Although
When
If
Unless
Because

Unless a cure is discovered, many more people will die of the disease.
       Dependent clause   +   Independent clause

Sample relative pronouns:
Who
Whom
Which
That

The White House has an official website, which contains press releases, news updates, and biographies of the President and Vice-President.
(Independent clause + relative pronoun + relative dependent clause)

Misplaced and Dangling Modifiers

Particular phrases that are not placed near the one word they modify often result in misplaced modifiers. Particular phrases that do not relate to the subject being modified result in dangling modifiers.

Error: Weighing the options carefully, a decision was made regarding the punishment of the convicted murderer.

Problem: Who is weighing the options? No one capable of weighing is named in the sentence; thus, the participle phrase weighing the options carefully dangles. This problem can be corrected by adding a subject of the sentence capable of doing the action.

Correction: Weighing the options carefully, the judge made a decision regarding the punishment of the convicted murderer.

Error: Returning to my favorite watering hole, brought back many fond memories.

Problem: The person who returned is never indicated, and the participle phrase dangles. This problem can be corrected by creating a dependent clause from the modifying phrase.

Correction: When I returned to my favorite watering hole, many fond memories came back to me.

Error: One damaged house stood only to remind townspeople of the hurricane.

Problem: The placement of the misplaced modifier only suggests that the sole reason the house remained was to serve as a reminder. The faulty modifier creates ambiguity.

Correction: Only one damaged house stood, reminding townspeople of the hurricane.

Spelling

Concentration in this section will be on spelling plurals and possessives. The multiplicity and complexity of spelling rules based on phonics, letter doubling, and exceptions to rules - not mastered by adulthood - should be replaced by a good dictionary. As spelling mastery is also difficult for adolescents, our recommendation is the same. Learning the use of a dictionary and thesaurus will be a more rewarding use of time.

Most plurals of nouns that end in hard consonants or hard consonant sounds followed by a silent *e* are made by adding *s*. Some words ending in vowels only add *s*.

fingers, numerals, banks, bugs, riots, homes, gates, radios, bananas

Nouns that end in soft consonant sounds *s, j, x, z, ch,* and *sh*, add *es*. Some nouns ending in *o* add es.

dresses, waxes, churches, brushes, tomatoes, potatoes

Nouns ending in *y* preceded by a vowel just add *s*.

boys, alleys

Nouns ending in *y* preceded by a consonant change the *y* to *i* and add *es*.

babies, corollaries, frugalities, poppies

Some nouns plurals are formed irregularly or remain the same.

sheep, deer, children, leaves, oxen

Some nouns derived from foreign words, especially Latin, may make their plurals in two different ways - one of them Anglicized. Sometimes, the meanings are the same; other times, the two plurals are used in slightly different contexts. It is always wise to consult the dictionary.

appendices, appendixes	criterion, criteria
indexes, indices	crisis, crises

Make the plurals of closed (solid) compound words in the usual way except for words ending in *ful* which make their plurals on the root word.

timelines, hairpins, cupsful

Make the plurals of open or hyphenated compounds by adding the change in inflection to the word that changes in number.

fathers-in-law, courts-martial, masters of art, doctors of medicine

Make the plurals of letters, numbers, and abbreviations by adding *s.*

fives and tens, IBMs, 1990s, *p*s and *q*s (Note that letters are italicized.)

Skill 6.4 Revising nonstandard capitalization and punctuation.

Capitalization

Capitalize all proper names of persons (including specific organizations or agencies of government); places (countries, states, cities, parks, and specific geographical areas); and things (political parties, structures, historical and cultural terms, and calendar and time designations); and religious terms (any deity, revered person or group, sacred writings).

Percy Bysshe Shelley, Argentina, Mount Rainier National Park, Grand Canyon, League of Nations, the Sears Tower, Birmingham, Lyric Theater, Americans, Midwesterners, Democrats, Renaissance, Boy Scouts of America, Easter, God, Bible, Dead Sea Scrolls, Koran

Capitalize proper adjectives and titles used with proper names.

California gold rush, President John Adams, French fries, Homeric epic, Romanesque architecture, Senator John Glenn

Note: Some words that represent titles and offices are not capitalized unless used with a proper name.

Capitalized	Not Capitalized
Congressman McKay	the congressman from Florida
Commander Alger	commander of the Pacific Fleet
Queen Elizabeth	the queen of England

Capitalize all main words in titles of works of literature, art, and music.

(See "Using Italics" in the Punctuation section.)

The candidate should be cognizant of proper rules and conventions of punctuation, capitalization, and spelling. Competency exams will generally test the ability to apply the more advanced skills; thus, a limited number of more frustrating rules is presented here. Rules should be applied according to the American style of English, i.e. spelling *theater* instead of *theatre* and placing terminal marks of punctuation almost exclusively within other marks of punctuation.

Punctuation

Using terminal punctuation in relation to quotation marks

In a quoted statement that is either declarative or imperative, place the period inside the closing quotation marks.

> "The airplane crashed on the runway during takeoff."

If the quotation is followed by other words in the sentence, place a comma inside the closing quotations marks and a period at the end of the sentence.

> "The airplane crashed on the runway during takeoff," said the announcer.

In most instances in which a quoted title or expression occurs at the end of a sentence, the period is placed before either the single or double quotation marks.

> "The middle school readers were unprepared to understand Bryant's poem 'Thanatopsis.'"

> Early book-length adventure stories like *Don Quixote* and *The Three Musketeers* were known as "picaresque novels."

There is an instance in which the final quotation mark would precede the period - if the content of the sentence were about a speech or quote so that the understanding of the meaning would be confused by the placement of the period.

> The first thing out of his mouth was "Hi, I'm home."
> *but*
> The first line of his speech began "I arrived home to an empty house".

In sentences that are interrogatory or exclamatory, the question mark or exclamation point should be positioned outside the closing quotation marks if the quote itself is a statement or command or cited title.

Who decided to lead us in the recitation of the "Pledge of Allegiance"?

Why was Tillie shaking as she began her recitation, "Once upon a midnight dreary..."?

I was embarrassed when Mrs. White said, "Your slip is showing"!

In sentences that are declarative but the quotation is a question or an exclamation, place the question mark or exclamation point inside the quotation marks.

The hall monitor yelled, "Fire! Fire!"

"Fire! Fire!" yelled the hall monitor.

Cory shrieked, "Is there a mouse in the room?" (In this instance, the question supersedes the exclamation.)

Using periods with parentheses or brackets

Place the period inside the parentheses or brackets if they enclose a complete sentence, independent of the other sentences around it.

Stephen Crane was a confirmed alcohol and drug addict. (He admitted as much to other journalists in Cuba.)

If the parenthetical expression is a statement inserted within another statement, the period in the enclosure is omitted.

Mark Twain used the character Indian Joe (He also appeared in *The Adventures of Tom Sawyer*) as a foil for Jim in *The Adventures of Huckleberry Finn*.

When enclosed matter comes at the end of a sentence requiring quotation marks, place the period outside the parentheses or brackets.

"The secretary of state consulted with the ambassador [Albright]."

Using commas

Separate two or more coordinate adjectives, modifying the same word and three or more nouns, phrases, or clauses in a list.

Maggie's hair was dull, dirty, and lice-ridden.

Dickens portrayed the Artful Dodger as skillful pickpocket, loyal follower of Fagin, and defendant of Oliver Twist.

Ellen daydreamed about getting out of the rain, taking a shower, and eating a hot dinner.

In Elizabethan England, Ben Johnson wrote comedy, Christopher Marlowe wrote tragedies, and William Shakespeare composed both.

Use commas to separate antithetical or complimentary expressions from the rest of the sentence.

The veterinarian, not his assistant, would perform the delicate surgery.

The more he knew about her, the less he wished he had known.

Randy hopes to, and probably will, get an appointment to the Naval Academy.

His thorough, though esoteric, scientific research could not easily be understood by high school students.

Using double quotation marks with other punctuation

Quotations - whether words, phrases, or clauses - should be punctuated according to the rules of the grammatical function they serve in the sentence.

The works of Shakespeare, "the bard of Avon," have been contested as originating with other authors.

"You'll get my money," the old man warned, "when 'Hell freezes over'."

Sheila cited the passage that began "Four score and seven years ago...." (Note the ellipsis followed by an enclosed period.)

"Old Ironsides" inspired the preservation of the U.S.S. Constitution. Use quotation marks to enclose the titles of shorter works: songs, short poems, short stories, essays, and chapters of books. (See "Using Italics" for punctuating longer titles.)

"The Tell-Tale Heart"   "Casey at the Bat"   "America the Beautiful"

Using semicolons

Use semicolons to separate independent clauses when the second clause is introduced by a transitional adverb. (These clauses may also be written as separate sentences, preferably by placing the adverb within the second sentence.)

> The Elizabethans modified the rhyme scheme of the sonnet; thus, it was called the English sonnet.
>
> *or*
>
> The Elizabethans modified the rhyme scheme of the sonnet. It thus was called the English sonnet.

Use semicolons to separate items in a series that are long and complex or have internal punctuation.

> The Italian Renaissance produced masters in the fine arts: Dante Alighieri, author of the *Divine Comedy;* Leonardo da Vinci, painter of *The Last Supper;* and Donatello, sculptor of the *Quattro Coronati*, the four saints.

> The leading scorers in the WNBA were Haizhaw Zheng, averaging 23.9 points per game; Lisa Leslie, 22; and Cynthia Cooper, 19.5.

Using colons

Place a colon at the beginning of a list of items. (Note its use in the sentence about Renaissance Italians on the previous page.)

> The teacher directed us to compare Faulkner's three symbolic novels: *Absalom, Absalom; As I Lay Dying;* and *Light in August.*

Do **not** use a comma if the list is preceded by a verb.

> Three of Faulkner's symbolic novels are *Absalom, Absalom; As I Lay Dying,* and *Light in August.*

Using dashes

Place dashes to denote sudden breaks in thought.

> Some periods in literature - the Romantic Age, for example - spanned different time periods in different countries.

Use dashes instead of commas if commas are already used elsewhere in the sentence for amplification or explanation.

The Fireside Poets included three Brahmans - James Russell Lowell, Henry David Wadsworth, Oliver Wendell Holmes - and John Greenleaf Whittier.

Use italics to punctuate the titles of long works of literature, names of periodical publications, musical scores, works of art and motion picture television, and radio programs. (When unable to write in italics, students should be instructed to underline in their own writing where italics would be appropriate.)

The Idylls of the King	*Hiawatha*	*The Sound and the Fury*
Mary Poppins	*Newsweek*	*The Nutcracker Suite*

Skill 6.5 Applying appropriate conventions for documenting primary and secondary sources.

- Keep a record of any sources consulted during the research process.
- As you take notes, avoid unintentional plagiarism.
- Summarize and paraphrase in your own words without the source in front of you.
- Cite anything that is not common knowledge. This includes direct quotes as well as ideas or statistics.

Blueprint for Standard Attribution:

1. Begin the sentence with, "According to _____,"
2. Proceed with the material being cited, followed by the page number in parentheses.
3. Include the source information in a bibliography or works cited page.
(Last name, first name. *Book Title*. Location: Publisher, year.)

Example:

In-Text Citation-
According to Steve Mandel, "our average conversational rate of speech is about 125 words per minute" (78).

Works Cited Entry-
Mandel, Steve. *Effective Presentation Skills*. Menlo Park, California: Crisp
    Publications, 1993.

Skill 6.6 Recognizing the uses of word-processing technologies to revise texts.

In learning to write and in improving one's writing, the most useful exercise is editing/revising. Extensive revision is the hallmark of most successful writers. In the past, writers, student writers in particular, have been reluctant to revise because it meant beginning over to prepare the document for final presentation. However, that time is long gone. The writing of graduate dissertations took on a whole new dimension after the creation of the word processor and before long, classroom writing teachers were able to use this function to help students improve their writing.

Requiring extensive revision in writing classrooms nowadays is not unreasonable and can be an important stage in the production of papers. Microsoft Word has had a "tracking" capability in its last several upgrades, which carries revision a step further. Now the teacher and student can carry on a dialogue on the paper itself. The teacher's deletions and additions can be tracked, the student can respond, and the tracking will be facilitated by automatically putting the changes in a different color. The "comment" function makes it possible for both teacher and student to write notes at the exactly relevant point in the manuscript.

Skill 6.7 Recognizing strategies for self-editing and peer editing.

Viewing writing as a process allows teachers and students to see the writing classroom as a cooperative workshop where students and teachers encourage and support each other in each writing endeavor. Listed below are some techniques that help teachers to facilitate and create a supportive classroom environment.

1.   Create peer response/support groups that are working on similar writing assignments. The members help each other in all stages of the writing process-from prewriting, writing, revising, editing, and publishing.

2.   Provide several prompts to give students the freedom to write on a topic of their own. Writing should be generated out of personal experience and students should be introduced to in-class journals. One effective way to get into writing is to let them write often and freely about their own lives, without having to worry about grades or evaluation.

3.   Respond in the form of a question whenever possible. Teacher/facilitator should respond noncritically and use positive, supportive language.

4.   Respond to formal writing acknowledging the student's strengths and focusing on the composition skills demonstrated by the writing. A response should encourage the student by offering praise for what the student has done well. Give the student a focus for revision and

demonstrate that the process of revision has applications in many other writing situations.

5.   Provide students with readers' checklists so that students can write observational critiques of others' drafts, and then they can revise their own papers at home using the checklists as a guide.

6.   Pair students so that they can give and receive responses. Pairing students keeps them aware of the role of an audience in the composing process and in evaluating stylistic effects.

7.   Focus critical comments on aspects of the writing that can be observed in the writing. Comments like "I noticed you use the word 'is' frequently" will be more helpful than "Your introduction is dull" and will not demoralize the writer.

8.   Provide the group with a series of questions to guide them through the group writing sessions.

COMPETENCY 7.0 UNDERSTAND WRITING FOR INFORMATION AND UNDERSTANDING

Skill 7.1 Evaluating the appropriateness of language for various audiences and purposes.

Listening to students sitting on the steps that lead into the building that houses their classrooms, teachers will hear dialogue that may not even be understandable to them. The student who is writing to his peers will need to know and understand the peculiarities of that discourse in order to be very effective with them. This is a good example for students of what it means to tailor language for a particular audience and for a particular person.

This is a good time to teach the concept of jargon. Writing to be read by a lawyer is a different thing from writing to be read by a medical doctor. Writing to be read by parents is different from writing to be read by the administrator of the school. Not only are the vocabularies different, but the formality/informality of the discourse will need to be adjusted.

The things to be aware of in determining what the language should be for a particular audience, then, hinges on two things: vocabulary and formality/informality. The most formal language does not use contractions or slang. The most informal language will certainly use contractions and the slang that is appropriate for the particular audience. Formal language will use longer sentences and will not sound like a conversation. The most informal language will use shorter sentences—not necessarily simple sentences—but shorter constructions and will sound like a conversation.

Novels use formal language only when it is in the mouth of a character who would speak that way, such as a lawyer or a school superintendent. It's jarring to read a novel that has a construction worker using formal language. Using examples of various characters and their dialogues from fiction is useful in helping students understand this crucial aspect of writing.

Skill 7.2 Evaluating alternative thesis statements or organizational patterns for a formal essay or a research paper on a given topic.

Once a topic is assigned or chosen, the next step is to begin to gather supporting materials. Those materials may come from the writer's own experience, and the best way to collect them is in prewriting—simply putting on paper whatever is there by way of past experience relevant to the topic; observations concerning it; newspaper articles or books that have been read on the topic; and television or radio presentations that have to do with the topic. The writer needs to keep in mind the need to make a statement about the topic—to declare something about it. Very often, once the writer has gone through this exercise, getting his/her own ideas and thoughts down on paper, a thesis or several theses may emerge. If not, then it is time to do active research on the topic.

It's better to write more than one thesis statement before research begins if possible. However, a successful writer will set a point when a single one must be chosen so the development of the paper may proceed. Once that decision has been made, the narrowing process begins. The writer should be asking such questions as "Is the scope too broad to cover in a 500-word paper?" For example, if the thesis statement is "Democracy is the best form of government," it will take a book or even several books to develop. However, if the thesis statement is "Democracy is the best form of government for Iraq," then it begins to become more doable. Even so, some narrowing of the predicate may still be in order. "The development of a democratic government will solve the problems of cultural and religious divisions in Iraq" may be a thesis that could be developed in one classroom assignment.

Remembering that the introduction and conclusion should be written after the paper is developed so the writer will know what is being introduced and concluded. A decision should be made as to whether the reasoning will be inductive, from particular to general or deductive, general to particular. Will the pattern be inductive—evidence presented first and the thesis stated at the end? Will the thesis—the generalization—be presented first and then the proofs and evidence?

Will the introduction offer background information or be an anecdote or other device that will help lead the reader into the thesis and proofs? Or will it simply be designed to grab the reader's interest? It can also be used to establish the credibility of the writer. In the conclusion, will the reasoning be restated briefly with emphasis on the point of the paper, or will it also be anecdotal in nature? Whatever form it takes, it should reinforce the point the paper makes and leave the reader with a favorable impression.

Skill 7.3 Applying knowledge of writing techniques and styles used in journalism (inverted pyramid).

News reporters generally become excellent writers because they get a lot of practice, which is a principle most writing teachers try to employ with their students. Also, news writing is instructive in skills for writing clearly and coherently. Reporters generally write in two modes: straight reporting and feature writing. In both modes, the writer must be concerned with accuracy and objectivity. The reporter does not write his opinions. He/she does not write persuasive discourse. The topic is typically assigned, although some experienced reporters have the opportunity to seek out and develop their own stories.

Investigative reporting is sometimes seen as a distinct class although, technically, all reporters are "investigative." That is, they research the background of the story they're reporting, using as many means as are available. For example, the wife of a conservative, model minister murders him premeditatively and in cold blood. The reporter reports the murder and the arrest of the wife, but the story is far from complete until some questions are answered, the most obvious one being "why?" The reporter is obligated to try to answer that question and to do so will interview as many people as will talk to him about the lives of both minister and wife, their parents, members of the church, their neighbors, etc. The reporter will also look at newspaper archives in the town where the murder took place as well as in newspapers in any town the husband and/or wife has lived in previously. High-school yearbooks are a source that are often explored in these cases.

When Bob Woodward and Carl Bernstein, reporters for *The Washington Post,* began to break the Watergate story in 1972 and 1973, they set new standards for investigative reporting and had a strong influence on journalistic writing. Most reporters wanted to be Woodward and Bernstein and became more aggressive than reporters had been in the past. Even so, the basic techniques and principles still apply. The reporting of these two talented journalists demonstrated that while newspapers keep communities aware of what's going on, they also have the power to influence it.

A good news story is written as an "inverted pyramid." That is, the reasoning is deductive. The "thesis" or point is stated first and is supported with details. It reasons from general to specific. The lead sentence might be, "The body of John Smith was found in the street in front of his home with a bullet wound through his skull." The headline will be a trimmed-down version of that sentence and shaped to grab attention. It might read: "Murdered man found on Spruce Street." The news article might fill several columns, the first details having to do with the finding of the body, the next the role of the police; the third will spread out and include details about the victim's life, then the scope will broaden to details about his family, friends, neighbors, etc. If he held a position of prominence in the community, those details will broaden further and include information about his relationships to fellow-workers and his day-to-day contacts in the community. The successful reporter's skills include the ability to do thorough research, to maintain an objective stance (not to become involved personally in the story), and to write an effective "inverted pyramid."

Feature writing is more like an informative essay although it may also follow the inverted pyramid model. This form of reporting focuses on a topic designed to be interesting to at least one segment of the readership—possible sports enthusiasts, travelers, vacationers, families, women, food lovers, etc. The article will focus on one aspect of the area of interest such as a particular experience for the vacationing family.

The first sentence might read something like this: "Lake Lure offers a close-to-home relaxing weekend getaway for families in East Tennessee." The development can be an ever-widening pyramid of details focused particularly on what the family can experience at Lake Lure but also directions for how to get there.

While the headline is intended to contain in capsule form the point that an article makes, it is rarely written by the reporter. This can sometimes result in a disconnection between headline and article. Well-written headlines will provide a guide for the reader as to what is in the article; they will also be attention-grabbers. This requires a special kind of writing, quite different from the inverted pyramid that distinguishes these writers from the investigative or feature reporter.

Skill 7.4 Evaluating the appropriateness of language and formats for various products of expository writing (business letter or complaint, news article, formal essay).

It may seem sometimes that the **business letter** is a thing of the past. Although much business-letter writing has been relegated to email communications, letters are still a valuable and potentially valuable form of communication. A carefully-written letter can be powerful. It can alienate, convince, persuade, entice, motivate, and/or create good-will.

As with any other communication, it's worthwhile to learn as much as possible about the receiver. This may be complicated if there will be more than one receiver of the message; in these cases, it's best to aim for the lowest common denominator if that can be achieved without "writing down" to any of those who will read and be affected or influenced by the letter. It may be better to send more than one form of the letter to the various receivers in some cases.

Purpose is the most powerful factor in writing a business letter. What is the letter expected to accomplish? Is it intended to get the receiver to act or to act in a specific manner? Are you hoping to see some action take place as the result of the letter? If so, you should clearly define for yourself what the purpose is before you craft the letter, and it's good to include a time deadline for the response.

Reasons for choosing the letter as the channel of communication include the following:
1. It's easy to keep a record of the transaction.
2. The message can be edited and perfected before it is transmitted.
3. It facilitates the handling of details.
4. It's ideal for communicating complex information.
5. It's a good way to disseminate mass messages at a relatively low cost.

The parts of a business letter are as follow: date line, inside address, salutation, subject line*, body, complimentary close, company name*, signature block, reference initials*, enclosure notation*, copy notation*, and postscript*.

Business letters typically use formal language. They should be straightforward and courteous. The writing should be concise, and special care should be taken to leave no important information out. Clarity is very important; otherwise, it may take more than one exchange of letters or phone calls to get the message across.

A complaint is a different kind of business letter. It can come under the classification of a "bad news" business letter, and there are some guidelines that are helpful when writing this kind of letter. A positive writing style can overcome much of the inherent negativity of a letter of complaint. No matter how much in the right you may be, maintaining self-control and courtesy and avoiding demeaning or blaming language is more likely to be effective. Abruptness, condescension, or harshness of tone will not help achieve your purpose, particularly if you are requesting a positive response such as reimbursement for a bad product or some help in righting a wrong that may have been done to you. It's important to remember that you want to solve the specific problem and to retain the good will of the receiver if possible.

Induction is better than deduction for this type of communication. Beginning with the details and building to the statement of the problem generally has the effect of softening the bad news. It's also useful to begin with an opening that will serve as a buffer. The same is true for the closing. It's good to leave the reader with a favorable impression by writing a closing paragraph that will generate good will rather than bad.

News articles are written in the "inverted pyramid" format—they are deductive in nature: the opening statement is the point of the article; everything else is details. "Who, what, why, when, and where" are usually the questions to be answered in a news article.

A formal essay, on the other hand, may be persuasive, informative, descriptive, or narrative in nature. The purpose should be clearly defined, and development must be coherent and easy to follow.

Email has revolutionized business communications. It has most of the advantages of business letters and the added ones of immediacy, lower costs, and convenience. Even very long reports can be attached to an email. On the other hand, a two-line message can be sent and a response received immediately bringing together the features of a postal system and the telephone. Instant messaging goes even one step further. It can do all of the above—send messages, attach reports, etc.—and still have many of the advantages of a telephone conversation. Email has an unwritten code of behavior that includes restrictions on how informal the writing can be. The level of accepted business conversation is usually also acceptable in emails. Capital letters and bolding are considered shouting and are usually frowned on.

*not required but sometimes useful.

Skill 7.5 Applying knowledge of objective vs. subjective points of view (news stories vs. editorials).

Freedom of the press is essential to democracy. In this form of government, representatives are elected by the people, are responsible to them, and they are entitled to know what those representatives are doing. The only way that can happen is if the press is free to report the news in an unbiased manner. If the mayor of a city has a conflict of interest that is profiting him, the people need to know. If an elected representative is arrested for driving under the influence, that representative's constituency has a right to know. It's the only way unbiased management of the public interest can occur. For these reasons, news media have an obligation to keep themselves unencumbered and unbiased. Most news people pride themselves on their objectivity.

News stories are always assumed to be unbiased. It can be argued, of course, that no one can be entirely unbiased and that it's the nature of the written word that those biases may creep into the reporting of news. Even so, the professional reporter and/or editor will exercise the strength necessary to keep his or her own biases out of the reporting as much as possible.

Editorializing is an entirely different thing. Most newspapers, for instance, have an editorial position, which will often correspond to political parties. A newspaper may, for instance, declare itself to be Republican. This does not mean that the newspaper will favor the party of choice in news reporting. It does, however mean that editorial materials will probably be slanted in that direction. In a time of election, a newspaper will often come out for one candidate over another and try to influence its readership to follow suit. A newspaper will often take a side when an *issue* is on the docket at time of election or even at other times. An editorial will frequently state an opinion about a matter that concerns the newspaper's readership.

Skill 7.6 Revising drafts to improve their effectiveness.

Sometimes this exercise is seen by students as simply catching errors in spelling or word use. Students need to reframe their thinking about revising and editing. Some questions that need to be asked:

- Is the reasoning coherent?
- Is the point established?
- Does the introduction make the reader want to read this discourse?

- What is the thesis? Is it proven?
- What is the purpose? Is it clear? Is it useful, valuable, interesting?
- Is the style of writing so wordy that it exhausts the reader and interferes with engagement?
- Is the writing so spare that it is boring?
- Are the sentences too uniform in structure?
- Are there too many simple sentences?
- Are too many of the complex sentences the same structure?
- Are the compounds truly compounds or are they unbalanced?
- Are parallel structures truly parallel?
- If there are characters, are they believable?
- If there is dialogue, is it natural or stilted?
- Is the title appropriate?
- Does the writing show creativity or is it boring?
- Is the language appropriate? Is it too formal? Too informal? If jargon is used, is it appropriate?

Studies have clearly demonstrated that the most fertile area in teaching writing is this one. If students can learn to revise their own work effectively, they are well on their way to becoming effective, mature writers. Word processing is an important tool for teaching this stage in the writing process. Microsoft Word has tracking features that make the revision exchanges between teachers and students more effective than ever before.

Skill 7.7 Applying knowledge of strategies for incorporating information from charts, graphs, and tables into expository writing.

The old adage that a picture is worth a thousand words is never more evident than in the use of charts, graphs, and tables into expository writing. It's one thing to say that the GDP of the United States rose fifteen percentage points in the last five years, it's an entirely different thing to show a graph that depicts that rapid rise. If the point being made is that the increase in the GDP is better than it has ever been in the past fifty years, then a graph showing that growth cinches the point. If the point being made is that the growth in the GDP corresponds to the growth of the stock market for the same period, then that also can be graphed.

It's important that data in charts and graphs be simple and comprehensive. Also, it should only be used if it does, in fact, display the information more effectively than words alone can. However, it should also be able to stand alone. It should make the point by itself. If two or more charts or tables are used within a work, they should be consistent in style. Whatever graphic is used, elements of the same kind must always be represented in the same way. This is not a time to be artistic graphically; visual effects should be used only for the purpose of making the point, not for variety.

In graphs, both the horizontal and vertical axes should be labeled. In a column, both column heads and stubs should be labeled. In a graph, the vertical axis is always read from the bottom up and curves or bars should be graphically distinct (color or dotted lines, for example) and all elements should be clearly identified in a key. The title appears in a caption rather than as a title and is lowercased except for names that would normally be capitalized in the text. If abbreviations are used, care should be taken to make them easily recognizable unless they are explained in the key or in the caption.

A table can often give information that would take several paragraphs to present and can do so more clearly. Tables should be as simple as the material allows and should be understandable without explanation even to a reader who might be unfamiliar with the subject matter. Only necessary explanations should be presented in the text; the table should be able to stand alone.

The advent of word processing makes the creation and insertion of charts, graphs, and tables much more practical than ever before. It takes very little knowledge or skill to create these illustrative devices, and helping students develop those skills is a valuable enhancement to a writing course.

COMPETENCY 8.0 UNDERSTAND WRITING FOR LITERARY RESPONSE AND EXPRESSION

Skill 8.1 Evaluating the appropriateness of language for various audiences and purposes.

In the past teachers have assigned reports, paragraphs and essays that focused on the teacher as the audience with the purpose of explaining information. However, for students to be meaningfully engaged in their writing, they must write for a variety of reasons. Writing for different audiences and aims allows students to be more involved in their writing. If they write for the same audience and purpose, they will continue to see writing as just another assignment. Listed below are suggestions that give students an opportunity to write in more creative and critical ways.

* Write letters to the editor, to a college, to a friend, to another student that would be sent to the intended audience.

* Write stories that would be read aloud to a group (the class, another group of students, to a group of elementary school students) or published in a literary magazine or class anthology.

* Write plays that would be performed.

* Have students discuss the parallels between the different speech styles we use and writing styles for different readers or audiences.

* Allow students to write a particular piece for different audiences.

* Make sure students consider the following when analyzing the needs of their audience.

  1. Why is the audience reading my writing? Do they expect to be informed, amused or persuaded?
  2. What does my audience already know about my topic?
  3. What does the audience want or need to know? What will interest them?
  4. What type of language suits my readers?

* As part of the prewriting have students identify the audience.

  * Expose students to writing that is on the same topic but with a different audience and have them identify the variations in sentence structure and style.

* Remind your students that it is not necessary to identify all the specifics of the audience in the initial stage of the writing process but that at some point they must make some determinations about audience.

Skill 8.2 Applying strategies for writing a response to a literary selection by referring to the text, to other works, and to personal experience.

The first essential principle in the writing of an analysis of a literary selection is a thorough reading and understanding of the work. Once the writer feels that the author's intent is clearly understood, the thesis statement of the analysis must be determined. It will probably be a declaration of the purpose of the author in the work, itself. For example, if one were analyzing Mitch Albom's *The Five People You Meet in Heaven*, the thesis for the analysis might be as follows: "The theme of this story is that living to serve others gives meaning to the end of one's life."

However, the writer can make a point that is meaningful by focusing on other aspects of the story. For example, the *style* of a writer like Ernest Hemingway is so unusual and significant that the thesis might focus on that aspect of one of his stories. Setting may play a special role in a story and might make a good thesis for analysis. In fact, any aspect of the story can be useful for this kind of paper. This choice is important and will drive how the analysis is developed.

Once the thesis is decided, the next steps just naturally fall in line. The first step is a search for passages that support or relate to the theme idea. Even before the thesis has been decided upon, the writer should have been taking notes, possibly on the pages of the book itself. Once the thesis is determined, then he/she will go back through the work, looking at the notes already made but adding or adjusting them to make sure adequate material is available to support the thesis of the analysis. By this time, the notes should begin to be recorded on a sheet of paper or in the word processor. Specifics are important here as are details if the analysis is to be complete and effective. In this second reading, the thesis might change—either to an entirely different one or to a variation of the first one.

It's not enough to just present illustrative material; it must be organized in such a way that it is logical and reasonable to the reader of the analysis. In other words, a preliminary outline of the final paper should be determined here. The steps may be in a different order than the illustrations appear in the work itself. One from later in the book might be relevant to an earlier one. The earlier one might foreshadow a later one, for instance.

In referring to a work of fiction, the record should always be in the present tense. For example, instead of Eddie *worked* in a maintenance shop—spreading grease, tightening bolts, etc., it should be: Eddie works in a maintenance shop—spreading grease, tightening bolts, etc. Keeping the tenses in the present requires special care. This is a good exercise in verb tenses for students.

It should be remembered that this is a recursive process. Nothing is set in stone until the paper is ready to be handed in. Things will be seen on the second and third readings that were not apparent the first time through, and the writer must feel free to make changes that make the point clearer or stronger. Even the thesis or the aspect of the story that will be the focus of the analysis is open to change until the last stage of the writing process. Students sometimes have difficulty coming to a decision, so they should be encouraged to set time limits on themselves for making the decisions and completing the various steps required to write a successful paper.

Helping students become successful writers of literary analyses depends on several factors. They should have plenty of experience in analysis in class. The short story is a good way to help students develop the confidence that they can do this kind of writing, which requires independent reasoning. Using the short story as the basis for a writing course gives students more opportunities to go through the analyzing process and gives them more opportunities to practice their analytical skills. The role of the teacher is to continually teach the principles but also to encourage independent thinking in these matters, even to accept sometimes less-than-perfect analyses.

Ultimately, the analysis should be the convictions arrived upon as a result of the reading and understanding the text. This is a good opportunity to help students begin to take responsibility for what they write—an important objective for a writing course.

Skill 8.3 Applying strategies for writing an analysis of an author's use of literary elements (plot, characters, setting, theme, point of view).

Writing about an author's use of plot should begin with determining what the conflicts are. In a naturalist story, the conflicts may be between the protagonist and a hostile or indifferent world. Sometimes, the conflicts are between two characters, the protagonist and the antagonist; and sometimes the conflicts are internal—between two forces within an individual character that have created a dilemma. For example, a Catholic priest may be devoted and committed to his role in the Church that calls for a celibate life yet at the same time be deeply in love with a woman.

Once the conflicts have been determined, the pattern of action will hinge on how the story comes out. Who (or what) wins and who (or what) loses. If the protagonist struggles throughout the story but emerges triumphant in the end, the pattern is said to be rising. On the other hand, if the story is about the downfall of the major character, the story can be said to be falling. If there is no winner in the end, the pattern is flat. This is an important point for a writer to make because it is crucial to all other aspects of an analysis of a work of fiction.

Characters are developed in many ways. Sometimes the writer simply tells the reader what kind of person this is. More often, however, the reader is left to deduce the characteristics from dialogue with others; with what other characters think or say about him/her; with description—what the character looks like, tall, short, thin, plump, dark-haired, gray-haired, etc. The techniques a writer uses to define character are called characterization, and a writer will usually deal with these matters when writing an analysis.

Setting can be a period of time, the 1930s, for example. It can also be a place, either a real place like a particular city or a fictional place like a farm or a mansion. It can be emotional—some of Truman Capote's stories are set in an atmosphere of fear and danger, and the effectiveness of the story depends on that setting. An analysis should deal with the *function* of the setting in the story. For example, if it is set in a particular period of time as *The Great Gatsby* is, would it be a different story if it were set in a different period of time? A setting can sometimes function as a symbol, so the writer should be looking for that as a possibility.

Theme in a work of fiction is similar to a thesis in an essay. It's the *point* the story makes. In a story, it may possibly be spoken by one of the characters; but more often, it is left to the writer to determine. This requires careful reading and should take into account the other aspects of the story before a firm decision is made with regard to the point of the story. Different analysts will come to different conclusions about what a story means. Very often the thesis of an analytical essay will be the writer's declaration of the theme according to his/her own well-reasoned opinion.

Point of view seems simple on the surface, but it rarely is in a story. In fact, Wallace Hildick wrote *Thirteen Types of Narrative* to explain point of view in literature. The most common ones are first person narrator objective in which the person telling the story only records his/her observations of what is happening. In this point of view, the only clues as to what the characters are like come from the narrator. The attitude of the narrator toward the theme or the characters will be an important part of the story and should be dealt with in an analysis. Sometimes, its' apparent that the narrator's view does not square with reality, in which the narrator becomes unreliable and the reader must make an effort to determine what is real and what is not. If a writer uses this device, it's extremely important that the analyst point it out and analyze what it does for the story.

The first person narrator may know what one or more of the characters is thinking and that will be important to the analysis of the story. If the narrator knows this, how did he/she acquire the knowledge? The most logical way is that the story was told to the narrator in the first place by that character or those characters.

Third person objective is another common form of development. In this point of view, there is no narrator. The story is told by an unseen observer. The reader does not know what anyone is thinking, only what is being said and described.

Third person omniscient is also fairly common. In this point of view, the story is being told by an unseen observer, but the observer is able to know what at least one person is thinking, which is sometimes called limited omniscient point of view. The reader may also know what most or all of the characters are thinking, and this point of view is simply called third-person omniscient.

Point of view is extremely powerful in the way a story is perceived and must be dealt with in a written analysis.

Skill 8.4 Analyzing written interpretations that explicate multiple layers of meaning in literary texts.

To *interpret* means essentially to read with understanding and appreciation. It is not as daunting as it is made out to be. Simple techniques for interpreting literature are as follows:

- **Context:** This includes the author's feelings, beliefs, past experiences, goals, needs, and physical environment. Incorporate an understanding of how these elements may have affected the writing to enrich an interpretation of it.
- **Symbols:** Also referred to as a sign, a symbol designates something which stands for something else. In most cases, it is standing for something that has a deeper meaning than its literal denotation. Symbols can have personal, cultural, or universal associations. Use an understanding of symbols to unearth a meaning the author might have intended but not expressed, or even something the author never intended at all.
- **Questions:** Asking questions, such as "How would I react in this situation?" may shed further light on how you feel about the work.

Skill 8.5 Demonstrating knowledge of techniques for writing a variety of original imaginative works (stories, poems, plays) that observe conventions of genre and use inventive language and text structures. Stories.

It seems simplistic, yet it's an often-overlooked truism: the first and most important measure of a story is the story itself. *The story's the thing.* However, a good story must have certain characteristics. Without conflict there is no story, so determining what the conflicts are should be a priority for the writer. Once the conflicts are determined, the outcome of the story must be decided. Who wins? Who loses? And what factors go into making one side of the equation win out over the other one? The pattern of the plot is also an important consideration.

Where is the climax going to occur? Is denouement necessary? Does the reader need to see the unwinding of all the strands? Many stories fail because a denouement is needed but not supplied.

Characterization, the choice the writer makes about the devices he/she will use to reveal character, requires an understanding of human nature and the artistic skill to convey a personality to the reader. This is usually accomplished subtly through dialogue, interior monologue, description, and the character's actions and behavior. In some successful stories, the writer comes right out and tells the reader what this character is like. However, sometimes there will be discrepancies between what the narrator tells the reader about the character and what is revealed to be actual, in which case the narrator is unreliable, and that unreliability of the voice the reader must depend on becomes an important and significant device for understanding the story.

Point of view is a powerful tool not only for the writer but for the enjoyment and understanding of the reader. The writer must choose among several possibilities: first-person narrator objective, first-person narrator omniscient, third-person objective, third-person omniscient, and third-person limited omniscient. The most successful story-writers use point of view very creatively to accomplish their purposes. If a writer wishes to be successful, he/she must develop point-of-view skills.

Style—the unique way a writer uses language—is often the writer's signature. The reader does not need to be told that William Faulkner wrote a story to know it because his style is so distinctive that it is immediately recognizable. Even the writing of Toni Morrison, which could be said to be Faulknerian, cannot be mistaken for the work of Faulkner, himself. The writer must be cognizant of his/her own strengths and weaknesses and continually work to hone the way sentences are written, words are chosen, and descriptions are crafted until they are razor-sharp. The best advice to the aspiring writer: read the works of successful writers. If a writer wants to write a best-seller, then that writer needs to be reading best-sellers.

Poetry. Writing poetry in the 21st century is quite a different thing from writing it in earlier periods. There was a time when a poem was required to fit a certain pattern or scheme. Poetry was once defined as a piece of writing that was made up of end-rhymes. No more. The rhymed poem makes up only a small percentage of worthwhile and successful poems nowadays.

The first skill to work on for the budding poet is descriptive writing, defined as language that appeals to one or more of the five senses. A good poem makes it possible for the reader to experience an emotional event—seeing a mountain range as the sun dawns, watching small children on a playground, smelling the fragrance of a rose, hearing a carillon peal a religious tune at sunset, feeling fine silk under one's fingers.

Creating language that makes that experience available to the readers is only the first step, however, because the ultimate goal is to evoke an emotional response. Feeling the horror of the battleground, weeping with the mother whose child was drowned, exulting with a winning soccer team. It's not enough to tell the reader what it's like. It's the *showing* that is necessary.

The aspiring poet should know the possibilities as well as the limitations of this genre. A poem can tell a story, for instance, but the emotional response is more important than the story itself. Edgar Allen Poe, in an 1842 review of Hawthorne's *Twice-Told Tales* in *Graham's Magazine* had important advice for the writer of poetry: " . . . the unity of effect or impression is a point of the greatest importance." Even though he considered the tale or short story the best way to achieve this, he wrote several memorable poems and much of his prose writing is considered to be as close to poetry as to prose by most critics. He also wrote in 1847, in an expansion of his critique of Hawthorne's works, that " . . .true originality . . .is that which, in bringing out the half-formed, the reluctant, or the unexpressed fancies of mankind, or in exciting the more delicate pulses of the heart's passion, or in giving birth to some universal sentiment or instinct in embryo, thus combines with the pleasurable effect of *apparent* novelty, a real egoistic delight."

Play writing. Play writing uses many of the same skills that are necessary to successful story writing. However, in addition to those skills, there are many more required of the writer who wishes his/her story to be told on stage or on film. The point of view, of course, is always objective unless the writers uses the Shakespearean device of the soliloquy, where a player steps forward and gives information about what's going on. The audience must figure out the meaning of the play on the basis of the actions and speeches of the actors.

A successful playwright is expert in characterization as described above under **Story**. What a character is like is determined by dialogue, appearance (costume, etc.), behavior, actions. A successful playwright also understands motivation. If a character's behavior cannot be traced to motivating circumstances, the audience will probably find the action incoherent—a major barrier to positive reception of the play.

The writing must be very carefully honed. Absolutely no excess of words can be found in a successful play. It takes very little time to lose an audience; every word counts. The playwright should concentrate on saying the most possible with the fewest words possible.

Setting is an important feature of the play. Most plays have only one because changing settings in the middle is difficult and disrupting. This calls for a very special kind of writing. The entire action of the play must either take place within the setting or be brought forth in that setting by the reporting or recounting of what is going on outside of the setting by one or more of the characters.

The writer must determine what the setting will be. The actual building and creation of the set is in the hands of another kind of artist—one who specializes in settings.

The plot of most plays is rising; that is, the conflicts are introduced early in the play and continue to develop and intensify over the life of the play. As a general rule, the climax is the last thing that happens before the final curtain falls, but not necessarily. Plots of plays demonstrate the same breadth of patterns that are true of stories. For example, a play may end with nothing resolved. Denouement is less likely to follow a climax in a play than in a story, but epilogues do sometimes occur.

Skill 8.6 Demonstrating awareness of voice in writing for literary response and expression.

There are at least thirteen possible choices for point of view (voice) in literature as demonstrated and explained by Wallace Hildick in his *13 Types of Narrative* (London: MacMillan and Co., 1968). However, for purposes of helping students write essays about literature, three, or possibly four, are adequate. The importance of teaching students to use this aspect of a piece of literature to write about it is not just as an analytic exercise but also should help them think about how a writer's choices impact the overall effect of the work.

Point of view or voice is essentially through whose eyes the reader sees the action. The most common is the third-person objective. If the story is seen from this point of view, the reader watches the action, hears the dialogue, reads descriptions and from all of those must deduce characterization—what sort of person a character is. In this point of view, an unseen narrator tells the reader what is happening, using the third person, he, she, it, they. The effect of this point of view is usually a feeling of distance from the plot. More responsibility is on the reader to make judgments than in other points of view. However, the author may intrude and evaluate or comment on the characters or the action.

The voice of the first-person narrator is often used also. The reader sees the action through the eyes of an actor in the story who is also telling the story. In writing about a story that uses this voice, the narrator must be analyzed as a character. What sort of person is this? What is this character's position in the story—observer, commentator, actor? Can the narrator be believed, or is he/she biased? The value of this voice is that, while the reader is able to follow the narrator around and see what is happening through that character's eyes, the reader is also able to feel what the narrator feels. For this reason, the writer can involve the reader more intensely in the story itself and move the reader by invoking feelings—pity, sorrow, anger, hate, confusion, disgust, etc. Many of the most memorable novels are written in this point of view.

Another voice often used may best be titled "omniscient" because the reader is able to get into the mind of more than one character or sometimes all the characters. This point of view can also bring greater involvement of the reader in the story. By knowing what a character is thinking and feeling, the reader is able to empathize when a character feels great pain and sorrow, which tends to make a work memorable. On the other hand, knowing what a character is thinking makes it possible to get into the mind of a pathological murderer and may elicit horror or disgust.

"Omniscient" can be broken down into third-person omniscient or first-person omniscient. In third-person omniscient, the narrator is not seen or known or acting in the story but is able to watch and record not only what is happening or being said, but what characters are thinking. In first-person omniscient on the other hand, the narrator plays a role in the story but can also record what other characters are thinking. It is possible, of course, that the narrator is the pathological murderer, which creates an effect quite different than a story where the thoughts of the murderer are known but the narrator is standing back and reporting his behavior, thoughts, and intents.

Point of view or voice is a powerful tool in the hands of a skillful writer. The questions to be answered in writing an essay about a literary work are: What point of view has this author used? What effect does it have on the story? If it had been written in a different voice, how would the story be different?

Most credible literary works are consistent in point of view but not always, so consistency is another aspect that should be analyzed. Does the point of view change? Where does it vary? Does it help or hurt the effect of the story?

COMPTENCY 9.0 UNDERSTAND WRITING FOR CRITICAL ANALYSIS, EVALUATION, AND PERSUASION

Skill 9.1 Evaluating the appropriateness of language for various audiences and purposes.

- **Values**- What is important to this group of people? What is their background and how will that affect their perception of your speech?
- **Needs**- Find out in advance what the audience's needs are. Why are they listening to you? Find a way to satisfy their needs.
- **Constraints**- What might hold the audience back from being fully engaged in what you are saying, or agreeing with your point of view, or processing what you are trying to say? These could be political reasons, which make them wary of your presentation's ideology from the start, or knowledge reasons, in which the audience lacks the appropriate background information to grasp your ideas. Avoid this last constraint by staying away from technical terminology, slang, or abbreviations that may be unclear to your audience.
- **Demographic Information**- Take the audience's size into account, as well as the location of the presentation.

Start where the listeners are, and then take them where you want to go!

Skill 9.2 Analyzing the organization of an editorial or argumentative essay on a given topic.

A logical argument consists of three stages. First of all, the propositions which are necessary for the argument to continue are stated. These are called the premises of the argument. They are the evidence or reasons for accepting the argument and its conclusions.

Premises (or assertions) are often indicated by phrases such as "because", "since", "obviously" and so on. (The phrase "obviously" is often viewed with suspicion, as it can be used to intimidate others into accepting suspicious premises. If something doesn't seem obvious to you, don't be afraid to question it. You can always say "Oh, yes, you're right, it is obvious" when you've heard the explanation.)

Next, the premises are used to derive further propositions by a process known as inference. In inference, one proposition is arrived at on the basis of one or more other propositions already accepted. There are various forms of valid inference.

The propositions arrived at by inference may then be used in further inference. Inference is often denoted by phrases such as "implies that" or "therefore".

Finally, we arrive at the conclusion of the argument -- the proposition which is affirmed on the basis of the premises and inference. Conclusions are often indicated by phrases such as "therefore", "it follows that", "we conclude" and so on. The conclusion is often stated as the final stage of inference.

Classical Argument

In its simplest form, the classical argument has five main parts:

The **introduction**, which warms up the audience, establishes goodwill and rapport with the readers, and announces the general theme or thesis of the argument.

The **narration**, which summarizes relevant background material, provides any information the audience needs to know about the environment and circumstances that produce the argument, and set up the stakes–what's at risk in this question.

The **confirmation**, which lays out in a logical order (usually strongest to weakest or most obvious to most subtle) the claims that support the thesis, providing evidence for each claim.

The **refutation and concession**, which looks at opposing viewpoints to the writer's claims, anticipating objections from the audience, and allowing as much of the opposing viewpoints as possible without weakening the thesis.

The **summation**, which provides a strong conclusion, amplifying the force of the argument, and showing the readers that this solution is the best at meeting the circumstances.

Skill 9.3 Distinguishing reasons, examples, or details that support a given argument or opinion.

Once a thesis is put forth, there are various ways to support it. The most obvious one is reasons. Usually a reason will answer the question why. Another technique is to give examples. A third is to give details.

The presentation of a prosecutor in a court trial is a good example of an argument that uses all of these.

The **thesis** of the prosecutor may be: John O'Hara stole construction materials from a house being built at 223 Hudson Ave. by the Jones Construction Company. As a **reason**, he might cite the following:

He is building his own home on Green Street and needs materials and tools. This will answer the question why. He might give **examples**: 20 bags of concrete disappeared the night before Mr. O'Hara poured the basement for his house on Green Street. The electronic nail-setter disappeared from the building site on Hudson Ave. the day before Mr. O'Hara began to erect the frame of his house on Green Street. He might fill in the **details**: Mr. O'Hara's truck was observed by a witness on Hudson Ave. in the vicinity of the Jones Construction Company site the night the concrete disappeared. Mr. O'Hara's truck was observed again on that street by a witness the night the nail-setter disappeared.

Another example of a trial might be: **Thesis**, Adam Andrews murdered Joan Rogers in cold blood on the night of December 20. **Reason #1**: She was about to reveal their affair to his wife. **Reason #2**: Andrews' wife would inherit half of his sizeable estate in case of a divorce since there is no prenuptial agreement. **Example #1**: Rogers has demonstrated that he is capable of violence in an incident with a partner in his firm. **Example #2**: Rogers has had previous affairs where he was accused of violence. **Detail #1**: Andrews' wife once called the police and signed a warrant. **Detail #2**: A previous lover sought police protection from Andrews.

An **opinion** is a thesis and requires support. It can also use reasons, examples, and details.

For example:

Opinion: Our borders must be protected.

Reason #1: Terrorists can get into the country undetected. **Example #1**: An Iranian national was able to cross the Mexican border and live in this country for years before being detected. **Detail**: The Iranian national came up through Central America to Mexico then followed the route that Mexican illegal immigrants regularly took. **Example #2**: a group of Middle Eastern terrorists were arrested in Oregon after they had crossed the Canadian border. **Detail**: There was no screening at that border.

Reason #2: Illegal aliens are an enormous drain on resources such as health care. **Example**: The states of California and Texas bear enormous burdens for health care and education for illegal immigrants. **Detail**: Legal citizens are often denied care in those states because resources are stretched so thin.

Skill 9.4 Identifying and analyzing techniques for expressing point of view and avoiding bias in persuasive writing.

It's not necessary to write "I believe that . . . ." for a statement to be attributed to the writer. The very fact that it comes from him or her assumes that. The judgment should be stated simply and positively rather than negatively.

If the statement has multiple phrases and clauses, developing it will be complicated. A simple, straightforward statement is better. For example: "The Mexican border should be closed." If another clause is added: "The Mexican border should be closed and all illegal immigrants should be sent home," then both issues must be proven and substantiated, and the reasoning tends to become confusing and muddy.

Once a position is taken, then reasons must be formulated: Terrorists can come across the open border; finding solutions to the increasing numbers of illegal immigrants becomes more difficult every year; it will be possible to control immigration with a closed border. Each of those points can be developed with reasoning and examples.

To avoid bias, all points of view must be taken into account. A good exercise is to argue the opposing point of view in order to understand the opposition. Also, establishing one's own credibility in a paper where there will be a strong counter-argument is helpful. The writer can demonstrate why he/she has no personal interest in either side, which will focus the writing on the reasoning rather than on the writer.

Skill 9.5 Recognizing how to use transitions to enhance the clarity of a line of argument.

A mark of maturity in writing is the effective use of transitional devices at all levels. For example, a topic sentence can be used to establish continuity, especially if it is positioned at the beginning of a paragraph. The most common use would be to refer to what has preceded, repeat it, or summarize it and then go on to introduce a new topic. An essay by W. H. Hudson uses this device: "Although the potato was very much to me in those early years, it grew to be more when I heard its history." It summarizes what has preceded, makes a comment on the author's interest, and introduces a new topic: the history of the potato.

Another example of a transitional sentence could be, "Not all matters end so happily." This refers to the previous information and prepares for the next paragraph, which will be about matters that do not end happily. This transitional sentence is a little more forthright: "The increase in drug use in our community leads us to another general question."

Another fairly simple and straightforward transitional device is the use of numbers or their approximation: "First, I want to talk about the dangers of immigration; second, I will discuss the enormity of the problem; third, I will propose a reasonable solution."

An entire paragraph may be transitional in purpose and form. In "Darwiniana," Thomas Huxley used a transitional paragraph:

So much, then, by way of proof that the method of establishing laws in science is exactly the same as that pursued in common life. Let us now turn to another matter (though really it is but another phase of the same question), and that is, the method by which, from the relations of certain phenomena, we prove that some stand in the position of causes toward the others.

The most common transitional device is a single word. Some examples: *and, furthermore, next, moreover, in addition, again, also, likewise, similarly, finally, second*, etc. There are many.

In marking student papers, a teacher can encourage a student to think in terms of moving coherently from one idea to the next by making transitions between the two. If the shift from one thought to another is too abrupt, the student can be asked to provide a transitional paragraph. Lists of possible transitions can be put on a handout and students can be encouraged to have the list at hand when composing essays. These are good tools for nudging students to more mature writing styles.

Skill 9.6 Analyzing fallacies in logic and other forms of weak reasoning in a piece of persuasive writing.

See Skill 3.2.

Skill 9.7 Demonstrating awareness of voice in writing for critical analysis, evaluation, and persuasion.

See Skill 8.6.

COMPETENCY 10.0 UNDERSTAND WRITING FOR PERSONAL EXPRESSION AND SOCIAL INTERACTION

Skill 10.1 Demonstrating awareness of connotation and figurative meaning in selecting language for a given expressive purpose.

To effectively teach language, it is necessary to understand that, as human beings acquire language, they realize that words have <u>denotative</u> and <u>connotative</u> meanings. Generally, denotative words point to things and connotative words deal with mental suggestions that the words convey. The word *skunk* has a denotative meaning if the speaker can point to the actual animal as he speaks the word and intends the word to identify the animal. *Skunk* has connotative meaning depending upon the tone of delivery, the socially acceptable attitudes about the animal, and the speaker's personal feelings about the animal.

Informative connotations

Informative connotations are definitions agreed upon by the society in which the learner operates. A *skunk* is "a black and white mammal of the weasel family with a pair of perineal glands which secrete a pungent odor." The *Merriam Webster Collegiate Dictionary* adds "...and offensive" odor. Identification of the color, species, and glandular characteristics are informative. The interpretation of the odor as *offensive* is affective.

Affective connotations

Affective connotations are the personal feelings a word arouses. A child who has no personal experience with a skunk and its odor or has had a pet skunk will feel differently about the word *skunk* than a child who has smelled the spray or been conditioned vicariously to associate offensiveness with the animal denoted *skunk*. The very fact that our society views a skunk as an animal to be avoided will affect the child's interpretation of the word. In fact, it is not necessary for one to have actually seen a skunk (that is, have a denotative understanding) to use the word in either connotative expression. For example, one child might call another child a skunk, connoting an unpleasant reaction (affective use) or, seeing another small black and white animal, call it a skunk based on the definition (informative use).

Using connotations

In everyday language, we attach affective meanings to words unconsciously; we exercise more conscious control of informative connotations. In the process of language development, the leaner must come not only to grasp the definitions of words but also to become more conscious of the affective connotations and how his listeners process these connotations. Gaining this conscious control over language makes it possible to use language appropriately in various situations and to evaluate its uses in literature and other forms of communication.

The manipulation of language for a variety of purposes is the goal of language instruction. Advertisers and satirists are especially conscious of the effect word choice has on their audiences. By evoking the proper responses from readers/listeners, we can prompt them to take action.

Choice of the medium through which the message is delivered to the receiver is a significant factor in controlling language. Spoken language relies as much on the gestures, facial expression, and tone of voice of the speaker as on the words he speaks. Slapstick comics can evoke laughter without speaking a word. Young children use body language overtly and older children more subtly to convey messages. These refinings of body language are paralleled by an ability to recognize and apply the nuances of spoken language. To work strictly with the written work, the writer must use words to imply the body language.

Skill 10.2 Analyzing problems relating to the effectiveness of narrative or descriptive materials and identifying appropriate revisions.

Some people say that God is in the details; others say that the devil is in the details. Either way, the message is the same with regards to vivid, informative writing: details are the key. Before assigning other written work, ask students to evaluate and analyze sentences such as the following for clarity and comprehensiveness.

- While walking I saw an accident.
- While walking to the store I saw a car accident.
- While walking to the drugstore last night, I saw a bad three-car accident in front of the gas station.

Each of these sentences report on the same event but only the last one meets the informative standard—the "journalistic guidelines"—explained in **Skill 6.2**. This sentence provides information that answers the who, what, where, and when aspects of the writer's chosen subject. Review the significance of this with students, then assign homework/class work accordingly.

Students also need to be aware of the pitfalls of providing too much information, especially redundant, marginal or irrelevant information, as in the following examples or ones like them. Have students point out, in writing, whatever is wrong with each example. Then have them revise each one.

- Last night 30 cm of cold white snow fell from the clouds in the sky above us.
- Before you swallow your food down into your stomach, you should chew it with your teeth.
- The great novelist hand-wrote his masterpiece novel on paper.

Students must also be made aware of how to "manage topic and time" in their writings. For example, in a 400-word essay assignment a topic such as "my year as a foreign exchange student in Germany" cannot likely be done justice: the timeframe is too long and the topic too broad for 400 words. Instead, encourage students to focus on smaller, more manageable topics. For example: "one big difference between German and American life," "a memorable day in my German neighborhood," etc. Less can be more. Emphasize this prior to assigning any written work.

Encourage students to write about what they know: the people in their lives, their personal experiences, opinions, their hobbies and interests, favorite literary works or music, sports, the future, etc. Assign written work accordingly.

Students who should an aptitude or interest for longer, even book-length, writing should be encouraged to take on larger topics and timeframes, perhaps as extra credit assignments.

Emphasize to students the importance of avoiding certain words and expressions that can either overstate a case, or leave no room for exceptions to it. Avoid readily falsifiable statements such as:

- "No-one thinks the way you do."
- "That's the way it's always been."
- "Everyone has always loved this song."

Have students revise all of the above into readily defensible statements. Teachers may also wish to provide students with a list of words to be especially careful with, lest a statement become an overstatement:

- always, never, forever, every time, any time
- no-one, nobody, none, all, every, everyone, everybody
- anywhere, everywhere, nowhere
- without exception, without a doubt

Skill 10.3 Applying strategies for using a variety of print and electronic formats for social communication (social notes, letters, e-mail).

The Internet has transformed all kinds of communications all over the world. Very few people write letters in the 21st century that will be delivered physically to an individual's mailbox. However, there are still important reasons for writing letters. For one thing, they are more personal and convey a quite different message from an e-mail, especially if they are handwritten. For another, not everybody has and uses e-mail regularly.

An electronic mailbox will retain what has been sent and received, sometimes to the writer's regret; even so, those messages and exchanges will not endure in the way that paper letters sometimes do over long periods. A husband and wife who married in 1954 always corresponded with his parents by mail approximately once a week in the first thirty years of their marriage. The three children often included a note of their own. It was before the long-distance call became routine and affordable. After the grandmother and grandfather had died, the family discovered that they had kept all of those letters. It's a priceless record of a period in the family's life. If that correspondence had occurred via e-mail, it would be lost to history.

Sometimes there's a business reason for a paper letter. It may contain a receipt or legal information that needs to be retained. For those people who do not yet have a computer or access to e-mail, paper letters are necessary. Sometimes a company or organization wishes to advertise a product or even issue invitations to an event when not all e-mail addresses are known. Mass-mailings can be sent quite easily to make sure that everyone on the list can be reached. Advertisers, of course, use mass-mail more than anyone else because they do not even need to know the addresses to get their literature into all the mailboxes in a zip code.

Sometimes courtesy requires a personally written letter either typed or handwritten. If a person in high office has taken the time to do something for an individual, certainly a handwritten letter of thanks would be in order. In the U.S., the form of the letter can be full block (all lines blocked at the left margin); modified block (all lines blocked at the left margin except the date and closing lines, which begin at the center point); and semi-block (same as modified block except that the first lines of paragraphs are indented by five points). Microsoft Word's letter wizard will automatically format a business letter according to these three styles.

Social notes should be handwritten on note paper, which varies in size but is smaller than letter-sized paper. They should be courteous and brief and should be specific about what is intended. For example, if the note is to say thank you, then the gift or favor should be specifically acknowledged in the note. If the note is an invitation, the same rule applies: the language should be courteous, the place and time specified, and any useful information such as "casual dress" or parking recommendations should be included.

A high percentage of communications between individuals, groups, and businesses is conducted nowadays over the Internet. It has even replaced many telephone calls. Internet language should be courteous, free of words that might be offensive, and clear. In the early days of e-mail, a writer was censured for using bold or capital letters. That has relaxed somewhat. Nowadays, almost anything goes although it's generally accepted that restrained language is assumed for business people and personal communications. The blog, where a person has his/her own website and uses it to send messages, is a new wrinkle.

Chat is available on most blogs as well as other Internet sites. The language and the messages tend to be unrestrained there.

Some people use the same styles for letters via e-mail that are recommended for paper letters; however, the formatting has tended to become less and less formal. It is not uncommon for thank-you letters and invitations to be sent via e-mail. One important feature of the Internet that makes it so valuable is that it reaches everywhere—to small communities, all the way across the country, and overseas. It's possible to dash off an e-mail note to a person or business or several persons or businesses in Europe as quickly as to a person in the next office, and it costs no extra money beyond the cost of equipment and Internet services.

The fax machine is yet another dimension of electronic communications. At first, it was used primarily by businesses, but it has become so affordable that many people have them in their homes. The fax makes possible an actual picture of a document. This may be preferable to retyping it or sending it by paper mail because it can go immediately. Sometimes people who are exchanging contracts will use the fax to cut down on the time it takes to get them signed and sent back and forth. The scanner will do the same thing but will produce a document that can be e-mailed.

Skill 10.4 Demonstrating awareness of voice in writing for personal expression and social interaction (in personal narratives, journals).

When writing personal notes or letters, the writer needs to keep the following key matters in mind:
- Once the topic is determined, the writer must determine the appropriate tone to introduce and express it. Is humor appropriate? Seriousness? Bluntness or subtlety? Does the situation call for formal or informal language? The answers to these questions will depend, in good part, on the writer's relationship to the reader. Plan appropriately regarding situation and audience.
- Does the writer's introduction clearly explain the topic/situation to a reader who doesn't know or feel everything that the reader knows or feels? Don't assume that the writer and reader are "on the same page." Make a checklist to make sure that all key information is clearly and concisely expressed.
- If a note or letter involves a request, what type of response/result does the writer desire? Devise a strategy or strategies for achieving a desired outcome.
- If a note or letter involves a complaint about the reader, the writer will need to decide whether to ask for particular amends or to let the reader decide what, if anything, to do. If no amends are requested, the writer may wish to suggest ideas that would help to avoid similar conflicts in the future. Asking the reader for his or her opinions is also a possibility.

- If a timely response to any note or letter is needed, the writer must mention this.

Give students in-class opportunities to write a variety of personal notes and letters, whether involving "real life" or hypothetical situations. Invitations, thank-you notes, complaints, requests for favors, or personal updates are a few of the options available. Have students experiment with a variety of tones and strategies on a particular piece of personal correspondence, e.g., write a complaint letter in a blunt tone, then write the same complaint in a humorous tone; compare and contrast the drafts. Structure in-class activities to allow for peer feedback.

A final note: Remind students that e-mail messages, even if intended for just one reader, may eventually reach a much wider audience. In recent years there have been numerous instances of writers finding themselves in embarrassing situations or legal troubles due to their personal e-mails being circulated on the internet. If a writer is addressing a sensitive, unpleasant or controversial matter, he or she should consult state laws to determine whether or not personal correspondence is protected by privacy laws. If the law does protect such correspondence from being circulated by the addressee, then the writer may wish to mention this in his or her message. Otherwise, clarity, concision, and civility in written works provide a writer all the protection that he or she will likely need.

Skill 10.5 Demonstrating awareness of techniques to expand text with appropriate details.

See Skill 9.3.

DOMAIN 3. READING

COMPETENCY 11.0 UNDERSTAND THE USE OF READING COMPREHENSION STRATEGIES

Skill 11.1 Recognizing how to vary reading strategies for different texts and purposes (skimming, scanning, in-depth reading, rereading).

The question to be asked first when approaching a reading task is what is my objective? What do I want to achieve from this reading? How will I use the information I gain from this reading? Do I only need to grasp the gist of the piece? Do I need to know the line of reasoning—not only the thesis but the subpoints? Will I be reporting important and significant details orally or in a written document?

A written document can be expected to have a thesis—either expressed or derived. To discover the thesis, the reader needs to ask what point the writer intended to make? The writing can also be expected to be organized in some logical way and to have subpoints that support or establish that the thesis is valid. It is also reasonable to expect that there will be details or examples that will support the subpoints. Knowing this, the reader can make a decision about reading techniques required for the purpose that has already been established.

If the reader only needs to know the gist of a written document, speed-reading skimming techniques may be sufficient by using the forefinger, moving the eyes down the page, picking up the important statements in each paragraph and deducing mentally that this piece is about such-and-such. If the reader needs to a little better grasp of how the writer achieved his/her purpose in the document, a quick and cursory glance—a skimming—of each paragraph will yield what the subpoints are, the topic sentences of the paragraphs, and how the thesis is developed, yielding a greater understanding of the author's purpose and method of development.

In-depth reading requires the scrutiny of each phrase and sentence with care, looking for the thesis first of all and then the topic sentences in the paragraphs that provide the development of the thesis, also looking for connections such as transitional devices that provide clues to the direction the reasoning is taking.

Sometimes rereading is necessary in order to make use of a piece of writing for an oral or written report upon a document. If this is the purpose of reading it, the first reading should provide a map for the rereading or second reading. The second time through should follow this map, and those points that are going to be used in a report or analysis will be focused upon on more carefully. Some new understandings may occur in this rereading, and it may become apparent that the "map" that was derived from the first reading will need to be adjusted. If this

English   71

rereading is for the purpose of writing an analysis or using material for a report, either highlighting or note-taking is advisable.

Skill 11.2 Demonstrating knowledge of strategies to use before and after reading to enhance comprehension (developing background knowledge, previewing the text, using text features such as bold print and heading, making predictions about a text, using K-W-L charts and other graphic organizers, taking notes, outlining, discussing).

Reading literature involves a reciprocal interaction between the reader and the text.

Types of responses

Emotional

The reader can identify with the characters and situations so as to project himself into the story. The reader feels a sense of satisfaction by associating aspects of his own life with the people, places, and events in the literature. Emotional responses are observed in a reader's verbal and non-verbal reactions - laughter, comments on its effects, and retelling or dramatizing the action.

Interpretive

Interpretive responses result in inferences about character development, setting, or plot; analysis of style elements - metaphor, simile, allusion, rhythm, tone; outcomes derivable from information provided in the narrative; and assessment of the author's intent. Interpretive responses are made verbally or in writing.

Critical

Critical responses involve making value judgments about the quality of a piece of literature. Reactions to the effectiveness of the writer's style and language use are observed through discussion and written reactions.

Evaluative

Some reading response theory researchers also add a response that considers the readers considerations of such factors as how well the piece of literature represents its genre, how well it reflects the social/ethical mores of society, and how well the author has approached the subject for freshness and slant.

Middle school readers will exhibit both emotional and interpretive responses.

Naturally, making interpretive responses depends on the degree of knowledge the student has of literary elements. A child's being able to say why a particular book was boring or why a particular poem made him sad evidences critical reactions on a fundamental level. Adolescents in ninth and tenth grades should begin to make critical responses by addressing the specific language and genre characteristics of literature. Evaluative responses are harder to detect and are rarely made by any but a few advanced high school students. However, if the teacher knows what to listen for, she can recognize evaluative responses and incorporate them into discussions.

For example, if a student says, "I don't understand why that character is doing that," he is making an interpretive response to character motivation. However, if he goes on to say, "What good is that action?" he is giving an evaluative response that should be explored in terms of "What good should it do and why isn't that positive action happening?"

At the emotional level, the student says, "I almost broke into a sweat when he was describing the heat in the burning house." An interpretive response says, "The author used descriptive adjectives to bring his setting to life." Critically, the student adds, "The author's use of descriptive language contributes to the success of the narrative and maintains reader interest through the whole story." If he goes on to wonder why the author allowed the grandmother in the story to die in the fire, he is making an evaluative response.

Levels of response

The levels of reader response will depend largely on the reader's level of social, psychological, and intellectual development. Most middle school students have progressed beyond merely involving themselves in the story enough to be able to retell the events in some logical sequence or describe the feeling that the story evoked. They are aware to some degree that the feeling evoked was the result of a careful manipulation of good elements of fiction writing. They may not explain that awareness as successfully as a high school student, but they are beginning to grasp the concepts and not just the personal reactions. They are beginning to differentiate between responding to the story itself and responding a literary creation.

Fostering self-esteem and empathy for others and the world in which one lives

All-important is the use of literature as bibliotherapy that allows the reader to identify with others and become aware of alternatives, yet not feeling directly betrayed or threatened. For the high school student the ability to empathize is an evaluative response, a much desired outcome of literature studies. Use of these books either individually or as a thematic unit of study allows for discussion or writing. The titles are grouped by theme, not by reading level.

ABUSE:

Blair, Maury and Brendel, Doug. *Maury, Wednesday's Child*

Dizenzo, Patricia. *Why Me?*

Parrot, Andrea. *Coping with Date Rape and Acquaintance Rape*

NATURAL WORLD CONCERNS:

Caduto, M. and Bruchac, J. *Keeper's of Earth*

Gay, Kathlyn. *Greenhouse Effect*

Johnson, Daenis. *Fiskadaro*

Madison, Arnold. *It Can't Happen to Me*

EATING DISORDERS:

Arnold, Caroline. *Too Fat, Too Thin, Do I Have a Choice?*

DeClements, Barthe. *Nothing's Fair in Fifth Grade*

Snyder, Anne. *Goodbye, Paper Doll*

FAMILY

Chopin, Kate. *The Runner*

Cormier, Robert. *Tunes for Bears to Dance to*

Danzinger, Paula. *The Divorce Express*

Neufield, John. *Sunday Father*

Okimoto, Jean Davies. *Molly by any Other Name*

Peck, Richard. *Don't Look and It Won't Hurt*

Zindel, Paul. *I Never Loved Your Mind*

STEREOTYPING:

Baklanov, Grigory. (Trans. by Antonina W. Bouis) *Forever Nineteen*

Kerr, M.E. *Gentle Hands*

Greene, Betty. *Summer of My German Soldier*

Reiss, Johanna. *The Upstairs Room*

Taylor, Mildred D. *Roll of Thunder, Hear Me Cry*

Wakatsuki-Houston, Jeanne and Houston, James D. *Farewell to Manzanar*

SUICIDE AND DEATH:

Blume, Judy. *Tiger Eyes*

Bunting, Eve. *If I Asked You, Would You Stay?*

Gunther, John. *Death Be Not Proud*

Mazer, Harry. *When the Phone Rings*

Peck, Richard. *Remembering the Good Times*

Richter, Elizabeth. *Losing Someone You Love*

Strasser, Todd. *Friends Till the End*

Cautions

There is always a caution when reading materials of a sensitive or controversial nature. The teacher must be cognizant of the happenings in the school and outside community to spare students undue suffering. A child who has known a recent death in his family or circle of friends may need to distance himself from classroom discussion. Whenever open discussion of a topic brings pain or embarrassment, the child should not be further subjected. Older children and young adults will be able to discuss issues with greater objectivity and without making blurted, insensitive comments. The teacher must be able to gauge the level of emotional development of her students when selecting subject matter and the strategies for studying it. The student or his parents may consider some material objectionable. Should a student choose not to read an assigned material, it is the teacher's responsibility to allow the student to select an alternate title. It is always advisable to notify parents if a particularly sensitive piece is to be studied.

Skill 11.3 Recognizing methods for monitoring comprehension while reading (recalling prior knowledge related to a topic, think-alouds, self-questioning strategies).

Reading emphasis in middle school
Reading for comprehension of factual material - content area textbooks, reference books, and newspapers - is closely related to study strategies in the middle/junior high.

Organized study models, such as the SQ3R method, a technique that makes it possible and feasible to learn the content of even large amounts of text (Survey, Question, Read, Recite, and Review Studying), teach students to locate main ideas and supporting details, to recognize sequential order, to distinguish fact from opinion, and to determine cause/ effect relationships.

Strategies

1. Teacher-guided activities that require students to organize and to summarize information based on the author's explicit intent are pertinent strategies in middle grades. Evaluation techniques include oral and written responses to standardized or teacher-made worksheets.

2. Reading of fiction introduces and reinforces skills in inferring meaning from narration and description. Teaching-guided activities in the process of reading for meaning should be followed by cooperative planning of the skills to be studied and of the selection of reading resources. Many printed reading for comprehension instruments as well as individualized computer software programs exist to monitor the progress of acquiring comprehension skills.

3. Older middle school students should be given opportunities for more student-centered activities - individual and collaborative selection of reading choices based on student interest, small group discussions of selected works, and greater written expression. Evaluation techniques include teacher monitoring and observation of discussions and written work samples.

4. Certain students may begin some fundamental critical interpretation - recognizing fallacious reasoning in news media, examining the accuracy of news reports and advertising, explaining their reasons for preferring one author's writing to another's. Development of these skills may require a more learning-centered approach in which the teacher identifies a number of objectives and suggested resources from which the student may choose his course of study. Self-evaluation through a reading diary should be stressed. Teacher and peer evaluation of creative projects resulting from such study is encouraged.

5. Reading aloud before the entire class as a formal means of teacher evaluation should be phased out in favor of one-to-one tutoring or peer-assisted reading. Occasional sharing of favored selections by both teacher and willing students is a good oral interpretation basic.

Reading emphasis in high school

Students in high school literature classes should focus on interpretive and critical reading.

Teachers should guide the study of the elements of inferential (interpretive) reading - drawing conclusions, predicting outcomes, and recognizing examples of specific genre characteristics, for example - and critical reading to judge the quality of the writer's work against recognized standards.

At this level students should understand the skills of language and reading that they are expected to master and be able to evaluate their own progress.

Strategies

1. The teacher becomes more facilitator than instructor - helping the student to make a diagnosis of his own strengths and weaknesses, keeping a record of progress, and interacting with other students and the teacher in practicing skills.

2. Despite the requisites and prerequisites of most literature courses, students should be encouraged to pursue independent study and enrichment reading.

3. Ample opportunities should be provided for oral interpretation of literature, special projects in creative dramatics, writing for publication in school literary magazines or newspapers, and speech/debate activities. A student portfolio provides for teacher and peer evaluation.

Skill 11.4 Demonstrating knowledge of techniques for identifying and using common text structures (cause and effect, compare and contrast, problem and solution) to improve comprehension.

Organizational Structures

Authors use a particular organization to best present the concepts which they are writing about. Teaching students to recognize organizational structures helps them to understand authors' literary intentions, and helps them in deciding which structure to use in their own writing.

Cause and Effect: When writing about *why* things happen, as well as *what* happens, authors commonly use the cause and effect structure. For example, when writing about how he became so successful, a CEO might talk about how he excelled in math in high school, moved to New York after college, and stuck to his goals even after multiple failures. These are all *causes* that lead to the *effect*, or result, of him becoming a wealthy and powerful businessman.

Compare and Contrast: When examining the merits of multiple concepts or products, compare and contrast lends itself easily to organization of ideas. For example, a person writing about foreign policy in different countries will put them against each other to point out differences and similarities, easily highlighting the concepts the author wishes to emphasize.

Problem and Solution: This structure is used in a lot of handbooks and manuals. Anything organized around procedure-oriented tasks, such as a computer repair manual, gravitates toward a problem and solution format, because it offers such clear, sequential text organization.

Skill 11.5 Recognizing how to trace an idea through a passage by identifying patterns of repeated words and phrases (key words and their synonyms, transitional words and phrases).

Tracing an idea through a passage goes much better if a strategy if developed for doing so. Good readers usually have these strategies even though they might not be aware of them. A good way to start is by looking for words or phrases that appear more than once or even many times. Following those key words and phrases will make it possible to observe a picture of the idea as it appears in the piece of writing.

Also, most published writers avoid repetition. For that reason, key words in a piece of writing will probably have several synonyms or even more. In strategizing for reading materials for comprehension, this device can be very useful. By focusing on the key words and thinking about their meanings, following the idea will be expedited.

Transitional words and phrases are designed to lead the reader forward and through a piece of writing. Such words as therefore, however, even so, although, etc. are clues to connections between one part of the writing and another and the nature of the connection. Phrases sometimes substitute for words. Some examples, as a matter of fact, in the long run, looking back, etc.

Skill 11.6 Demonstrating knowledge of the ways in which proficient readers use word identification strategies (knowledge of roots, affixes, and cognates) to improve comprehension by analyzing the denotative and connotative meanings of words in given contexts.

Identification of common morphemes, prefixes, and suffixes

This aspect of vocabulary development is to help students look for structural elements within words which they can use independently to help them determine meaning.

The terms listed below are generally recognized as the key structural analysis components.

Root words: A root word is a word from which another word is developed. The second word can be said to have its "root" in the first. This structural component nicely lends itself to a tree with roots illustration which can concretize the meaning for students.

Students may also want to literally construct root words using cardboard trees and/or actual roots from plants to create word family models. This is a lovely way to help students own their root words.

Base words: A stand-alone linguistic unit which can not be deconstructed or broken down into smaller words. For example, in the word "re-tell," the base word is "tell."

Contractions: These are shortened forms of two words in which a letter or letters have been deleted. These deleted letter have been replaced by an apostrophe.

Prefixes: These are beginning units of meaning which can be added (the vocabulary word for this type of structural adding is "affixed") to a base word or root word. They can not stand alone. They are also sometimes known as "bound morphemes," meaning that they can not stand alone as a base word.

Suffixes: These are ending units of meaning which can be "affixed" or added on to the ends of root or base words. Suffixes transform the original meanings of base and root words. Like prefixes, they are also known as "bound morphemes," because they can not stand alone as words.

Compound words: Occur when two or more base words are connected to form a new word. The meaning of the new word is in some way connected with that of the base word.

Inflectional endings: Are types are suffixes that impart a new meaning to the base or root word. These endings in particular change the gender, number, tense, or form of the base or root words. Just like other suffixes, these are also termed "bound morphemes."

COMPETENCY 12.0 UNDERSTAND READING FOR INFORMATION AND UNDERSTANDING

Skill 12.1 Demonstrating the ability to gather, synthesize, and evaluate information from a variety of printed texts and electronic sources.

The best place to start research is usually at your local library. Not only does it have numerous books, videos, and periodicals to use for references, the librarian is always a valuable resource for information, or where to get that information.

"Those who declared librarians obsolete when the internet rage first appeared are now red-faced. We need them more than ever. The internet is full of 'stuff' but its value and readability is often questionable. 'Stuff' doesn't give you a competitive edge, high-quality related information does."
    -Patricia Schroeder, President of the Association of American Publishers

The internet is a multi-faceted goldmine of information, but you must be careful to discriminate between reliable and unreliable sources. Stick to sites that are associated with an academic institution, whether it be a college or university or a scholarly organization.

Keep **content** and **context** in mind when researching. Don't be so wrapped up how you are going to apply your resource to your project that you miss the author's entire purpose or message. Remember that there are multiple ways to get the information you need. Read an encyclopedia article about your topic to get a general overview, and then focus in from there. Note important names of people associated with your subject, time periods, and geographic areas. Make a list of key words and their synonyms to use while searching for information. And finally, don't forget about articles in magazines and newspapers, or even personal interviews with experts related to your field of interest!

Skill 12.2 Identifying and applying distinctions between general statements and specific details.

From general to specific is a continuum. In other words, a term or phrase may be more specific than another term or more general than another one. For example, car is about the middle of the continuum; however, if I mention John Smith's car, it has become more specific. The most specific is a unique item: John Smith's 2007 Lexus, serial #000000000. Cars is a general term that can be narrowed and narrowed and narrowed to suit whatever purposes the writer has for the term. For instance, it would be possible to make a statement about all the cars in the United States, which has been narrowed somewhat from cars. It is, however, a very general term. A thesis statement is typically a generality: All the cars in the United States run on gasoline. Then specifics would be needed to prove that generalization.

In developing a line of reasoning, the choice will be either inductive, going from the specific to the general, or deductive, going from the general to the specific. Inductive reasoning might be as follows: "I tasted a green apple from my grandfather's yard when I was five years old, and it was sour. I also tasted a green apple that my friend brought to school in his lunchbox when I was eight years old, and it was sour. I was in Browns' roadside market and bought some green Granny Smith apples last week, and they were sour." This is a series of specifics. From those specifics, I might draw a conclusion—a generalization—all apples are sour, and I would have reasoned inductively to arrive at that generalization.

The same simplistic argument developed deductively would begin with the generalization: all apples are sour. Then specifics would be offered to support that generalization: the sour green apple I tasted in my grandfather's orchard, the sour green apple in my friend's lunchbox, the Granny Smith apples from the market.

When reasoning is this simple and straightforward, it's easy to follow, but it's also easy to see fallacies. For example, this person hasn't tasted all the green apples in the world; and, in fact, some green apples are not sour. However, it's rarely that easy to see the generalizations and the specifics. In determining whether a point has been proven, it's necessary to do that.

Sometimes generalizations are cited on the assumption that they are commonly accepted and do not need to be supported. An example: all men die sooner or later. Examples wouldn't be needed because that is commonly accepted. Now, some people might require that "die" be defined, but even the definition of "die" is assumed in this generalization.

Some current generalizations that may assume common acceptance: Providing healthcare for all citizens is the responsibility of the government. All true patriots will support any war the government declares.

Flaws in argument, either intended or unintended, frequently have to do with generalizations and specifics. Are the specifics sufficient to prove the truth of the generality? Does a particular specific actually apply to this generalization? Many times it will depend on definitions. The question can always be asked: has the writer (or speaker) established the generalization?

Skill 12.3 Applying inferential comprehension skills to draw conclusions from a given passage and interpret implied information (causal relations) in a given passage.

A common fallacy in reasoning is the *post hoc ergo propter hoc* ("after this, therefore because of this") or the false-cause fallacy. These occur in cause/effect reasoning, which may either go from cause to effect or effect to cause.

They happen when an inadequate cause is offered for a particular effect; when the possibility of more than one cause is ignored; and when a connection between a particular cause and a particular effect is not made.

An example of a *post hoc*: Our sales shot up thirty-five percent after we ran that television campaign; therefore the campaign caused the increase in sales. It might have been a cause, of course, but more evidence is needed to prove it.

An example of an inadequate cause for a particular effect: An Iraqi truck driver reported that Saddam Hussein had nuclear weapons; therefore, Saddam Hussein is a threat to world security. More causes are needed to prove the conclusion.

An example of ignoring the possibility of more than one possible cause: John Brown was caught out in a thunderstorm and his clothes were wet before he was rescued; therefore, he developed influenza the next day was because he got wet. Being chilled may have played a role in the illness, but Brown would have had to contract the influenza virus before he would come down with it whether or not he had gotten wet.

An example of failing to make a connection between a particular cause and an effect assigned to it. Anna fell into a putrid pond on Saturday; on Monday she came down with polio; therefore, the polio was caused by the pond. This, of course, is not acceptable unless the polio virus is found in a sample of water from the pond. A connection must be proven.

Skill 12.4 Demonstrating an understanding of techniques for summarizing or paraphrasing a given passage.

Paraphrasing is the art of rewording text. The goal is to maintain the original purpose of the statement while translating it into your own words. Your newly generated sentence can be longer or shorter than the original. Concentrate on the meaning, not on the words. Do not change concept words, special terms, or proper names. There are numerous ways to effectively paraphrase:

- Change the key words' form or part of speech. Example: "American news **coverage** is frequently **biased** in favor of Western views," becomes "When American journalists **cover** events, they often display a Western **bias**."
- Use synonyms of "relationship words." Look for a relationship word, such as **contrast, cause,** or **effect,** and replace it with a word that conveys a similar meaning, thus creating a different structure for your sentence. Example: "**Unlike** many cats, Purrdy can sit on command," becomes "Most cats are not able to be trained, **but** Purrdy can sit on command."

- Use synonyms of phrases and words. Example: "The Beatnik writers were relatively unknown at **the start of the decade**," becomes "**Around the early 1950s**, the Beatnik writers were still relatively unknown."
- Change passive voice to active voice or move phrases and modifiers. Example: "Not to be outdone by the third graders, the fourth grade class added a musical medley to their Christmas performance," becomes "The fourth grade class added a musical medley to their Christmas performance to avoid being showed up by the third graders."
- Use reversals or negatives that do not change the meaning of the sentence. Example: "That burger chain is only found in California," becomes "That burger chain is not found on the east coast."

Skill 12.5 Analyzing information from texts containing tables, charts, graphs, maps, and other illustrations.

Tables that simply store descriptive information in a form available for general use are called repository tables. They usually contain primary data, which simply summarize raw data. They are not intended to analyze the data, so any analysis is left to the reader or user of the table. A good example of a repository table would be a report of birth statistics by the federal Health and Human Services Department. An analytical table, on the other hand, is constructed from some sort of analysis of primary or secondary data, possibly from a repository table or from the raw data itself. An example of an analytical table would be one that compares birth statistics in 1980 to birth statistics in 2005 for the country at large. It might also break the data down into comparisons by state.

Graphs also present data in visual form. Whereas tables are useful for showing large numbers of specific, related facts or statistics in a brief space, trends, movements, distributions and cycles are more readily apparent in a graph. However, although graphs can present statistics in a more interesting and comprehensible form than tables, they are less accurate. For this reason, the two will often be shown together.

While the most obvious use for **maps** is to locate places geographically, they can also show specific geographic features such as roads, mountains, rivers, etc. The can also show information according to geographic distribution such as population, housing, manufacturing centers, etc.

A wide range of **illustrations** may be used to illuminate the text in a document. They may also be a part of a graphic layout designed to make the page more attractive.

Some possibilities for the analysis of data whether presented in tables, charts, graphs, maps, or other illustrations are as follow:
Qualitative descriptions—drawing conclusions about the quality of a particular treatment, course of action as revealed by the illustration.

Quantitative descriptions—how much do the results of one particular treatment or course of action differ from another one, and is that variation significant?
Classification—is worthwhile information derived from breaking the information down into classifications?
Estimations—is it possible to estimate future performance on the basis of the information in the illustration?
Comparisons—is it useful to make comparisons based on the data?
Relationships—are relationships between components revealed by the scrutiny of the data?
Cause-and-effect relationships—is it suggested by the data that there were cause-and-effect relationships that were not previously apparent?
Mapping and modeling—if the data were mapped and a model drawn up, would the point of the document be demonstrated or refuted?

Questions to ask regarding an illustration: Why is it in this document? What was the writer's purpose in putting it in the document and why at this particular place? Does it make a point clearer? What implications are inherent in a table that shows birth statistics in all states or even in some selected states? What does that have to do with the point and purpose of this piece of writing? Is there adequate preparation in the text for the inclusion of the illustration? Does the illustration underscore or clarify any of the points made in the text? Is there a clear connection between the illustration and the subject matter of the text?

COMPETENCY 13.0 UNDERSTAND READING FOR LITERARY RESPONSE, PERSONAL ENJOYMENT, AND SOCIAL INTERACTION

Skill 13.1 Analyzing the use of language elements to develop a plot, portray character, describe setting, or create a mood in a given passage.

It's no accident that **plot** is sometimes called action. If the plot does not *move*, the story quickly dies. Therefore, the successful writer of stories uses a wide variety of active verbs in creative and unusual ways. If a reader is kept on his/her toes by the movement of the story, the experience of reading it will be pleasurable. That reader will probably want to read more of this author's work. Careful, unique, and unusual choices of active verbs will bring about that effect. William Faulkner is a good example of a successful writer whose stories are lively and memorable because of his use of unusual active verbs. In analyzing the development of plot, it's wise to look at the verbs. However, the development of believable conflicts is also vital. If there is no conflict, there is no story. What devices does a writer use to develop the conflicts, and are they real and believable?

Character is portrayed in many ways: description of physical characteristics, dialogue, interior monologue, the thoughts of the character, the attitudes of other characters toward this one, etc. Descriptive language depends on the ability to recreate a sensory experience for the reader. If the description of the character's appearance is a visual one, then the reader must be able to *see* the character. What's the shape of the nose? What color are the eyes? How tall or how short is this character? Thin or chubby? How does the character move? How does the character walk? Terms must be chosen that will create a picture for the reader. It's not enough to say the eyes are blue, for example. What blue? Often the color of eyes is compared to something else to enhance the readers' ability to visualize the character. A good test of characterization is the level of emotional involvement of the reader in the character. If the reader is to become involved, the description must provide an actual experience—seeing, smelling, hearing, tasting, or feeling.

Dialogue will reflect characteristics. Is it clipped? Is it highly dialectal? Does a character use a lot of colloquialisms? The ability to portray the speech of a character can make or break a story. The kind of person the character is in the mind of the reader is dependent on impressions created by description and dialogue. How do other characters feel about this one as revealed by their treatment of him/her, their discussions of him/her with each other, or their overt descriptions of the character. For example, "John, of course, can't be trusted with another person's possessions." In analyzing a story, it's useful to discuss the devices used to produce character.

Setting may be visual, temporal, psychological, or social. Descriptive words are often used here also. In Edgar Allan Poe's description of the house in "The Fall of the House of Usher" as the protagonist/narrator approaches it, the air of dread and gloom that pervades the story is caught in the setting and sets the stage for the story. A setting may also be symbolic, as it is in Poe's story, where the house is a symbol of the family that lives in it. As the house disintegrates, so does the family.

The language used in all of these aspects of a story—plot, character, and setting—work together to create the **mood** of a story. Poe's first sentence establishes the mood of the story: "During the whole of a dull, dark, and soundless day in the autumn of the year, when the clouds hung oppressively low in the heavens, I had been passing alone, on horseback, through a singularly dreary tract of country; and at length found myself, as the shades of the evening drew on, within view of the melancholy House of Usher."

Skill 13.2 Analyzing an author's use of ambiguity, connotation, or symbolism in language to convey such effects as ironic undertones, sensory impressions, or emotions.

- **Ambiguity:** Ambiguity is any writing whose meaning cannot be determined by its context. Ambiguity may be introduced accidentally, confusing the readers and disrupting the flow of reading. If a sentence or paragraph jars upon reading, there is lurking ambiguity. It is particularly difficult to spot your own ambiguities, since authors tend to see what they mean rather than what they say.

- **Connotation:** Connotation refers to the ripple effect surrounding the implications and associations of a given word, distinct from the denotative, or literal meaning. For example, "Good night, sweet prince, and flights of angels sing thee to thy rest," refers to a burial. Connotation is used when a subtle tone is preferred. It may stir up a more effective emotional response than if the author had used blunt, insensitive diction.

- **Symbolism:** Also referred to as a sign, a symbol designates something which stands for something else. In most cases, it is standing for something that has a deeper meaning than its literal denotation. Symbols can have personal, cultural, or universal associations. An understanding of symbols can be used to unearth a meaning the author might have intended but not expressed, or even something the author never intended at all.

Skill 13.3 Interpreting the use of such techniques as rhythm, rhyme, diction, or imagery to evoke a response in the reader.

- **Rhythm:** Writing can be compared to dancing, in that it is a balance between words and flow.

- Rhythm refers to the harmony between the words chosen and the smoothness, rapidity, or disjointedness of the way those words are written. Sentences that are too long may disrupt the rhythm of a piece. Reading text out loud is an easy way to impart understanding of literary rhythm.
- **Rhyme:** Writing with rhyme can be especially effective on reader response. Think about the success Dr. Suess had with his rhyming style. Rhyme is tricky though; used ineffectively or unnecessarily, it can break up the entire rhythm of the piece or fog the reader's understanding of it. Rhyme should be used when it is purely beneficial to the format of the piece. Make sure it is not forcing you to use more words than needed, and that each verse is moving the story forward.
- **Diction:** Diction is simply the right word in the right spot for the right purpose. The hallmark of a great writer is precise, unusual, and memorable diction.
- **Imagery:** Imagery involves engaging one or more of your five senses in your writing. An author might use imagery to give the reader a greater, more real picture of the scene they are trying to depict. Imagery may conjure up a past experience that the reader had (the smell of the ocean, the feeling of their childhood blanket) thereby enriching their mental picture of the scene.

Skill 13.4 Modeling the lifelong value of reading independently for enjoyment and the benefits of participating in a community of readers.

Reading for enjoyment makes it possible to go to places in the world we will never be able to visit, or perhaps when we learn about the enchantments of a particular place, we will set a goal of going there someday. When *Under the Tuscan Sun* by Frances Mayes was published, it became a best seller. It also increased tourism to Italy. Many of the readers of that book visited Italy for the first time in their lives.

In fiction, we can live through experiences that we will never encounter. We delve into feelings that are similar to our own or are so far removed from our own that we are filled with wonder and curiosity. In fact, we read because we're curious—curious to visit, experience, and know new and different things. The reader lives with a crowd of people and a vast landscape. Life is constantly being enriched by the reading, and the mind is constantly being expanded. To read is to grow. Sometimes the experience of reading a particular book or story is so delicious that we go back and read it again and again, such as the works of Jane Austen. We keep track of what is truly happening in the world when we read current best-sellers because they not only reflect what everyone else is interested in right now, they can influence trends. We can know in-depth what television news cannot cram in by reading publications like *Time* and *Newsweek*.

How do we model this wonderful gift for our students?

We can bring those interesting stories into our classrooms and share the excitement we feel when we discover them. We can relate things that make us laugh so students may see the humor and laugh with us. We can vary the established curriculum to include something we are reading that we want to share. The tendency of students nowadays is to receive all of their information from television or the internet. It's important for the teacher to help students understand that television and the internet are not substitutes for reading. They should be an accessory, an extension, a springboard for reading.

Another thing teachers can do to inspire students to become readers is to assign a book that you have never read before and read along with them, chapter by chapter. Run a contest and the winner gets to pick a book that you and they will read chapter by chapter. If you are excited about it and are experiencing satisfaction from the reading, that excitement will be contagious. Be sure that the discussion sessions allow for students to relate what they are thinking and feeling about what they are reading. Lively discussions and the opportunity to express their own feelings will lead to more spontaneous reading.

You can also hand out a reading list of your favorite books and spend some time telling the students what you liked about each. Make sure the list is diverse. It's good to include nonfiction along with fiction. Don't forget that a good biography or autobiography may encourage students to read beyond thrillers and detective stories.

When the class is discussing the latest movie, whether formally as a part of the curriculum or informally and incidentally, if the movie is based on a book, this is a good opportunity to demonstrate how much more can be derived from the reading than from the watching. Or how the two combined make the experience more satisfying and worthwhile.

Share with your students the excitement you have for reading. Successful writers are usually good readers. The two go hand-in-hand.

COMPETENCY 14.0 UNDERSTAND READING FOR CRITICAL ANALYSIS AND EVALUATION

Skill 14.1 Distinguishing opinion from fact, conclusion, or inference in a passage.

Facts are statements that are verifiable. Opinions are statements that must be supported in order to be accepted. Facts are used to support opinions. For example, "Jane is a bad girl" is an opinion. However, "Jane hit her sister with a baseball bat" is a *fact* upon which the opinion is based. Judgments are opinions—decisions or declarations based on observation or reasoning that express approval or disapproval. Facts report what has happened or exists and come from observation, measurement, or calculation. Facts can be tested and verified whereas opinions and judgments cannot. They can only be supported with facts.

Most statements cannot be so clearly distinguished. "I believe that Jane is a bad girl" is a fact. The speaker knows what he/she believes. However, it obviously includes a judgment that could be disputed by another person who might believe otherwise. Judgments are not usually so firm. They are, rather, plausible opinions that provoke thought or lead to factual development.

Conclusions are drawn as a result of a line of reasoning. Inductive reasoning begins with particulars and reasons to a generality. For example: "When I was a child, I bit into a green apple from my grandfather's orchard, and it was sour" (specific fact #1). "I once bought green apples from a roadside vendor, and when I bit into one, it was sour" (specific fact #2). "My grocery store had a sale on green Granny Smith apples last week, and I bought several only to find that they were sour when I bit into one" (specific fact #3). Conclusion: All green apples are sour. While this is an example of inductive reasoning, it is also an example of the weakness of such reasoning. The speaker has not tasted all the green apples in the world, and there very well may be some apples that are green that are not sour.

Deductive reasoning begins with the generalization: "Green apples are sour" and supports that generalization with the specifics.

An inference is drawn from an inductive line of reasoning. The most famous one is "all men are mortal," which is drawn from the observation that everyone a person knows has died or will die and that everyone else concurs in that judgment. It is assumed to be true and for that reason can be used as proof of another conclusion: "Socrates is a man; therefore, he will die."

Sometimes the inference is assumed to be proven when it is not reliably true in all cases, such as "aging brings physical and mental infirmity." Reasoning from that *inference*, many companies will not hire anyone above a certain age.

Actually, being old does not necessarily imply physical and/or mental impairment. There are many instances where elderly people have made important contributions that require exceptional ability.

Skill 14.2 Judging the accuracy, relevance, importance, or sufficiency of facts in a writer's argument.

An argument is a generalization that is proven or supported with facts. If the facts are not accurate, the generalization remains unproven. Using inaccurate "facts" to support an argument is called a *fallacy* in reasoning. Some factors to consider in judging whether the facts used to support an argument are accurate are as follow:

1. Are the facts current or are they out of date? For example, if the proposition "birth defects in babies born to drug-using mothers are increasing," then the data must include the latest that is available.
2. Another important factor to consider in judging the accuracy of a fact is its source. Where was the data obtained, and is that source reliable?
3. The calculations on which the facts are based may be unreliable. It's a good idea to run one's own calculations before using a piece of derived information.

Even facts that are true and have a sharp impact on the argument may not be relevant to the case at hand.

1. Health statistics from an entire state may have no relevance, or little relevance, to a particular county or zip code. Statistics from an entire country cannot be used to prove very much about a particular state or county.
2. An analogy can be useful in making a point, but the comparison must match up in all characteristics or it will not be relevant. Analogy should be used very carefully. It is often just as likely to destroy an argument as it is to strengthen it.

The importance or significance of a fact may not be sufficient to strengthen an argument. For example, of the millions of immigrants in the U.S., using a single family to support a solution to the immigration problem will not make much difference overall even though those single-example arguments are often used to support one approach or another. They may achieve a positive reaction, but they will not prove that one solution is better than another. If enough cases were cited from a variety of geographical locations, the information might be significant.

How much is enough? Generally speaking, three strong supporting facts are sufficient to establish the thesis of an argument. For example:

Conclusion: All green apples are sour.

- When I was a child, I bit into a green apple from my grandfather's orchard, and it was sour.
- I once bought green apples from a roadside vendor, and when I bit into one, it was sour.
- My grocery store had a sale on green Granny Smith apples last week, and I bought several only to find that they were sour when I bit into one.

The fallacy in the above argument is that the sample was insufficient. A more exhaustive search of literature, etc., will probably turn up some green apples that are not sour.

Sometimes more than three arguments are too many. On the other hand, it's not unusual to hear public speakers, particularly politicians, who will cite a long litany of facts to support their positions.

Skill 14.3 Recognizing the deliberate omission of facts in an argument.

A very good example of the omission of facts in an argument is the resumé of an applicant for a job. The applicant is arguing that he/she should be chosen to be awarded a particular job. The application form will ask for information about past employment, and unfavorable dismissals from jobs in the past may just be omitted. Employers are usually suspicious of periods of time when the applicant has not listed an employer.

A writer makes choices about which facts will be used and which will be discarded in developing an argument. Those choices may exclude anything that is not supportive of the point of view the arguer is taking. It's always a good idea for the reader to do some research to spot the omissions and to ask whether they have impact on acceptance of the point of view presented in the argument.

No judgment is either black or white. If the argument seems too neat or too compelling, there are probably facts that might be relevant that have not been included.

Skill 14.4 Assessing the credibility or objectivity of information from print and electronic sources.

Before accepting as gospel anything that is printed in a newspaper or advertising or presented on radio, television, or the Internet, it is wise to first of all consider the source. Even though news reporters and editors claim to be unbiased in the presentation of news, they usually take an editorial point of view. A newspaper may avow that it is Republican or conservative and may even make recommendations at election time, but it will still claim to present the news without bias. Sometimes this is true, and sometimes it is not. For example, Fox News declares itself to be conservative and to support the Republican party.

Its presentation of news often reveals that bias. When Vice President Cheney made a statement about his shooting of a friend in a duck-hunting accident, it was only made available to Fox News.

On the other hand, CBS has tended to favor more liberal politicians although it avows that it is even-handed in its coverage. Dan Rather presented a story critical of President Bush's military service that was based on a document that could not be validated. His failure to play by the rules of certification of evidence cost him his job and his career. Even with authentication, such a story would not have gotten past the editors of a conservative-leaning news system.

Even politicians usually play by the rules of fairness in the choices they make about going public. They usually try to be even-handed. However, some channels and networks will show deference to one politician over another.

Advertising, whether in print or electronic media is another thing. Will using a certain tooth paste improve a person's love life? Is a dish better than cable? The best recourse a reader/viewer has is to ask around and find someone who has experience that is relevant or conduct research and conduct interviews of users of both.

Skill 14.5 Determining how the author uses tone and style to present a particular point of view.

A piece of writing is an integrated whole. It's not enough to just look at the various parts; the total entity must be examined. It should be considered in two ways:
- As an emotional expression of the author
- As an artistic embodiment of a meaning or set of meanings.

This is what is sometimes called "**tone**" in literary criticism.

It's important to remember that the writer is a human being with his/her own individual bents, prejudices, and emotions. A writer is telling the readers about the world as he/she sees it and will give voice to certain phases of his/her own personality. By reading a writer's works, we can know the personal qualities and emotions of the writer embodied in the work itself. However, it's important to remember that not all the writer's characteristics will be revealed in a single work. People change and may have very different attitudes at different times in their lives. Sometimes, a writer will be influenced by a desire to have a piece of work accepted or to appear to be current or by the interests and desires of the readers he/she hopes to attract. It can destroy a work or make it less than it might be. Sometimes the best works are not commercial successes in the generation when they were written but are discovered at a later time and by another generation.

There are three places to look for tone:

- Choice of form: tragedy or comedy; melodrama or farce; parody or sober lyric.
- Choice of materials: characters that have human qualities that are attractive; others that are repugnant. What an author shows in a setting will often indicate what his/her interests are.
- The writer's interpretation: it may be explicit—telling us how he/she feels.
- The writer's implicit interpretations: the author's feelings for a character come through in the description. For example, the use of "smirked" instead of "laughed"; "minced," "stalked," "marched," instead of walked.

The reader is asked to join the writer in the feelings expressed about the world and the things that happen in it. The tone of a piece of writing is important in a critical review of it.

Style, in literature, means a distinctive manner of expression and applies to all levels of language, beginning at the phonemic level—word choices, alliteration, assonance, etc.; the syntactic level—length of sentences, choice of structure and phraseology, patterns, etc.; and extends even beyond the sentence to paragraphs and chapters. What is distinctive about this writer's use of these elements?

In Steinbeck's *Grapes of Wrath*, for instance, the style is quite simple in the narrative sections and the dialogue is dialectal. Because the emphasis is on the story—the narrative—his style is straightforward, for the most part. He just tells the story.

However, there are inter chapters where he varies his style. He uses symbols and combines them with description that is realistic. He sometimes shifts to a crisp, repetitive pattern to underscore the beeping and speeding of cars. By contrast, some of those inter chapters are lyrical, almost poetic.

These shifts in style reflect the attitude of the author toward the subject matter. He intends to make a statement, and he uses a variety of styles to strengthen the point.

Skill 14.6 Recognizing fallacies in logic.

See Skill 3.2.

DOMAIN 4. FUNDAMENTALS OF LITERATURE

COMPETENCY 15.0 UNDERSTAND THE HISTORICAL, SOCIAL, AND CULTURAL ASPECTS OF LITERATURE, INCLUDING THE WAYS IN WHICH LITERARY WORKS AND MOVEMENTS BOTH REFLECT AND SHAPE CULTURE AND HISTORY.

Skill 15.1 Applying knowledge of the characteristics and significance of mythology and folk literature of a variety of cultures.

Literary allusions are drawn from classic mythology, national folklore, and religious writings that are supposed to have such familiarity to the reader that he can recognize the comparison between the subject of the allusion and the person, place, or event in the current reading. Children and adolescents who have knowledge of proverbs, fables, myths, epics, and the *Bible* can understand these allusions and thereby appreciate their reading to a greater degree than those who cannot recognize them.

Fables and folktales

This literary group of stories and legends was originally orally transmitted to the common populace to provide models of exemplary behavior or deeds worthy of recognition and homage.

In fables, animals talk, feel, and behave like human beings. The fable always has a moral and the animals illustrate specific people or groups without directly identifying them. For example, in Aesop's *Fables,* the lion is the "King" and the wolf is the cruel, often unfeeling, "noble class." In the fable of "The Lion and the Mouse" the moral is that "Little friends may prove to be great friends." In "The Lion's Share" it is "Might makes right." Many British folktales - *How Robin Became an Outlaw* and *St. George - Slaying of the Dragon* - stress the correlation between power and right.

Classical mythology

Much of the mythology that produces allusions in modern English writings is a product of ancient Greece and Rome because these myths have been more liberally translated. Some Norse myths are also well known. Children are fond of myths because those ancient people were seeking explanations for those elements in their lives that predated scientific knowledge just as children seek explanations for the occurrences in their lives. These stories provide insight into the order and ethics of life as ancient heroes overcome the terrors of the unknown and bring meaning to the thunder and lightning, to the changing of the seasons, to the magical creatures of the forests and seas, and to the myriad of natural phenomena that can frighten mankind.

There is often a childlike quality in the emotions of supernatural beings with which children can identify. Many good translations of myths exist for readers of varying abilities, but Edith Hamilton's *Mythology* is the most definitive reading for adolescents.

Fairy tales

Fairy tales are lively fictional stories involving children or animals that come in contact with super-beings via magic. They provide happy solutions to human dilemmas. The fairy tales of many nations are peopled by trolls, elves, dwarfs, and pixies, child-sized beings capable of fantastic accomplishments.

Among the most famous are "Beauty and the Beast," "Cinderella," "Hansel and Gretel," "Snow White and the Seven Dwarfs," "Rumplestiltskin," and "Tom Thumb." In each tale, the protagonist survives prejudice, imprisonment, ridicule, and even death to receive justice in a cruel world.

Older readers encounter a kind of fairy tale world in Shakespeare's *The Tempest* and *A Midsummer Night's Dream*, which use pixies and fairies as characters. Adolescent readers today are as fascinated by the creations of fantasy realms in the works of Piers Anthony, Ursula LeGuin, and Anne McCaffrey. An extension of interest in the supernatural is the popularity of science fiction that allows us to use current knowledge to predict the possible course of the future.

Angels (or sometimes fairy godmothers) play a role in some fairy tales, and Milton in Paradise Lost and Paradise Regained also used symbolic angels and devils.

Biblical stories provide many allusions. Parables, moralistic like fables but having human characters, include the stories of the Good Samaritan and the Prodigal Son. References to the treachery of Cain and the betrayal of Christ by Judas Iscariot are oft-cited examples.

American folk tales

American folktales are divided into two categories.

Imaginary tales, also called tall tales (humorous tales based on non-existent, fictional characters developed through blatant exaggeration)

> John Henry is a two-fisted steel driver who beats out a steam drill in competition.

> Rip Van Winkle sleeps for twenty years in the Catskill Mountains and upon awakening cannot understand why no one recognizes him.

Paul Bunyan, a giant lumberjack, owns a great blue ox named Babe and has extraordinary physical strength. He is said to have plowed the Mississippi River while the impression of Babe's hoof prints created the Great Lakes.

Real tales, also called legends (based on real persons who accomplished the feats that are attributed to them even if they are slightly exaggerated)

For more than forty years, Johnny Appleseed (John Chapman) roamed Ohio and Indiana planting apple seeds.

Daniel Boone - scout, adventurer, and pioneer - blazed the Wilderness Trail and made Kentucky safe for settlers.

Paul Revere, an colonial patriot, rode through the New England countryside warning of the approach of British troops.

George Washington cut down a cherry tree, which he could not deny, or did he?

Skill 15.2 Analyzing the expression of values and ideas (including regional, cultural, ethnic, historical) through literature.

Literature is powerful in influencing the thinking of individual readers and all of society. Waves of philosophical ideas have swept over the reading world almost from the time of the invention of the printing press. It's possible to trace the emergence of a particular set of values over centuries. Feminism is a case in point. While the matter of women's rights didn't reach a boiling point until the 1960s, it can be traced through history for many years.

For example, Empress Theodora of Byzantium was a proponent of legislation that would afford greater protections and freedoms to her female subjects, and Christine de Pizan, the first professional female writer, advanced many feminist ideas as early as the 1300s in the face of attempts to restrict female inheritance and guild membership. In 1869, John Stuart Mill published *The Subjection of Women* to demonstrate that "the legal subordination of one sex to the other is wrong…and…one of the chief hindrances to human improvement." Norwegian playwright Henrik Ibsen wrote the highly controversial play, *A Doll's House,* in 1879, a scathing criticism of the traditional roles of men and women in Victorian marriages. These and many other works with feminist themes led to changes in the way society viewed women throughout the civilized world. The impact of the literature and the changes in thinking on this issue led to many countries' granting of the vote to women in the late 1800s and the early years of the 20th century.

Regional literature has played an important role in the themes of popular literature, particularly in American literature. The best-known of the regional American writers is Samuel Langhorne Clemens, better known as Mark Twain with his stories about the Mississippi River and the state of Missouri. Although his home state was a slave state and considered by many to be part of the South, it declined to join the Confederacy and remained loyal to the union. He wrote sympathetic slave characters in many of his stories.

Some regional American writers:
Harriet Beecher Stowe
Sarah Orne Jewett
George Washington Cable
Joel Chandler Harris
Edward Eggleston
James Whitcomb Riley
Bret Harte

Ethnic themes are also very popular in American literature. Toni Morrison, who writes African-American stories, is considered to be the most important American writer of the last 25 years and won the Nobel Prize for Literature in 1993 for her collected works. Saul Bellow wrote of his own Jewish backgrounds and also won the Nobel Prize in 1976.

James Michener wrote history as fiction in his many novels: *Tales of the South Pacific* (for which he won the Pulitzer Prize for Fiction in 1948), *Hawaii*, *The Drifters*, *Centennial*, *The Source*, *The Fires of Spring*, *Chesapeake*, *Caribbean*, *Caravans*, *Alaska*, *Texas*, and *Poland*.

Literature about a particular period has also been very popular with American writers. The Civil War era has been a very successful subject for novelists, most notable of which is *Gone With the Wind* by Margaret Mitchell.

Some novels about the American Civil War:
- *The Red Badge of Courage* by Stephen Crane
- *Cold Mountain* by Charles Frazier
- *Love and War* by John Jakes
- *Gods and Generals*; *The Last Full Measure* by Jeffrey Shaara
- *By Valour and Arms* by James Street
- *Fort Pillow* by Harry Turtledove
- *Lincoln* by Gore Vidal

Skill 15.3 Analyzing the role of diverse authors in influencing public opinion about and understanding of social issues.

Writers, from the time of the invention of the printing press, have played important roles in shaping public opinion, not only in their own countries but also around the world.

Worldwide philosophical trends can be traced to the literature that was popular in a particular period of time. America has always been a nation of readers. With the development of theaters and ultimately movies and television that often dramatized popular novels, the power of the written word has increased.

John Steinbeck's *Grapes of Wrath* focused the attention of Americans on the plight of the common people who suffered more than anyone else because of the Great Depression. His revelation that Americans were starving to death in a land of great abundance still resonates with the public. Members of the "establishment" in the farms and towns of California are revealed as callous and greedy. Church members, particularly clergy and leaders, don't come off much better in his revealing story. Steinbeck lived with some of the migrants so he could write authentically and with first-hand knowledge. Many of the writers who have influenced public opinion write from personal experience.

The feminist movement has virtually been fueled by literature going back several hundred years. Although the organized movement began with the first women's rights convention at Seneca Falls, New York, in 1948, in 1869, John Stuart Mill had already published *The Subjection of Women* to demonstrate that the legal subordination of one sex to the other is wrong. Virginia Woolf's essay, *A Room of One's Own*, first published in 1929, had a strong influence on how women were beginning to see their roles.

However, in the crusade that was ignited by the Civil Rights movement of the 1960s, Betty Friedan's book, *The Feminine Mystique*, published in 1963, was very popular and influenced many women to become involved, both in changes in their own outlooks and behaviors, but also in the movement at large as activists. Feminism has been so much a part of the thinking throughout the world that it should always be included in the potential themes one looks for when writing a critique of a literary work.

Uncle Tom's Cabin broke new ground in literature on social injustice and was very powerful in influencing the thinking of American people about slavery. It was the best-selling novel of the 19th century and is credited with helping to fuel the abolitionist cause prior to the American Civil War. Written by Harriet Beecher Stowe and published in 1852, slavery is its central theme.

The Vietnam War inspired many novels although most were written after the war was over. However, the attitudes of Americans about the war have been influenced by these novels, and for many, they have formed the concept they carry with them about the conflict.

Some examples of novels about the Vietnam War:
- *Apocalypse Now*
- *Full Metal Jacket*
- *Platoon*

- *Good Morning Vietnam*
- *The Deer Hunter*
- *Born on the Fourth of July*
- *Hamburger Hill*

Skill 15.4 Applying criteria for evaluating literary merit based on an understanding of genre, literary elements, and literary period and tradition.

There are many ways to talk about the merit of a particular piece of literature. Making the New York Times best-seller list is a pinnacle that most novel writers hope to achieve although those that make the list are not necessarily very highly rated by literary critics. Longevity may be the only true test of the merit of a writer's works. The Nobel Prize for Literature is coveted by serious writers and the recipients are usually considered to be writing valuable and worthwhile works. However, in looking at a particular work and making judgments about its merit, genre must be taken into account. A list of all the possible genres is very long and will include not only romance novels but a long list of subgenres under it, which is indicative of the complications involved in determining the genre a particular piece might fit into and what other works it can reasonably be compared to.

Encyclopedia Britannica points out that even in the oral literature of preliterate people, the important literary genres all existed: heroic epic; songs in praise of priests and kings; stories of mystery and the supernatural; love lyrics; personal songs; love stories; tales of adventure and heroism; satire; satirical combats; ballads; folktales of tragedy and murder; folk stories; animal fables; riddles, proverbs, and philosophical observations; hymns, incantations, and mysterious songs of priests; and mythology.

It's inevitable with all of the writing and publishing going on now that subdivisions have developed in all of these major genres, so for an individual critic to determine exactly what subgenre a particular work appears in can be difficult. Even so, works must be judged against the standards for their genres. Comparing a mystery novel to a romantic novel is not very useful.

At the most basic level, all poetry can be measured by certain standards: A bad poem tends to be stereotyped; an excellent poem unique. What is it trying to do and be and does it succeed? Before judging a poem, one must understand it, although an obscure poem that demands much from the reader may be worthwhile for that very reason. Thomas Aquinas' definition of beauty, "wholeness, harmony, and radiance," are useful in determining whether a poem is successful, valuable, and worthwhile. A good poem should have a significant theme although that is not enough to make it great. Even not-so-good poems can have admirable themes. A great poem shocks us into another order of perception, helps us know ourselves, and points beyond words to something still more essential.

The best poem ushers us into an experience so profoundly moving that we feel changed. A bad or indifferent poem fails to do so. Different periods will judge the same poem differently. It's useful to read what earlier critics have said about a poem and measure their conclusions against those of a different era and of the current understanding of what is valuable and what is not.

Much of the same can be said of the novel. While the novel existed before the 18th century, it was during that period that it came into its own. Pierre Daniel Huet published a treatise on the analysis of the novel in 1670 in which he recommended the following questions: What did the fictional work of a foreign culture or distant period tell us about those who constructed the fiction? What were the cultural needs such stories answered? Are there fundamental anthropological premises which make us create fictional worlds? Did these fictions entertain, divert and instruct? Did they—as one could assume when reading ancient and medieval myths—just provide a substitute for better, more scientific knowledge, or did they add to the luxuries of life a particular culture enjoyed?

Suddenly, reading a novel became more than just getting lost in a dream world of romance; the potential for adding to the readers' store of knowledge about earlier and foreign cultures was an acceptable reason for reading. Literary criticism, critical discussions of poetry and fiction did not come into being until the second half of the eighteenth century. This threw a whole new light on writing. Now novelists could write to be criticized, and the public could observe the interaction between critics and authors. The result was a division into popular fictions and literary production, the latter deemed worthy of discussion and criticism. The Romantic Movement, which began in the 1770s ushered in the *avant garde* novel, where emotions found their test cases. The *Bildungsroman*, a novel of personal development, emerged during this time. For the most part, these novels are too sentimental to pass muster with a 21st century reader or reviewer.

Toward the end of the 18th century, the gothic novel was born. In these novels the sublime (or awful) was juxtaposed with the beautiful. The beautiful heroine's susceptibility to supernatural elements is featured in these novels, designed to scare and terrify readers. By the beginning of the 19th century, the gothic novel had run its course. Jane Austen's *Northanger Abbey* (1803) parodied the gothic novel, reflecting its death. Austen introduced the comedy of manners—novels that were funny but also scathingly critical of the restrictive rural culture of the early 19th century. Before the end of the 19th century, novels had begun to be separated into high and low forms, which continues into the 21st century. The high forms are those that are worthy of criticism; the low forms do not achieve that distinction.

The "low" novelist is usually preoccupied with plot whereas the writer of novels that are adjudged to be "high" enough for criticism are usually concerned with the convolutions of the human personality.

The experiences that are the basis for the conflicts in the story are carefully crafted and are the chief preoccupation. A character may or may not be a human being. In some novels, the conflicts are between non-human elements—the setting or even an animal as in Jack London's *Call of the Wild*. If the characters claim readers' interest, they may be willing to put up with other elements that may be less than perfect. If the character or characters are memorable, the reader tends to see the novel as a good one. If the character seems to have a life beyond the book, the author tends to be better regarded than others.

A novel must be adjudged by the period in which it was created. The sentimentalism of an earlier period might not be appealing to a 21st century reader or critic; nevertheless, they were probably appropriate in the period in which they were written. If they have endured and have continued to be read and enjoyed, then time has proven their worth.

Skill 15.5 Demonstrating awareness of the issue of censorship in relation to literature provided for, or selected by, adolescent readers.

In Rome, the censor had two duties: to count the citizens and to supervise their morals. Today's teacher sometimes fits that definition. However, "supervising morals" becomes increasingly complicated as heated discussions over the role of religion in the classroom, freedom of speech, and maintaining discipline in the classroom mount.

Censorship-of-curriculum issues are usually decided by the administrators and sometimes by the board members of a particular school. Issues involved in making those decisions are religion, race, sex, and politics. Government money is not to be used to promote a particular religion. Even so, any definition of "promote" is debatable. Does a reference to the history of a particular religion fall under the definition? How about an objective comparison of religions? Does the very mention of the names of particular religious figures constitute promotion?

Is it permissible for a student to refer to his own religion in a discussion of literature? Is it permissible for a student to refer to a religion not his own in such a discussion? If students are asked to select a work of literature for a report, is it permissible for that work to reflect a particular religion?

Young people are often very sensitive to issues regarding race and may perceive that there is discrimination where none exists. Nevertheless, a work of literature that seems to present a character of a particular race in a demeaning or critical way should be avoided. Students should be advised of these matters when they are allowed to select what they will read and report on.

Knowing what is too mature sexually for students of a particular age is problematical. Most popular literature includes sexually explicit treatment of characters, plot, conflicts, etc. The safest course is to avoid these resources as much as possible, which amounts to downright censorship. What is lost if this is the course that is taken? Overprotecting students may not be the best preparation for the world they live in or will be moving into as adults. Discussions of some of these matters may be useful in helping them grow and understand what is going on in their lives. Children are becoming sexually active at much earlier ages than ever in the history of public education and must be taken into account. If material that is sexually explicit is used in the classroom, there are sure to be some parents who will object. Carefully following the guidelines of a particular school or school district is the safest route to take.

Skill 15.6 Interpreting a literary passage from a given critical perspective.

To *interpret* means essentially to read with understanding and appreciation. It is not as daunting as it is made out to be. Simple techniques for interpreting literature are as follows:

- **Context:** This includes the author's feelings, beliefs, past experiences, goals, needs, and physical environment. Incorporate an understanding of how these elements may have affected the writing to enrich an interpretation of it.
- **Symbols:** Also referred to as a sign, a symbol designates something which stands for something else. In most cases, it is standing for something that has a deeper meaning than its literal denotation. Symbols can have personal, cultural, or universal associations. Use an understanding of symbols to unearth a meaning the author might have intended but not expressed, or even something the author never intended at all.
- **Questions:** Asking questions, such as "How would I react in this situation?" may shed further light on how you feel about the work.

COMPETENCY 16.0 UNDERSTAND THE CHARACTERISTICS FEATURES OF VARIOUS GENRES OF FICTION, INCLUDING DRAMA.

Skill 16.1 Analyzing elements of fiction (plot, character, setting, theme, point of view) in a passage context.

Essential terminology and literary devices germane to literary analysis include alliteration, allusion, antithesis, aphorism, apostrophe, assonance, blank verse, caesura, conceit, connotation, consonance, couplet, denotation, diction, epiphany, exposition, figurative language, free verse, hyperbole, iambic pentameter, inversion, irony, kenning, metaphor, metaphysical poetry, metonymy, motif, onomatopoeia, octava rima, oxymoron, paradox, parallelism personification, quatrain, scansion, simile, soliloquy, Spenserian stanza, synecdoche, terza rima, tone, and wit.

The more basic terms and devices, such as alliteration, allusion, analogy, aside, assonance, atmosphere, climax, consonance, denouement, elegy, foil, foreshadowing, metaphor, simile, setting, symbol, and theme are defined and exemplified in the English 5-9 Study Guide.

Antithesis: Balanced writing about conflicting ideas, usually expressed in sentence form. Some examples are expanding from the center, shedding old habits, and searching never finding.

Aphorism: A focused, succinct expression about life from a sagacious viewpoint. Writings by Ben Franklin, Sir Francis Bacon, and Alexander Pope contain many aphorisms. "Whatever is begun in anger ends in shame" is an aphorism.

Apostrophe: Literary device of addressing an absent or dead person, an abstract idea, or an inanimate object. Sonneteers, such as Sir Thomas Wyatt, John Keats, and William Wordsworth, address the moon, stars, and the dead Milton. For example, in William Shakespeare's *Julius Caesar*, Mark Antony addresses the corpse of Caesar in the speech that begins: "O, pardon me, thou bleeding piece of earth, That I am meek and gentle with these butchers! Thou art the ruins of the noblest man That ever lived in the tide of times. Woe to the hand that shed this costly blood!"

Blank Verse: Poetry written in iambic pentameter but unrhymed. Works by Shakespeare and Milton are epitomes of blank verse. Milton's Paradise Lost states, "Illumine, what is low raise and support, That to the highth of this great argument I may assert Eternal Providence And justify the ways of God to men."

Caesura: A pause, usually signaled by punctuation, in a line of poetry. The earliest usage occurs in *Beowulf*, the first English epic dating from the Anglo-Saxon era. 'To err is human, // to forgive, divine' (Pope).

Conceit: A comparison, usually in verse, between seemingly disparate objects or concepts. John Donne's metaphysical poetry contains many clever conceits. For instance, Donne's "The Flea" (1633) compares a flea bite to the act of love; and in "A Valediction: Forbidding Mourning" (1633) separated lovers are likened to the legs of a compass, the leg drawing the circle eventually returning home to "the fixed foot."

Connotation: The ripple effect surrounding the implications and associations of a given word, distinct from the denotative, or literal meaning. For example, "Good night, sweet prince, and flights of angels sing thee to thy rest," refers to a burial.

Consonance: The repeated usage of similar consonant sounds, most often used in poetry. "Sally sat sifting seashells by the seashore" is a familiar example.

Couplet: Two rhyming lines of poetry. Shakespeare's sonnets end in heroic couplets written in iambic pentameter. Pope is also a master of the couplet. His *Rape of the Lock* is written entirely in heroic couplets.

Denotation: What a word literally means, as opposed to its connotative meaning. For example, "Good night, sweet prince, and flights of angels sing thee to thy *rest"* refers to sleep.

Diction: The right word in the right spot for the right purpose. The hallmark of a great writer is precise, unusual, and memorable diction.

Epiphany: The moment when the proverbial light bulb goes off in one's head and comprehension sets in.

Exposition: Fill-in or background information about characters meant to clarify and add to the narrative; the initial plot element which precedes the buildup of conflict.

Figurative Language: Not meant in a literal sense, but to be interpreted through symbolism. Figurative language is made up of such literary devices as hyperbole, metonymy, synecdoche, and oxymoron. A synecdoche is a figure of speech in which the word for part of something is used to mean the whole; for example, "sail" for "boat," or vice versa.

Free Verse: Poetry that does not have any predictable meter or patterning. Margaret Atwood, e. e. cummings, and Ted Hughes write in this form.

Hyperbole: Exaggeration for a specific effect. For example, "I'm so hungry that I could eat a million of these."

Iambic Pentameter: The two elements in a set five-foot line of poetry. An iamb is two syllables, unaccented and accented, per foot or measure. Pentameter means five feet of these iambs per line or ten syllables.

Inversion: A typical sentence order to create a given effect or interest. Bacon's and Milton's work use inversion successfully. Emily Dickinson was fond of arranging words outside of their familiar order. For example in "Chartless" she writes "Yet know I how the heather looks" and "Yet certain am I of the spot." Instead of saying "Yet I know" and "Yet I am certain" she reverses the usual order and shifts the emphasis to the more important words.

Irony: An unexpected disparity between what is written or stated and what is really meant or implied by the author. Verbal, situational, and dramatic are the three literary ironies. Verbal irony is when an author says one thing and means something else. Dramatic irony is when an audience perceives something that a character in the literature does not know. Irony of situation is a discrepancy between the expected result and actual results. Shakespeare's plays contain numerous and highly effective use of irony. O. Henry's short stories have ironic endings.

Kenning: Another way to describe a person, place, or thing so as to avoid prosaic repetition. The earliest examples can be found in Anglo-Saxon literature such as *Beowulf* and "The Seafarer." Instead of writing King Hrothgar, the anonymous monk wrote, great Ring-Giver, or Father of his people. A lake becomes the swans' way, and the ocean or sea becomes the great whale's way. In ancient Greek literature, this device was called an "epithet."

Metaphysical Poetry: Verse characterization by ingenious wit, unparalleled imagery, and clever conceits. The greatest metaphysical poet is John Donne. Henry Vaughn and other 17th century British poets contributed to this movement as in *Words*, "I saw eternity the other night, like a great being of pure and endless light."

Metonymy: Use of an object or idea closely identified with another object or idea to represent the second. "Hit the books" means "go study." Washington, D.C. means the U.S. government and the White House means the U.S. President.

Motif: A key, oft-repeated phrase, name, or idea in a literary work. Dorset/Wessex in Hardy's novels and the moors and the harsh weather in the Bronte sisters' novels are effective use of motifs. Shakespeare's *Romeo and Juliet* represents the ill-fated young lovers' motif.

Onomatopoeia: Word used to evoke the sound in its meaning. The early Batman series used *pow, zap, whop, zonk* and *eek* in an onomatopoetic way.

Octava rima: A specific eight-line stanza of poetry whose rhyme scheme is abababcc. Lord Byron's mock epic, *Don Juan*, is written in this poetic way.

Oxymoron: A contradictory form of speech, such as jumbo shrimp, unkindly kind, or singer John Mellencamp's "It hurts so good."

Paradox: Seemingly untrue statement, which when examined more closely proves to be true. John Donne's sonnet "Death Be Not Proud" postulates that death shall die and humans will triumph over death, at first thought not true, but ultimately explained and proven in this sonnet.

Parallelism: A type of close repetition of clauses or phrases that emphasize key topics or ideas in writing. The psalms in the King James Version of the *Bible* contain many examples.

Personification: Giving human characteristics to inanimate objects or concepts. Great writers, with few exceptions, are masters of this literary device.

Quatrain: A poetic stanza composed of four lines. A Shakespearean or Elizabethan sonnet is made up of three quatrains and ends with a heroic couplet.

Scansion: The two-part analysis of a poetic line. Count the number of syllables per line and determine where the accents fall. Divide the line into metric feet. Name the meter by the type and number of feet. Much is written about scanning poetry. Try not to inundate your students with this jargon; rather allow them to feel the power of the poets' words, ideas, and images instead.

Soliloquy: A highlighted speech, in drama, usually delivered by a major character expounding on the author's philosophy or expressing, at times, universal truths. This is done with the character alone on the stage.

Spenserian Stanza: Invented by Sir Edmund Spenser for usage in *The Fairie Queene*, his epic poem honoring Queen Elizabeth I. Each stanza consists of nine lines, eight in iambic parameter. The ninth line, called an alexandrine, has two extra syllables or one additional foot.

Sprung Rhythm: Invented and used extensively by the poet, Gerard Manley Hopkins. It consists of variable meter, which combines stressed and unstressed syllables fashioned by the author. See "Pied Beauty" or "God's Grandeur."

Stream of Consciousness: A style of writing which reflects the mental processes of the characters expressing, at times, jumbled memories, feelings, and dreams. "Big time players" in this type of expression are James Joyce, Virginia Woolf, and William Faulkner.

Terza Rima: A series of poetic stanzas utilizing the recurrent rhyme scheme of aba, bcb, cdc, ded, and so forth. The second-generation Romantic poets - Keats, Byron, Shelley, and, to a lesser degree, Yeats - used this Italian verse form, especially in their odes. Dante used this stanza in *The Divine Comedy*.

Tone: The discernible attitude inherent in an author's work regarding the subject, readership, or characters. Swift's or Pope's tone is satirical. Boswell's tone toward Johnson is admiring.

Wit: Writing of genius, keenness, and sagacity expressed through clever use of language. Alexander Pope and the Augustans wrote about and were themselves said to possess wit.

Skill 16.2 Comparing the characteristics of types of fictional narratives (Fable, folk legend, fantasy, realistic novel).

The major literary genres include allegory, ballad, drama, epic, epistle, essay, fable, novel, poem, romance, and the short story.

Allegory: A story in verse or prose with characters representing virtues and vices. There are two meanings, symbolic and literal. John Bunyan's *The Pilgrim's Progress* is the most renowned of this genre.

Ballad: An *in medias res* story told or sung, usually in verse and accompanied by music. Literary devices found in ballads include the refrain, or repeated section, and incremental repetition, or anaphora, for effect. Earliest forms were anonymous folk ballads. Later forms include Coleridge's Romantic masterpiece, "The Rime of the Ancient Mariner."

Drama: Plays – comedy, modern, or tragedy - typically in five acts. Traditionalists and neoclassicists adhere to Aristotle's unities of time, place and action. Plot development is advanced via dialogue. Literary devices include asides, soliloquies and the chorus representing public opinion. Greatest of all dramatists/playwrights is William Shakespeare. Other dramaturges include Ibsen, Williams, Miller, Shaw, Stoppard, Racine, Moliére, Sophocles, Aeschylus, Euripides, and Aristophanes.

Epic: Long poem usually of book length reflecting values inherent in the generative society. Epic devices include an invocation to a Muse for inspiration, purpose for writing, universal setting, protagonist and antagonist who possess supernatural strength and acumen, and interventions of a God or the gods. Understandably, there are very few epics: Homer's *Iliad* and *Odyssey*, Virgil's *Aeneid*, Milton's *Paradise Lost*, Spenser's *The Fairie Queene*, Barrett Browning's *Aurora Leigh*, and Pope's mock-epic, *The Rape of the Lock*.

Epistle: A letter that is not always originally intended for public distribution, but due to the fame of the sender and/or recipient, becomes public domain. Paul wrote epistles that were later placed in the <u>Bible</u>.

Essay: Typically a limited length prose work focusing on a topic and propounding a definite point of view and authoritative tone. Great essayists include Carlyle, Lamb, DeQuincy, Emerson and Montaigne, who is credited with defining this genre.

Fable: Terse tale offering up a moral or exemplum. Chaucer's "The Nun's Priest's Tale" is a fine example of a *bete fabliau* or beast fable in which animals speak and act characteristically human, illustrating human foibles.

Legend: A traditional narrative or collection of related narratives, popularly regarded as historically factual but actually a mixture of fact and fiction.

Myth: Stories that are more or less universally shared within a culture to explain its history and traditions.

Novel: The longest form of fictional prose containing a variety of characterizations, settings, local color and regionalism. Most have complex plots, expanded description, and attention to detail. Some of the great novelists include Austin, the Brontes, Twain, Tolstoy, Hugo, Hardy, Dickens, Hawthorne, Forster, and Flaubert.

Poem: The only requirement is rhythm. Sub-genres include fixed types of literature such as the sonnet, elegy, ode, pastoral, and villanelle. Unfixed types of literature include blank verse and dramatic monologue.

Romance: A highly imaginative tale set in a fantastical realm dealing with the conflicts between heroes, villains and/or monsters. "The Knight's Tale" from Chaucer's *Canterbury Tales*, *Sir Gawain and the Green Knight* and Keats' "The Eve of St. Agnes" are prime representatives.

Short Story: Typically a terse narrative, with less developmental background about characters. May include description, author's point of view, and tone. Poe emphasized that a successful short story should create one focused impact. Considered to be great short story writers are Hemingway, Faulkner, Twain, Joyce, Shirley Jackson, Flannery O'Connor, de Maupasssant, Saki, Edgar Allen Poe, and Pushkin.

Skill 16.3 Identifying types of drama (comedy, tragedy) and applying knowledge of dramatic structure (introduction, rising action, climax, falling action, conclusion) and common dramatic devices (irony, suspense, soliloquy, aside).

Comedy: The comedic form of dramatic literature is meant to amuse, and often ends happily. It uses techniques such as satire or parody, and can take many forms, from farce to burlesque. Examples include Dante Alighieri's *The Divine Comedy,* Noel Coward's play *Private Lives,* and some of Geoffrey Chaucer's *Canterbury Tales* and William Shakespeare's plays.

Tragedy: Tragedy is comedy's other half. It is defined as a work of drama written in either prose or poetry, telling the story of a brave, noble hero who, because of some tragic character flaw, brings ruin upon himself. It is characterized by serious, poetic language that evokes pity and fear.

In modern times, dramatists have tried to update its image by drawing its main characters from the middle class and showing their nobility through their nature instead of their standing. The classic example of tragedy is Sophocles' *Oedipus Rex*, while Henrik Ibsen and Arthur Miller epitomize modern tragedy.

Drama: In its most general sense, a drama is any work that is designed to be performed by actors onstage. It can also refer to the broad literary genre that includes comedy and tragedy. Contemporary usage, however, denotes drama as a work that treats serious subjects and themes but does not aim for the same grandeur as tragedy. Drama usually deals with characters of a less stately nature than tragedy. A classical example is Sophocles' tragedy *Oedipus Rex,* while Eugene O'Neill's *The Iceman Cometh* represents modern drama.

Dramatic Monologue: A dramatic monologue is a speech given by an actor, usually intended for themselves, but with the intended audience in mind. It reveals key aspects of the character's psyche and sheds insight on the situation at hand. The audience takes the part of the silent listener, passing judgment and giving sympathy at the same time. This form was invented and used predominantly by Victorian poet Robert Browning.

Tempo

Interpretation of dialogue must be connected to motivation and detail. During this time, the director is also concerned with pace and seeks a variation of tempo. If the overall pace is too slow, then the action becomes dull and dragging. If the overall pace is too fast, then the audience will not be able to understand what is going on, for they are being hit with too much information to process.

Dramatic Arc

Good drama is built on conflict of some kind — an opposition of forces or desires that must be resolved by the end of the story. The conflict can be internal, involving emotional and psychological pressures, or it can be external, drawing the characters into tumultuous events. These themes are presented to the audience in a narrative arc that looks roughly like this:

English   109

Following the Arc

Although any performance may have a series of rising and falling levels of intensity, in general the opening should set in motion the events which will generate an emotional high toward the middle or end of the story. Then, regardless of whether the ending is happy, sad, bittersweet, or despairing, the resolution eases the audience down from those heights and establishes some sense of closure. Reaching the climax too soon undermines the dramatic impact of the remaining portion of the performance, whereas reaching it too late rushes the ending and creates a jarringly abrupt end to events.

Skill 16.4 Recognizing the challenges of interpreting a dramatic text when the text is read rather than performed.

The playwright does many of the things the novelist does. The play will have conflicts, characters, plot, setting, climax, and possibly denouement just as a novel does. However, some parts of the play are not written into the story, such as setting and the personal characteristics of the characters, which will be supplied by a staged setting and the actors, who will be adding their own interpretations. The characterization of a rounded character in a novel requires creating pictures for the reader. Those pictures are not provided in a drama—they are supplied in the acting out of the play itself.

The playwright will write stage directions, which are intended to provide visual clues for the audience. Even if those directions are included in the reading of the play, there is often a disconnect between what is mentally envisioned and what would actually be a factor in the effect of the play on an audience. In a play by Shakespeare, those stage directions will be difficult to understand because the theaters they were written for were very different from modern ones.

If a play is assigned to be read, students should be advised of these deficiencies and suggestions made for compensating for them to include visualizing setting and actor interpretation. Certainly, plot can be derived from a reading of a play and there are clues to what the characters will be like. The theme or point of the story can usually be derived form a reading. Even so, a fully-developed critique can only come from viewing it dramatized.

The plays of Shakespeare are often read, but seeing one of those plays acted out is an entirely different experience. If students are reading a Shakespearean play, it is helpful to obtain a recording of a dramatized one so students can see the difference. It often leads to a lifetime of enthusiasm for and enjoyment of good drama, a valuable objective for a literature class.

COMPETENCY 17.0 UNDERSTAND THE CHARACTERISTIC FEATURES OF VARIOUS TYPES OF NONFICTION

Skill 17.1 Comparing and contrasting characteristics of various types of nonfiction (biographies, autobiographies, essays, journals, letters, memoirs, informational books and articles, newspaper accounts of events).

Biography: A form of nonfictional literature, the subject of which is the life of an individual. The earliest biographical writings were probably funeral speeches and inscriptions, usually praising the life and example of the deceased. Early biographies evolved from this and were almost invariably uncritical, even distorted, and always laudatory. Beginning in the 18th century, this form of literature saw major development; an eminent example is James Boswell's *Life of Johnson*, which is very detailed and even records conversations. Eventually, the antithesis of the grossly exaggerated tomes praising an individual, usually a person of circumstance, developed. This form is denunciatory, debunking, and often inflammatory. A famous modern example is Lytton Strachey's *Eminent Victorians* (1918).

Autobiography: A form of biography, but it is written by the subject himself or herself. Autobiographies can range from the very formal to intimate writings made during one's life that were not intended for publication. These include letters, diaries, journals, memoirs, and reminiscences. Autobiography, generally speaking, began in the 15th century; one of the first examples is one written in England by Margery Kempe. There are four kinds of autobiography: thematic, religious, intellectual, and fictionalized. Some "novels" may be thinly disguised autobiography, such as the novels of Thomas Wolfe.

Informational books and articles: Make up much of the reading of modern Americans. Magazines began to be popular in the 19th century in this country, and while many of the contributors to those publications intended to influence the political/social/religious convictions of their readers, many also simply intended to pass on information. A book or article whose purpose is simply to be informative, that is, not to persuade, is called exposition (adjectival form: expository). An example of an expository book is the *MLA Style Manual*. The writers do not intend to persuade their readers to use the recommended stylistic features in their writing; they are simply making them available in case a reader needs such a guide. Articles in magazines such as *Time* may be persuasive in purpose, such as Joe Klein's regular column, but for the most part they are expository, giving information that television coverage of a news story might not have time to include.

Newspaper accounts of events: Expository in nature, of course, a reporting of a happening. That happening might be a school board meeting, an automobile accident that sent several people to a hospital and accounted for the death of a passenger, or the election of the mayor.

They are not intended to be persuasive although the bias of a reporter or of an editor must be factored in. A newspapers' editorial stance is often openly declared, and it may be reflected in such things as news reports. Reporters are expected to be unbiased in their coverage and most of them will defend their disinterest fiercely, but what a writer *sees* in an event is inevitably shaped to some extent by the writer's beliefs and experiences.

Skill 17.2 Comparing and contrasting characteristics of fiction and nonfiction.

Fiction is the opposite of fact, and, simple as that may seem, it's the major distinction between fictional works and nonfictional works. The earliest nonfiction came in the form of cave-paintings, the record of what prehistoric man caught on hunting trips. On the other hand, we don't know that some of it might be fiction—that is, what they would like to catch on future hunting trips. Cuneiform inscriptions, which hold the earliest writings, are probably nonfiction, about conveying goods such as oxen and barley and dealing with the buying and selling of these items. It's easy to assume that nonfiction, then, is pretty boring, since it simply serves the purpose of recording everyday facts. Fiction, on the other hand, is the result of imagination and is recorded for the purpose of entertainment. If a work of nonfiction endures beyond its original time, it tends to be viewed as either exceptionally well made or perfectly embodying the ideas, manners, and attitudes of the time when it was produced.

Some (not all) types of nonfiction:
- Almanac
- Autobiography
- Biography
- Blueprint
- Book report
- Diary
- Dictionary
- Documentary film
- Encyclopedia
- Essay
- History
- Journal
- Letter
- Philosophy
- Science book
- Textbook
- User manual

These can also be called genres of nonfiction—divisions of a particular art according to criteria particular to that form.

How these divisions are formed is vague. There are actually no fixed boundaries for either fiction or nonfiction. They are formed by sets of conventions and many works cross into multiple genres by way of borrowing and recombining these conventions.

Some genres of fiction (not all):

- Action-adventure
- Crime
- Detective
- Erotica
- Fantasy
- Horror
- Mystery
- Romance
- Science fiction
- Thriller
- Western

A *bildungsroman* (from the German) means "novel of education" or "novel of formation" and is a novel that traces the spiritual, moral, psychological, or social development and growth of the main character from childhood to maturity. Dickens' *David Copperfield* (1850) represents this genre as does Thomas Wolfe's *Look Homeward Angel* (1929).

A work of fiction typically has a central character, called the protagonist, and a character that stands in opposition, called the antagonist. The antagonist might be something other than a person. In Stephen Crane's short story, *The Open Boat*, for example, the antagonist is a hostile environment, a stormy sea. Conflicts between protagonist and antagonist are typical of a work of fiction, and climax is the point at which those conflicts are resolved. The plot has to do with the form or shape that the conflicts take as they move toward resolution. A fiction writer artistically uses devices labeled characterization to reveal character. Characterization can depend on dialogue, description, or the attitude or attitudes of one or more characters toward another.

Enjoying fiction depends upon the ability of the reader to suspend belief, to some extent. The reader makes a deal with the writer that for the time it takes to read the story, his/her own belief will be put aside, replaced by the convictions and reality that the writer has written into the story. This is not true in nonfiction. The writer of nonfiction declares in the choice of that genre that the work is reliably based upon reality. The *MLA Style Manual*, for instance, can be relied upon because it is not the result of someone's imagination.

Skill 17.3 Analyzing the author's point of view, tone, and style in nonfiction works.

See Skill 14.5.

Skill 17.4 Analyzing the use of common patterns of organization in nonfiction works of various types.

An easy and effective way of organizing information to be used in a work of nonfiction is by asking specific questions that are geared towards a particular mode of presentation. An example of these questions follows:

Useful research questions:

What is it?

It is the process of thinking up and writing down a set of questions that you want to answer about the research topic you have selected.

Why should I do it?

It will keep you from getting lost or off-track when looking for information. You will try to find the answers to these questions when you do your research.

When do I do it?

After you have written your statement of purpose, and have a focused topic to ask questions about, begin research.

How do I do it?

Make two lists of questions. Label one "factual" questions and one "interpretive" questions. The answers to factual questions will give your reader the basic background information they need to understand your topic. The answers to interpretive questions show your creative thinking in your project and can become the basis for your thesis statement.

Asking factual questions:

Assume your reader knows nothing about your subject. Make an effort to tell them everything they need to know to understand what you will say in your project.

Make a list of specific questions that ask: Who? What? When? Where?

Example: For a report about President Abraham Lincoln's attitude and policies towards slavery, people will have to know; Who was Abraham Lincoln? Where and when was he born? What political party did he belong to? When was he elected president? What were the attitudes and laws about slavery during his lifetime? How did his actions affect slavery?

Asking Interpretive Questions:

These kinds of questions are the result of your own original thinking. They can be based on the preliminary research you have done on your chosen topic. Select one or two to answer in your presentation. They can be the basis of forming a thesis statement.

- **Hypothetical**: How would things be different today if something in the past had been different?

Example: How would our lives be different today if the Confederate (southern) states had won the United States Civil War? What would have happened to the course of World War Two if the Atomic Bomb hadn't been dropped on Hiroshima and Nagasaki?

- **Prediction**: How will something look or be in the future, based on the way it is now?

Example: What will happen to sea levels if global warming due to ozone layer depletion continues and the polar caps melt significantly? If the population of China continues to grow at the current rate for the next fifty years, how will that impact its role in world politics?

- **Solution**: What solutions can be offered to a problem that exists today?

Example: How could global warming be stopped? What can be done to stop the spread of sexually transmitted diseases among teenagers?

- **Comparison or Analogy**: Find the similarities and differences between your main subject and a similar subject, or with another subject in the same time period or place.

Example: In what ways is the Civil War in the former Yugoslavia similar to (or different from) the United States Civil War?
What is the difference in performance between a Porsche and a Lamborghini?

- **Judgment**: Based on the information you find, what can you say as your informed opinion about the subject?

Example: How does tobacco advertising affect teen cigarette smoking? What are the major causes of eating disorders among young women? How does teen parenthood affect the future lives of young women and men?

Skill 17.5 Applying knowledge of criteria for evaluating nonfiction (point of view, objectivity, subjectivity, bias).

See Competency 14.0.

COMPETENCY 18.0 UNDERSTAND THE CHARACTERISTIC FEATURES OF VARIOUS FORMS OF POETRY

Skill 18.1 Analyzing the relationship between the form and meaning of a poetic text.

When we speak of *form* with regard to poetry, we usually mean one of three things:
1. The pattern of the sound and rhythm
2. The visible shape it takes
3. Rhyme or free verse

1. The pattern of the sound and rhythm

It helps to know the history of this peculiarity of poetry. History was passed down in oral form almost exclusively until the invention of the printing press and was often set to music. A rhymed story is much easier to commit to memory. Adding a tune makes it even easier to remember, so it's not a surprise that much of the earliest literature—epics, odes, etc., are rhymed and were probably sung. When we speak of the pattern of sound and rhythm, we are referring to two things: verse form and stanza form.

The verse form is the rhythmic pattern of a single verse. An example would be any meter: blank verse, for instance, is iambic pentameter. A stanza is a group of a certain number of verses (lines), having a rhyme scheme. If the poem is written, there is usually white space between the verses although a short poem may be only one stanza. If the poem is spoken, there will be a pause between stanzas.

2. The visible shape it takes

In the seventeenth century, some poets shaped their poems to reflect the theme. A good example is George Herbert's *Easter Wings*. Since that time, poets have occasionally played with this device; it is, however, generally viewed as nothing more than a demonstration of ingenuity. The rhythm, effect, and meaning are often sacrificed to the forcing of the shape.

3. Rhyme and free verse

Poets also use devices to establish form that will underscore the meanings of their poems. A very common one is alliteration. When the poem is read (which poetry is usually intended to be), the repetition of a sound may not only underscore the meaning, it may also pleasure to the reading. Following a strict rhyming pattern can add intensity to the meaning of the poem in the hands of a skilled and creative poet. On the other hand, the meaning can be drowned out by the steady beat-beat-beat of it.

Shakespeare very skillfully used the regularity of rhyme in his poetry, breaking the rhythm at certain points to very effectively underscore a point. For example, in Sonnet #130, "My mistress' eyes are nothing like the sun," the rhythm is primarily iambic pentameter. It lulls the reader (or listener) to accept that this poet is following the standard conventions for love poetry, which in that day reliably used rhyme and more often than not iambic pentameter to express feelings of romantic love along conventional lines. However, in Sonnet #130, the last two lines sharply break from the monotonous pattern, forcing reader or speaker to pause:

> And yet, by heaven, I think my love as rare
> As any she belied with false compare

Shakespeare's purpose is clear: he is not writing a conventional love poem; the object of his love is not the red-and-white conventional woman written about in other poems of the period. This is a good example where a poet uses form to underscore meaning.

Poets eventually began to feel constricted by the rhyming conventions and began to break away and make new rules for poetry. When poetry was only rhymed, it was easy to define it. When free verse, or poetry written in a flexible form, came upon the scene in France in the 1880s, it quickly began to influence English-language poets such as T. S. Eliot, whose memorable poem, *The Wasteland*, had an alarming but desolate message for the modern world. It's impossible to imagine that it could have been written in the soothing, lulling rhymed verse of previous periods. Those who first began writing in free verse in English were responding to the influence of the French *vers libre*. However, it should be noted that it could be loosely applied to the poetry of Walt Whitman, writing in the mid-nineteenth century, as can be seen in the first stanza of *Son of Myself*:

> I celebrate myself, and sing myself,
> And what I assume you shall assume,
> For every atom belonging to me as good belongs to you.

When poetry was no longer defined as a piece of writing arranged in verses that had a rhyme-scheme of some sort, distinguishing poetry from prose became a point of discussion. Merriam Webster's *Encyclopedia of Literature* defines poetry as follows: "Writing that formulates a concentrated imaginative awareness of experience in language chosen and arranged to create a specific emotional response through its meaning, sound and rhythm."

A poet chooses the form of his poetry deliberately, based upon the emotional response he hopes to evoke and the meaning he wishes to convey. Robert Frost, a twentieth-century poet who chose to use conventional rhyming verse to make his point is a memorable and often-quoted modern poet. Who can forget his closing lines in "Stopping by Woods"?

> And miles to go before I sleep,
> And miles to go before I sleep.

Would they be as memorable if the poem had been written in free verse?

Skill 18.2 Applying knowledge of formal rhyme schemes and other poetic techniques related to the sounds of words (slant rhyme, alliteration, assonance, onomatopoeia).

Slant Rhyme: Occurs when the final consonant sounds are the same, but the vowels are different. Occurs frequently in Irish, Welsh, and Icelandic verse. Examples include: green and gone, that and hit, ill and shell.

Alliteration: Alliteration occurs when the initial sounds of a word, beginning either with a consonant or a vowel, are repeated in close succession. Examples include: Athena and Apollo, Nate never knows, People who pen poetry.

Note that the words only have to be close to one another: Alliteration that repeats and attempts to connect a number of words is little more than a tongue-twister.

The function of alliteration, like rhyme, might be to accentuate the beauty of language in a given context, or to unite words or concepts through a kind of repetition. Alliteration, like rhyme, can follow specific patterns. Sometimes the consonants aren't always the initial ones, but they are generally the stressed syllables. Alliteration is less common than rhyme, but because it is less common, it can call our attention to a word or line in a poem that might not have the same emphasis otherwise.

Assonance: If alliteration occurs at the beginning of a word and rhyme at the end, assonance takes the middle territory. Assonance occurs when the vowel sound within a word matches the same sound in a nearby word, but the surrounding consonant sounds are different. "Tune" and "June" are rhymes; "tune" and "food" are assonant. The function of assonance is frequently the same as end rhyme or alliteration; all serve to give a sense of continuity or fluidity to the verse. Assonance might be especially effective when rhyme is absent: It gives the poet more flexibility, and it is not typically used as part of a predetermined pattern. Like alliteration, it does not so much determine the structure or form of a poem; rather, it is more ornamental.

Onomatopoeia: Word used to evoke the sound in its meaning. The early Batman series used *pow, zap, whop, zonk* and *eek* in an onomatopoetic way.

Skill 18.3 Demonstrating knowledge of poetic meter and stanza structures.

Rhythm in poetry refers to the recurrence of stresses at equal intervals. A stress (accent) is a greater amount of force given to one syllable in speaking than is given to another. For example, we put the stress on the first syllable of such words as father, mother, daughter, children. The unstressed or unaccented syllable is sometimes called a slack syllable. All English words carry at least one stress except articles and some prepositions such as by, from, at, etc. Indicating where stresses occur is to scan; doing this is called scansion.

Very little is gained in understanding a poem or making a statement about it by merely scanning it. The pattern of the rhythm—the meter—should be analyzed in terms of its overall relationship to the message and impression of the poem.

Slack syllables, when they recur in pairs cause rhythmic trippings and bouncings; on the other hand, recurrent pairs of stresses will create a heavier rocking effect. The rhythm is dependent on words to convey meaning. Alone, they communicate nothing. When examining the rhythm and meaning of a poem, a good question to ask is whether the rhythm is appropriate to the theme. A bouncing rhythm, for example, might be dissonant in a solemn elegy.

Stops are those places in a poem where the punctuation requires a pause. An end-stopped line is one that *ends* in a pause whereas one that has no punctuation at its end and is, therefore, read with only a slight pause after it is said to be run-on and the running on of its thought into the next line is called enjambment. These are used by a poet to underscore, intensify, communicate meaning.

Rhythm, then, is a *pattern of recurrence* and in poetry is made up of stressed and relatively unstressed syllables. The poet can manipulate the rhythm by making the intervals between his stresses regular or varied, by making his lines short or long, by end-stopping his lines or running them over, by choosing words that are easier or less easy to say, by choosing polysyllabic words or monosyllables. The most important thing to remember about rhythm is that it conveys meaning.

The basic unit of rhythm is called a foot and is usually one stressed syllable with one or two unstressed ones or two stressed syllables with one unstressed one. A foot made up of one unstressed syllable and one stressed one is called an iamb. If a line is made of five iambs, it is iambic pentameter. A rhymed poem typically establishes a pattern such as iambic pentameter, and even though there will be syllables that don't fit the pattern, the poem, nevertheless, will be said to be in iambic pentameter. In fact, a poem may be considered weak if the rhythm is too monotonous.

The most common kinds of feet in English poetry:

iamb: -'
anapest: --'
trochee: '-
dactyl: '--
Monosyllabic: '
Spondee: "
Pyrrhic foot: --

Iambic and anapestic are said to be rising because the movement is from slack to stressed syllables. Trochaic and dactylic are said to be falling.

Meters are named as follows:
Monometer: a line of one foot
Dimeter: a line of two feet
Trimeter: a line of three feet
Tetrameter: a line of four feet
Pentameter: a line of five feet
Hexameter: a line of six feet
Heptameter: a line of seven feet
Octameter: a line of eight feet

Longer lines are possible, but a reader will tend to break it up into shorter lengths.

A caesura is a definite pause within a line, in scansion indicated by a double line: ‖

A stanza is a group of a certain number of lines with a rhyme scheme or a particular rhythm or both, typically set off by white space.

Some typical patterns of English poetry:
Blank verse: unrhymed iambic pentameter.
Couplet: two-line stanza, usually rhymed and typically not separated by white space.
Heroic couplet or closed couplet: two rhymed lines of iambic pentameter, the first ending in a light pause, the second more heavily end-stopped.
Tercet: a three-line stanza, which, if rhymed, usually keeps to one rhyme sound.
Terza rima: the middle line of the tercet rhymes with the first and third lines of the next tercet.
The quatrain: four-line stanza, the most popular in English.
The ballad stanza: four iambic feet in lines 1 and 3, three in lines 2 and 4. Rhyming is abcb.
The refrain: a line or lines repeated in a ballad as a chorus.
Terminal refrain: follows a stanza in a ballad.
Five-line stanzas occur, but not frequently.
Six-line stanzas, more frequent than five-line ones.
The sestina: six six-line stanzas and a tercet. Repeats in each stanza the same six end-words in a different order.
Rime royal: seven-line stanza in iambic pentameter with rhyme ababbcc.
Ottava rima: eight-line stanza of iambic pentameter rhyming abababcc.
Spenserian stanza: nine lines, rhyming ababbcbcc for eight lines then concludes with an Alexandrine.
The Alexandrine: a line of iambic hexameter.
Free verse: no conventional patterns of rhyme, stanza, or meter.
Sonnet: a fourteen-line poem in iambic pentameter.
  1) English sonnet: sometimes called a Shakespearean sonnet. Rhymes cohere in four clusters: abab cdcd efef gg

2) Italian or Petrarchan sonnet: first eight lines (the octave), abbaabba; then the sestet, the last six lines add new rhyme sounds in almost any variation; does not end in a couplet.

Skill 18.4 Analyzing the use of imagery, symbolism, allusion, and figurative language in poetic texts.

Imagery can be described as a word or sequence of words that refers to any sensory experience—that is, anything that can be seen, tasted, smelled, heard, or felt on the skin or fingers. While writers of prose may also use these devices, it is most distinctive of poetry. The poet intends to make an experience available to the reader. In order to do that, he/she must appeal to one of the senses. The most-often-used one, of course, is the visual sense. The poet will deliberately paint a scene in such a way that the reader can see it. However, the purpose is not simply to stir the visceral feeling but also to stir the emotions. A good example is "The Piercing Chill" by Taniguchi Buson (1715-1783):

> The piercing chill I feel:
> My dead wife's comb, in our bedroom,
> Under my heel . . .

In only a few short words, the reader can feel many things: the shock that might come from touching the corpse, a literal sense of death, the contrast between her death and the memories he has of her when she was alive. Imagery might be defined as speaking of the abstract in concrete terms, a powerful device in the hands of a skillful poet.

A **symbol** is an object or action that can be observed with the senses in addition to its suggesting many other things. The lion is a symbol of courage; the cross a symbol of Christianity; the color green a symbol of envy. These can almost be defined as metaphors because society pretty much agrees on the one-to-one meaning of them. Symbols used in literature are usually of a different sort. They tend to be private and personal; their significance is only evident in the context of the work where they are used. A good example is the huge pair of spectacles on a sign board in Fitzgerald's *The Great Gatsby*. They are interesting as a part of the landscape, but they also symbolize divine myopia. A symbol can certainly have more than one meaning, and the meaning may be as personal as the memories and experiences of the particular reader. In analyzing a poem or a story, it's important to identify the symbols and their possible meanings.

Looking for symbols is often challenging, especially for novice poetry readers. However, these suggestions may be useful: First, pick out all the references to concrete objects such as a newspaper, black cats, etc. Note any that the poet emphasizes by describing in detail, by repeating, or by placing at the very beginning or ending of a poem. Ask yourself, what is the poem about? What does it add up to? Paraphrase the poem and determine whether or not the meaning depends upon certain concrete objects. Then ponder what the concrete object symbolizes in this particular poem.

Look for a character with the name of a prophet who does little but utter prophecy or a trio of women who resemble the Three Fates. A symbol may be a part of a person's body such as the eye of the murder victim in Poe's story *The Tell-Tale Heart* or a look, a voice, or a mannerism.

Some things a symbol is not: an abstraction such as truth, death, and love; in narrative, a well-developed character who is not at all mysterious; the second term in a metaphor. In Emily Dickenson's *The Lightning is a yellow Fork*, the symbol is the lightning, not the fork.

An **allusion** is very much like a symbol, and the two sometimes tend to run together. An allusion is defined by Merriam Webster's *Encyclopedia of Literature* as "an implied reference to a person, event, thing, or a part of another text." Allusions are based on the assumption that there is a common body of knowledge shared by poet and reader and that a reference to that body of knowledge will be immediately understood. Allusions to the Bible and classical mythology are common in western literature on the assumption that they will be immediately understood. This is not always the case, of course. T. S. Eliot's *The Wasteland* requires research and annotation for understanding. He assumed more background on the part of the average reader than actually exists. However, when Michael Moore on his web page headlines an article on the war in Iraq: "Déjà Fallouja: Ramadi surrounded, thousands of families trapped, no electricity or water, onslaught impending," we understand immediately that he is referring first of all to a repeat of the human disaster in New Orleans although the "onslaught" is not a storm but an invasion by American and Iraqi troops.

The use of allusion is a sort of shortcut for poets. They can use an economy of words and count on meaning to come from the reader's own experience.

Figurative language is also called figures of speech. If all figures of speech that have ever been identified were listed, it would be a very long list. However, for purposes of analyzing poetry, a few are sufficient.
1. Simile: Direct comparison between two things. "My love is like a red-red rose."
2. Metaphor: Indirect comparison between two things. The use of a word or phrase denoting one kind of object or action in place of another to suggest a comparison between them. While poets use them extensively, they are also integral to everyday speech. For example, chairs are said to have "legs" and "arms" although we know that it's humans and other animals that have these appendages.
3. Parallelism: The arrangement of ideas in phrases, sentences, and paragraphs that balance one element with another of equal importance and similar wording. An example from Francis Bacon's *Of Studies:* "Reading maketh a full man, conference a ready man, and writing an exact man."

4. Personification: Human characteristics are attributed to an inanimate object, an abstract quality, or animal. Examples: John Bunyan wrote characters named Death, Knowledge, Giant Despair, Sloth, and Piety in his *Pilgrim's Progress.* The metaphor of an arm of a chair is a form of personification.

5. Euphemism: The substitution of an agreeable or inoffensive term for one that might offend or suggest something unpleasant. Many euphemisms are used to refer to death to avoid using the real word such as "passed away," "crossed over," or nowadays "passed."

6. Hyperbole: Deliberate exaggeration for effect or comic effect. An example from Shakespeare's *The Merchant of Venice*:

> Why, if two gods should play some heavenly match
> And on the wager lay two earthly women,
> And Portia one, there must be something else
> Pawned with the other, for the poor rude world
> Hath not her fellow.

7. Climax: A number of phrases or sentences are arranged in ascending order of rhetorical forcefulness. Example from Melville's *Moby Dick*:

> All that most maddens and torments; all that stirs up the lees of things; all truth with malice in it; all that cracks the sinews and cakes the brain; all the subtle demonisms of life and thought; all evil, to crazy Ahab, were visibly personified and made practically assailable in Moby Dick.

8. Bathos: A ludicrous attempt to portray pathos—that is, to evoke pity, sympathy, or sorrow. It may result from inappropriately dignifying the commonplace, elevated language to describe something trivial, or greatly exaggerated pathos.

9. Oxymoron: A contradiction in terms deliberately employed for effect. It is usually seen in a qualifying adjective whose meaning is contrary to that of the noun it modifies such as wise folly.

10. Irony: Expressing something other than and particularly opposite the literal meaning such as words of praise when blame is intended. In poetry, it is often used as a sophisticated or resigned awareness of contrast between what is and what ought to be and expresses a controlled pathos without sentimentality. It is a form of indirection that avoids overt praise or censure. An early example: the Greek comic character Eiron, a clever underdog who by his wit repeatedly triumphs over the boastful character Alazon.

11. Alliteration: The repetition of consonant sounds in two or more neighboring words or syllables. In its simplest form, it reinforces one or two consonant sounds. Example: Shakespeare's Sonnet #12:

> When I do count the clock that tells the time.

Some poets have used more complex patterns of alliteration by creating consonants both at the beginning of words and at the beginning of stressed syllables within words. Example: Shelley's "Stanzas Written in Dejection Near Naples"

The City's voice itself is soft like Solitude's

12. Onomatopoeia: The naming of a thing or action by a vocal imitation of the sound associated with it such as buzz or hiss or the use of words whose sound suggests the sense. A good example: from "The Brook" by Tennyson:

> I chatter over stony ways,
> In little sharps and trebles,
> I bubble into eddying bays,
> I babble on the pebbles.

13. Malapropism: A verbal blunder in which one word is replaced by another similar in sound but different in meaning. Comes from Sheridan's Mrs. Malaprop in *The Rivals* (1775). Thinking of the geography of contiguous countries, she spoke of the "geometry" of "contagious countries."

Poets use figures of speech to sharpen the effect and meaning of their poems and to help readers see things in ways they have never seen them before. Marianne Moore observed that a fir tree has "an emerald turkey-foot at the top." Her poem makes us aware of something we probably had never noticed before. The sudden recognition of the likeness yields pleasure in the reading. Figurative language allows for the statement of truths that more literal language cannot. Skillfully used, a figure of speech will help the reader see more clearly and to focus upon particulars. Figures of speech add many dimensions of richness to our reading and understanding of a poem; they also allow many opportunities for worthwhile analysis. The approach to take in analyzing a poem on the basis of its figures of speech is to ask the question: What does it do for the poem? Does it underscore meaning? Does it intensify understanding? Does it increase the intensity of our response?

Skill 18.5 Analyzing the formal characteristics and distinctive content of narrative poetry.

The greatest difficulty in analyzing narrative poetry is that it partakes of many genres. It can have all the features of poetry: meter, rhyme, verses, stanzas, etc., but it can have all the features of prose, not only fictional prose but also nonfictional. It can have a protagonist, characters, conflicts, action, plot, climax, theme, and tone. It can also be a persuasive discourse and have a thesis (real or derived) and supporting points. The arrangement of an analysis will depend to a great extent upon the peculiarities of the poem itself.

In an epic, the conflicts take place in the social sphere rather than a personal life, and it will have a historical basis or one that is accepted as historical. The conflict will be between opposed nations or races and will involve diverging views of civilization that are the foundation of the challenge. Often it will involve the pitting of a group that conceives of itself as a higher civilization against a lower civilization and, more often than not, divine will determines that the higher one will win, exerting its force over the lower, barbarous, and profane enemy.

Examples are the conflict of Greece with Troy, the fates of Rome with the Carthaginian and the Italian, the Crusaders with the Saracen, or even of Milton's Omnipotent versus Satan. In analyzing these works, protagonist and antagonist need to be clearly identified, the conflicts established, the climax and an outcome that sets the world right in the mind of the writer clearly shown .

At the same time, the form of the epic as a poem must be considered. What meter, rhyme scheme, verse form, and stanza form have been chosen to tell this story. Is it consistent? If it varies, where does it vary and what does the varying do for the poem/story? What about figures of speech? Is there alliteration or onomatopoeia? Etc.

The epic is a major literary form historically although it had begun to fall out of favor by the end of the seventeenth century. There have been notable efforts to produce an American epic, but they always seem to slide over into prose. The short story and the novel began to take over the genre. Even so, some would say that *Moby Dick* is an American epic.

Narrative poetry has been very much a part of the output of modern American writers totally apart from attempts to write epics. Many of Emily Dickenson's poems are narrative in form and retain the features that we look for in the finest of American poetry. The first two verses of "A Narrow Fellow in the Grass" illustrate the use of narrative in a poem:

> A narrow fellow in the grass
> Occasionally rides;
> You may have met him—did you not?
> His notice sudden is.
>
> The grass divides as with a comb,
> A spotted shaft is seen;
> And then it closes at your feet
> And opens further on. . . .

This is certainly narrative in nature and has many of the aspects of prose narrative. At the same time, it is a poem with rhyme, meter, verses, stanzas, etc. and can be analyzed as such.

Skill 18.6 Analyzing various types of patterned lyric poetry (sonnet, limerick, cinquain, haiku).

The sonnet is a fixed-verse form of Italian origin, which consists of 14 lines that are typically five-foot iambics rhyming according to a prescribed scheme. Popular since its creation in the thirteenth century in Sicily, it spread at first to Tuscany, where it was adopted by Petrarch. The Petrarchan sonnet generally has a two-part theme. The first eight lines, the octave, state a problem, ask a question, or express an emotional tension.

The last six lines, the sestet, resolve the problem, answer the question, or relieve the tension. The rhyme scheme of the octave is abbaabba; that of the sestet varies.

Sir Thomas Wyatt and Henry Howard, Earl of Surrey, introduced this form into England in the sixteenth century. It played an important role in the development of Elizabethan lyric poetry, and a distinctive English sonnet developed, which was composed of three quatrains, each with an independent rhyme-scheme, and it ended with a rhymed couplet. A form of the English sonnet created by Edmond Spenser combines the English form and the Italian. The Spenserian sonnet follows the English quatrain and couplet pattern but resembles the Italian in its rhyme scheme, which is linked: abab bcbc cdcd ee. Many poets wrote sonnet sequences, where several sonnets were linked together, usually to tell a story. Considered to be the greatest of all sonnet sequences is one of Shakespeare's, which are addressed to a young man and a "dark lady" wherein the love story is overshadowed by the underlying reflections on time and art, growth and decay, and fame and fortune.

The sonnet continued to develop, more in topics than in form. When John Donne in the seventeenth century used the form for religious themes, some of which are almost sermons, or on personal reflections ("When I consider how my light is spent"), there were no longer any boundaries on the themes it could take.

That it is a flexible form is demonstrated in the wide range of themes and purposes it has been used for—all the way from more frivolous concerns to statements about time and death. Wordsworth, Keats, and Elizabeth Barrett Browning used the Petrarchan form of the sonnet. A well-known example is Wordsworth's "The World Is Too Much With Us." Rainer Maria Rilke's Sonnette an Orpheus (1922) is a well-known twentieth-century sonnet.

Analysis of a sonnet should focus on the form—does it fit a traditional pattern or does it break from tradition? If so, why did the poet choose to make that break? Does it reflect the purpose of the poem? What is the theme? What is the purpose? Is it narrative? If so, what story does it tell and is there an underlying meaning? Is the sonnet appropriate for the subject matter?

The limerick probably originated in County Limerick, Ireland, in the 18th century. It is a form of short, humorous verse, often nonsensical, and often ribald. Its five lines rhyme aabbaa with three feet in all lines except the third and fourth, which have only two. Rarely presented as serious poetry, this form is popular because almost anyone can write it.

Analysis of a limerick should focus on its form. Does it conform to a traditional pattern or does it break from the tradition? If so, what impact does that have on the meaning? Is the poem serious or frivolous? Is it funny?

Does it try to be funny but does not achieve its purpose? Is there a serious meaning underlying the frivolity?

A cinquain is a poem with a five-line stanza. Adelaide Crapsey (1878-1914) called a five-line verse form a cinquain and invented a particular meter for it. Similar to the haiku, there are two syllables in the first and last lines and four, six, and eight in the middle three lines. It has a mostly iambic cadence. Her poem, "November Night," is an example:

> Listen…
> With faint dry sound
> Like steps of passing ghosts,
> the leaves, frost-crisp'd, break from the trees
> And fall.

Haiku is a very popular unrhymed form that is limited to seventeen syllables arranged in three lines thus: five, seven, and five syllables. This verse form originated in Japan in the seventeenth century where it is accepted as serious poetry and is Japan's most popular form. Originally, it was to deal with the season, the time of day, and the landscape although as it has come into more common use, the subjects have become less restricted. The imagist poets and other English writers used the form or imitated it. It's a form much used in classrooms to introduce students to the writing of poetry.

Analysis of a cinquain and a haiku poem should focus on form first. Does the haiku poem conform to the seventeen-syllables requirement and are they arranged in a five, seven, and five pattern? For a cinquain, does it have only five lines? Does the poem distill the words so as much meaning as possible can be conveyed? Does it treat a serious subject? Is the theme discernable? Short forms like these seem simple to dash off; however, they are not effective unless the words are chosen and pared so the meaning intended is conveyed. The impact should be forceful, and that often takes more effort, skill, and creativity than longer forms. This should be taken into account in their analysis.

COMPETENCY 19.0 UNDERSTAND LITERATURE WRITTEN FOR ADOLESCENTS

Skill 19.1 Demonstrating knowledge of traditional and contemporary literature for adolescents.

Prior to twentieth century research on child development and child/adolescent literature's relationship to that development, books for adolescents were primarily didactic. They were designed to be instructive of history, manners, and morals.

Middle Ages

As early as the eleventh century, Anselm, the Archbishop of Canterbury, wrote an encyclopedia designed to instill in children the beliefs and principles of conduct acceptable to adults in medieval society. Early monastic translations of the *Bible* and other religious writings were written in Latin, for the edification of the upper class. Fifteenth century hornbooks were designed to teach reading and religious lessons. William Caxton printed English versions of *Aesop's Fables*, Malory's *Le Morte d'Arthur* and stories from Greek and Roman mythology. Though printed for adults, tales of adventures of Odysseus and the Arthurian knights were also popular with literate adolescents.

Renaissance

The Renaissance saw the introduction of the inexpensive chapbooks, small in size and 16-64 pages in length. Chapbooks were condensed versions of mythology and fairy tales. Designed for the common people, chapbooks were imperfect grammatically but were immensely popular because of their adventurous contents. Though most of the serious, educated adults frowned on the sometimes-vulgar little books, they received praise from Richard Steele of *Tatler* fame for inspiring his grandson's interest in reading and pursuing his other studies.

Meanwhile, the Puritans' three most popular reads were the *Bible*, John Foxe's *Book of Martyrs*, and John Bunyan's *Pilgrim's Progress*. Though venerating religious martyrs and preaching the moral propriety which was to lead to eternal happiness, the stories of the *Book of Martyrs* were often lurid in their descriptions of the fate of the damned. Not written for children and difficult reading even for adults, *Pilgrim's Progress* was as attractive to adolescents for its adventurous plot as for its moral outcome. In Puritan America, the *New England Primer* set forth the prayers, catechisms, *Bible* verses, and illustrations meant to instruct children in the Puritan ethic. The seventeenth-century French used fables and fairy tales to entertain adults, but children found them enjoyable as well.

Seventeenth century

The late seventeenth century brought the first concern with providing literature that specifically targeted the young. Pierre Perrault's *Fairy Tales*, Jean de la Fontaine's retellings of famous fables, Mme. d'Aulnoy's novels based on old folktales, and Mme. de Beaumont's "Beauty and the Beast" were written to delight as well as instruct young people. In England, publisher John Newbury was the first to publish a line for children. These include a translation of Perrault's *Tales of Mother Goose; A Little Pretty Pocket-Book*, "intended for instruction and amusement" but decidedly moralistic and bland in comparison to the previous century's chapbooks; and *The Renowned History of Little Goody Two Shoes*, allegedly written by Oliver Goldsmith for a juvenile audience.

Eighteenth century

By and large, however, into the eighteenth century adolescents were finding their reading pleasure in adult books: Daniel Defoe's *Robinson Crusoe*, Jonathan Swift's *Gulliver's Travels*, and Johann Wyss's *Swiss Family Robinson*. More books were being written for children, but the moral didacticism, though less religious, was nevertheless ever present. The short stories of Maria Edgeworth, the four-volume *The History of Sandford and Merton* by Thomas Day, and Martha Farquharson's twenty-six volume *Elsie Dinsmore* series dealt with pious protagonists who learned restraint, repentance, and rehabilitation from sin. Two bright spots in this period of didacticism were Jean Jacques Rousseau's *Emile* and *The Tales of Shakespeare*, Charles and Mary Lamb's simplified versions of Shakespeare's plays. Rousseau believed that a child's abilities were enhanced by a free, happy life, and the Lambs subscribed to the notion that children were entitled to more entertaining literature in language comprehensible to them.

Nineteenth century

Child/adolescent literature truly began its modern rise in nineteenth century Europe. Hans Christian Andersen's *Fairy Tales* were fanciful adaptations of the somber revisions of the Grimm brothers in the previous century. Andrew Lang's series of colorful fairy books contain the folklores of many nations and are still part of the collections of many modern libraries. Clement Moore's "A Visit from St. Nicholas" is a cheery, non-threatening child's view of the "night before Christmas." The humor of Lewis Carroll's books about Alice's adventures, Edward Lear's poems with caricatures, Lucretia Nole's stories of the Philadelphia Peterkin family, were full of fancy and not a smidgen of morality. Other popular Victorian novels introduced the modern fantasy and science fiction genres: William Makepeace Thackeray's *The Rose and the Ring*, Charles Dickens' *The Magic Fishbone*, and Jules Verne's *Twenty Thousand Leagues Under the Sea*.

Adventure to exotic places became a popular topic: Rudyard Kipling's *Jungle Books*, Verne's *Around the World in Eighty Days*, and Robert Louis Stevenson's *Treasure Island* and *Kidnapped*. In 1884, the first English translation Johanna Spyre's *Heidi* appeared.

North America was also finding its voices for adolescent readers. American Louisa May Alcott's *Little Women* and Canadian L.M. Montgomery's *Anne of Green Gables* ushered in the modern age of realistic fiction. American youth were enjoying the articles of Tom Sawyer and Huckleberry Finn. For the first time children were able to read books about real people just like themselves.

Twentieth century

The literature of the twentieth century is extensive and diverse, and as in previous centuries much influenced by the adults who write, edit, and select books for youth consumption. In the first third of the century, suitable adolescent literature dealt with children from good homes with large families. These books projected an image of a peaceful, rural existence. Though the characters and plots were more realistic, the stories maintained focus on topics that were considered emotionally and intellectually proper. Popular at this time were Laura Ingalls Wilder's Little House on the Prairie Series and Carl Sandburg's biography *Abe Lincoln Grows Up*. English author J.R.R. Tolkein's fantasy *The Hobbit* prefaced modern adolescent readers' fascination with the works of Piers Antony, Madelaine L'Engle, and Anne McCaffery.

Skill 19.2 Recognizing how major genres and topics in adolescent literature (contemporary problem novels, coming-of-age stories, biographies, science fiction/fantasy) may reflect issues of adolescent development.

The late nineteenth and early twentieth centuries' studies by behaviorists and developmental psychologists significantly affected the manner in which the education community and parents approached the selection of literature for children.

The cognitive development studies of Piaget, the epigenetic view of personality development by Erik Erikson, the formulation of Abraham Maslow's hierarchy of basic needs, and the social learning theory of behaviorists like Alfred Bandura contributed to a greater understanding of child/adolescent development even as these theorists contradicted each others findings. Though few educators today totally subscribe to Piaget's inflexible stages of mental development, his principles of both qualitative and quantitative mental capacity, his generalizations about the parallels between physical growth and thinking capacity, and his support of the adolescent's heightened moral perspective are still used as measures by which to evaluate child/adolescent literature.

Piaget's four stages of mental development:

- Sensimotor intelligence (birth to age two) deals with the pre-language period of development. The child is most concerned with coordinating movement and action. Words begin to represent people and things.

- Preoperational thought is the period spanning ages 2-12. It is broken into several substages.

    1. Preconceptual (2-4) phase - most behavior is based on subjective judgment.

    2. Intuitive (4-7) phase - children use language to verbalize their experiences and mental processes.

- Concrete operations (7-11) - children begin to apply logic to concrete things and experiences. They can combine performance and reasoning to solve problems.

- Formal operations (12-15) - adolescents begin to think beyond the immediate and to theorize. They apply formal logic to interpreting abstract constructions and to recognizing experiences that are contrary to fact.

Though Piaget presented these stages as progressing sequentially, a given child might enter any period earlier or later than most children. Furthermore, a child might perform at different levels in different situations. Thus, a fourteen year old female might be able to function at the formal operations stage in a literature class, but function at a concrete operations level in mathematical concepts.

Piaget's Theories Influence Literature

Most middle school students have reached the concrete operations level. By this time they have left behind their egocentrism for a need to understand the physical and social world around them. They become more interested in ways to relate to other people. Their favorite stories become those about real people rather than animals or fairy tale characters. The conflicts in their literature are internal as well as external. Books like Paula Fox's *The Stone-Faced Boy*, Betsy Byards' *The Midnight Fox*, and Lois Lenski's *Strawberry Girl* deal with a child's loneliness, confusion about identity or loyalty, and poverty. Pre-adolescents are becoming more cognizant of and interested in the past, thus their love of adventure stories about national heroes like Davy Crockett, Daniel Boone, and Abe Lincoln and biographies/autobiographies of real life heroes, like Jackie Robinson and Cesar Chevas. At this level, children also become interested in the future; thus, their love of both fantasy (most medieval in spirit) and science fiction.

The seven to eleven year olds also internalize moral values. They are concerned with their sense of self and are willing to question rules and adult authority. In books such as Beverly Cleary's *Henry Huggins* and *Mitch and Amy*, the protagonists are children pursuing their own desires with the same frustrations as other children. When these books were written in the 1960s, returning a found pet or overcoming a reading disability were common problems.

From twelve to fifteen, adolescents advance beyond the concrete operations level to begin developing communication skills that enable them to articulate attitudes/opinions and exchange knowledge. They can recognize and contrast historical fiction from pure history and biography. They can identify the elements of literature and their relationships within a specific story. As their thinking becomes more complex, early adolescents become more sensitive to others' emotions and reactions. They become better able to suspend their disbelief and enter the world of literature, thus expanding their perceptions of the real world.

In discussing the adolescent's moral judgment, Piaget noted that after age eleven, children stopped viewing actions as either "right" or "wrong." The older child considers both the intent and the behavior in its context. A younger child would view an accidental destruction of property in terms of the amount of damage. The older child would find the accident less wrong than minor damage done with intended malice.

Kohlberg's Theories of Moral Development

Expanding on Piaget's thinking, Lawrence Kohlberg developed a hierarchy of values. Though progressive, the stages of Kohlberg's hierarchy are not clearly aligned to chronological age. The six stages of development correlate to three levels of moral judgment.

Level I. Moral values reside in external acts rather than in persons or standards.

Stage 0. Premoral - No association of actions or needs with sense of right or wrong.

Stage 1. Obedience and punishment orientation. Child defers to adult authority. His actions are motivated by a desire to stay out of trouble.

Stage 2. Right action/self-interest orientation. Performance of right deeds results in needing satisfaction.

Level II. Moral values reside in maintaining conventions of right behavior.

Stage 3. Good person orientation. The child performs right actions to receive approval from others, conforming to the same standards.

Stage 4. Law and order orientation. Doing one's duty and showing respect for authority contributes to maintaining social order.

Level III. Moral values reside in principles separate in association from the persons or agencies that enforce these principles.

Stage 5. Legalistic orientation. The rules of society are accepted as correct but alterable. Privileges and duties are derived from social contact. Obedience to society's rules protects the rights of self and others.

Stage 6. Conscience orientation. Ethical standards, such as justice, equality, and respect for others, guide moral conduct more than legal rules.

Though these stages represent a natural progression of values to actions relationships, persons may regress to an earlier stage in certain situations. An adolescent already operating at Stage 5 may regress to Stage 3 in a classroom where consequences of non-conformity are met with disapproval or punishment. An adult operating at Stage 6 may regress to Stage 4 when obligated by military training or confronted with a conflict between self-preservation and the protection of others.

Values clarification education based on Piaget's and Kohlberg's theories imply that development is inherent in human socialization. Becoming a decent person is a natural result of human development.

Social Learning Theory

Much of traditional learning theory resulted from the work of early behaviorists, like B. F. Skinner, and has been refined by modern theorists such as Albert Bandura. Behaviorists believe that intellectual, and therefore behavioral, development cannot be divided into specific stages. They believe that behavior is the result of conditioning experiences, a continuum of rewards and punishments. Environmental conditions are viewed as greater stimuli than inherent qualities. Thus in social learning theory the consequences of behavior - that is, the rewards or punishments - are more significant in social development than are the motivations for the behavior.

Bandura also proposed that a child learns vicariously through observing the behavior of others, whereas the developmental psychologists presumed that children developed through the actual self-experience.

The Humanistic Theory of Development

No discussion of child development would be complete without a review of Abraham Maslow's hierarchy of needs, from basic physiological needs to the need for self-actualization. The following list represents those needs from the hierarchy that most affect children.

1. **Need for physical well-being**. In young children the provisions for shelter, food, clothing, and protection by significant adults satisfy this need. In older children, this satisfaction of physical comforts translates to a need for material security and may manifest itself in struggles to overcome poverty and maintain the integrity of home and family.

2. **Need for love**. The presumption is that every human being needs to love and be loved. With young children this reciprocal need is directed at and received from parents and other family members, pets, and friends. In older children and adolescents this need for love forms the basis for romance and peer acceptance.

3. **Need to belong**. Beyond the need for one-on-one relationships, a child needs the security of being an accepted member of a group. Young children identify with family, friends, and schoolmates. They are concerned with having happy experiences and being accepted by people they love and respect. Later, they associate with community, country, and perhaps world groups. Adolescents become more aware of a larger world order and thus develop concerns about issues facing society, such as political or social unrest, wars, discrimination, and environmental issues. They seek to establish themselves with groups who accept and share their values. They become more team oriented.

4. **Need to achieve competence**. A human's need to interact satisfactorily with his environment begins with the infant's exploration of his immediate surroundings. Visual and tactile identification of objects and persons provides confidence to perform further explorations. To become well adjusted, the child must achieve competence to feel satisfaction. Physical and intellectual achievements become measures of acceptance. Frustrations resulting from physical or mental handicaps are viewed as hurtles to be overcome if satisfaction is to be achieved. Older children view the courage-overcome obstacles as part of the maturing process.

5. **Need to know**. Curiosity is the basis of intelligence. The need to learn is persistent.

To maintain intellectual security, children must be able to find answers to their questions in order to stimulate further exploration of information to satisfy that persistent curiosity.

6. **Need for beauty and order**. Aesthetic satisfaction is as important as the need for factual information. Intellectual stimulation comes from satisfying curiosity about the fine, as well as the practical, arts. Acceptance for one's accomplishments in dance, music, drawing, writing, or performing/ appreciating any of the arts leads to a sense of accomplishment and self-actualization.

Theory of Psychosocial Development

Erik Erikson, a follower of Sigmund Freud, presented the theory that human development consists of maturation through a series of psychosocial crisis. The struggle to resolve these crises helps a person achieve individuality as he learns to function in society.

Maturation occurs as the individual moves through a progression of increasingly complex stages. The movement from one stage to the next hinges on the successful resolution of the conflicts encountered in each stage, and each of the stages represents a step in identity formation. Stage 1 (trust versus distrust), stage 2 (achieving autonomy), and stage 3 (developing initiative) relate to infants and young/middle children. Stages 4 and 5 relate to late childhood through adolescents.

Stage 4 - **Becoming Industrious**. Late childhood, according to Erikson, occurs between seven to eleven. Having already mastered conflicts that helped them overcome mistrust of unfamiliar persons, places, and things; that made them more independent in caring for themselves and their possessions; and that overcame their sense of guilt at behavior that creates opposition with others, children are ready to assert themselves in suppressing feelings of inferiority. Children at this stage learn to master independent tasks as well as to work cooperatively with other children. They increasingly measure their own competence by comparing themselves to their peers.

Stage 5 - **Establishing Identity**. From age eleven through the teen years, a person's conflicts arise from his search for identity, as an individual and a member of society. Because internal demands for independence and peer acceptance sometimes oppose external demands for conformity to rules and standards, friction with family, school, and society in general occur during these years. The adolescent must resolve issues such as the amount of control he will concede to family and other rule enforcing adults as he searches for other acceptance models. In his quest for self-identity, he experiments with adult behavior and attitudes. At the end of his teen years, he should have a well - established sense of identity.

Theory of multiple intelligences

Howard Gardner's research in the 1980s has been recently influential in helping teachers understand that human beings process information differently and, therefore, communicate their knowledge through different modes of operation. It is important to present language and literature in visual, auditory, tactile, and kinesthetic ways to allow every child to develop good skills through his own mode of learning. Then, the child himself must be allowed to perform through the strength of his intelligence. The movement toward learning academies in the practical and fine arts and in the sciences is a result of our growing understanding of all aspects of child development.

Modern society's role in child development

Despite their differences, there are many similarities in the theories of child development. However, most of these theories were developed prior to the social unrest of the 1970s. In industrialized Western society, children are increasingly excluded from the activities of work and play with adults and education has become their main occupation. This exclusion tends to prolong childhood and adolescents and thus inhibit development as visualized by theorists. For adolescents in America, this prolonging results in slower social and intellectual maturation, contrasted to increasing physical maturity. Adolescents today deal with drugs, violence, communicable diseases, and a host of social problems that were of minimal concerns thirty years ago. Even pre-adolescent children are dealing with poverty, disease, broken homes, abuse, and drugs.

Influence of Theories on Literature

All of these development theories and existing social conditions influence the literature created and selected for and by child/adolescent readers.

Child/adolescent literature has always been to some degree didactic, whether non-fiction or fiction. Until the twentieth century, "kiddie" lit was also morally prescriptive. Written by adults who determined either what they believed children needed or liked or what they should need or like, most books, stories, poems, and essays dealt with experiences or issues that would make children into better adults. The fables, fairy tales, and epics of old set the moral/social standards of their times while entertaining the child in every reader/listener. These tales are still popular because they have a universal appeal. Except for the rare exceptions discussed earlier in this section, most books were written for literate adults. Educated children found their pleasure in the literature that was available.

Benefits of research

One benefit of the child development and learning theory research is that they provide guidelines for writers, publishers, and educators to follow in the creation, marketing, and selection of good reading materials. MacMillan introduced children's literature as a separate publishing market in 1918. By the 1930s, most major publishers had a children's department. Though arguments have existed throughout this century about quality versus quantity, there is no doubt that children's literature is a significant slice of the market pie.

Another influence is that children's books are a reflection of both developmental theories and social changes. Reading provides children with the opportunity to become more aware of societal differences, to measure their behavior against the behavior of realistic fictional characters or the subjects of biographies, to become informed about events of the past and present that will affect their futures, and to acquire a genuine appreciation of literature.

Furthermore, there is an obligation for adults to provide instruction and entertainment that all children in our democratic society can use. As parents and educators we have a further obligation to guide children in the selection of books that are appropriate to their reading ability and interest levels. Of course, there is a fine line between guidance and censorship. As with discipline, parents learn that to make forbidden is to make more desirable. To publish a list of banned books is to make them suddenly attractive. Most children/adolescents left to their own selections will choose books on topics that interest them and are written in language they can understand.

Skill 19.3 Analyzing issues of culture, gender, ethnicity, and other personal characteristics reflected in adolescent literature.

The social changes of post-World War II significantly affected adolescent literature. The Civil Rights movement, feminism, the protest of the Vietnam Conflict, and issues surrounding homelessness, neglect, teen pregnancy, drugs, and violence have bred a new vein of contemporary fiction that helps adolescents understand and cope with the world they live in.

Popular books for preadolescents deal more with establishing relationships with members of the opposite sex (Sweet Valley High series) and learning to cope with their changing bodies, personalities, or life situations, as in Judy Blume's *Are You There, God? It's Me, Margaret.* Adolescents are still interested in the fantasy and science fiction genres as well as popular juvenile fiction. Middle school students still read the Little House on the Prairie series and the mysteries of the Hardy boys and Nancy Drew.

Teens value the works of Emily and Charlotte Bronte, Willa Cather, Jack London, William Shakespeare, and Mark Twain as much as those of Piers Anthony, S.E. Hinton, Madeleine L'Engle, Stephen King, and J.R.R. Tolkein, because they're fun to read whatever their underlying worth may be.

Older adolescents enjoy the writers in these genres.

1. Fantasy: Piers Anthony, Ursula LeGuin, Ann McCaffrey

2. Horror: V.C. Andrews, Stephen King

3. Juvenile fiction: Judy Blume, Robert Cormier, Rosa Guy, Virginia Hamilton, S.E. Hinton, M.E. Kerr, Harry Mazer, Norma Fox Mazer, Richard Newton Peck, Cynthia Voight, and Paul Zindel.

4. Science fiction: Isaac Asimov, Ray Bradbury, Arthur C. Clarke, Frank Herbert, Larry Niven, H.G. Wells.

Skill 19.4 Demonstrating knowledge of criteria for selecting and evaluating print and non-print texts for adolescents.

These classic and contemporary works combine the characteristics of multiple theories. Functioning at the concrete operations stage (Piaget), being of the "good person," orientation (Kohlberg), still highly dependent on external rewards (Bandura), and exhibiting all five needs previously discussed from Maslow's hierarchy, these eleven to twelve year olds should appreciate the following titles, grouped by reading level. These titles are also cited for interest at that grade level and do not reflect high-interest titles for older readers who do not read at grade level. Some high interest titles will be cited later.

Reading level 6.0 to 6.9

Barrett, William. *Lilies of the Field*
Cormier, Robert. *Other Bells for Us to Ring*
Dahl, Roald. *Danny, Champion of the World; Charlie and the Chocolate Factory*
Lindgren, Astrid. *Pippi Longstocking*
Lindbergh, Anne. *Three Lives to Live*
Lowry, Lois. *Rabble Starkey*
Naylor, Phyllis. *The Year of the Gopher, Reluctantly Alice*
Peck, Robert Newton. *Arly*
Speare, Elizabeth. *The Witch of Blackbird Pond*
Sleator, William. *The Boy Who Reversed Himself*

For seventh and eighth grades

Most seventh and eight grade students, according to learning theory, are still functioning cognitively, psychologically, and morally as sixth graders. As these are not inflexible standards, there are some twelve and thirteen year olds who are much more mature socially, intellectually, and physically than the younger children who share the same school. They are becoming concerned with establishing individual and peer group identities that presents conflicts with breaking from authority and the rigidity of rules. Some at this age are still tied firmly to the family and its expectations while others identify more with those their own age or older. Enrichment reading for this group must help them cope with life's rapid changes or provide escape and thus must be either realistic or fantastic depending on the child's needs. Adventures and mysteries (the Hardy Boys and Nancy Drew series) are still popular today. These preteens also become more interested in biographies of contemporary figures rather than legendary figures of the past.

Reading level 7.0 to 7.9

Armstrong, William. *Sounder*
Bagnold, Enid. *National Velvet*
Barrie, James. *Peter Pan*
London, Jack. *White Fang, Call of the Wild*
Lowry, Lois. *Taking Care of Terrific*
McCaffrey, Anne. The *Dragonsinger* series
Montgomery, L. M. *Anne of Green Gables* and sequels
Steinbeck, John. *The Pearl*
Tolkien, J. R. R. *The Hobbit*
Zindel, Paul. *The Pigman*

Reading level 8.0 to 8.9

Cormier, Robert. *I Am the Cheese*
McCullers, Carson. *The Member of the Wedding*
North, Sterling. *Rascal*
Twain, Mark. *The Adventures of Tom Sawyer*
Zindel, Paul. *My Darling , My Hamburger*

For ninth grade

Depending upon the school environment, a ninth grader may be top-dog in a junior high school or underdog in a high school. Much of his social development and thus his reading interests become motivated by his peer associations. He is technically an adolescent operating at the early stages of formal operations in cognitive development. His perception of his own identity is becoming well-defined and he is fully aware of the ethics required by society.

He is more receptive to the challenges of classic literature but still enjoys popular teen novels.

<u>Reading level 9.0 to 9.9</u>

Brown, Dee. *Bury My Heart at Wounded Knee*
Defoe, Daniel. *Robinson Crusoe*
Dickens, Charles. *David Copperfield*
Greenberg, Joanne. *I Never Promised You a Rose Garden*
Kipling, Rudyard. *Captains Courageous*
Mathabane, Mark. *Kaffir Boy*
Nordhoff, Charles. *Mutiny on the Bounty*
Shelley, Mary. *Frankenstein*
Washington, Booker T. *Up From Slavery*

For tenth - twelfth grades

All high school sophomores, juniors and seniors can handle most other literature except for a few of the very most difficult titles like *Moby Dick* or *Vanity Fair*. However, since many high school students do not progress to the eleventh or twelfth grade reading level, they will still have their favorites among authors whose writings they can understand. Many will struggle with assigned novels but still read high interest books for pleasure. A few high interest titles are listed below without reading level designations, though most are 6.0 to 7.9.

Bauer, Joan. *Squashed*
Borland, Hal. *When the Legends Die*
Danzinger, Paula. *Remember Me to Herald Square*
Duncan, Lois. *Stranger with my Face*
Hamilton, Virginia. *The Planet of Junior Brown*
Hinton, S. E. *The Outsiders*
Paterson, Katherine. *The Great Gilly Hopkins*

Teachers of students at all levels must be familiar with the materials offered by the libraries in their own schools. Only then can she guide her students into appropriate selections for their social age and reading level development.

Skill 19.5 Analyzing the themes of works targeted for adolescents.

Adolescent literature, because of the age range of readers, is extremely diverse. Fiction for the middle group, usually ages ten/eleven to fourteen/fifteen, deals with issues of coping with internal and external changes in their lives. Because children's writers in the twentieth century have produced increasingly realistic fiction, adolescents can now find problems dealt with honestly in novels.

Teachers of middle/junior high school students see the greatest change in interests and reading abilities. Fifth and sixth graders, included in elementary grades in many schools, are viewed as older children while seventh and eighth graders are preadolescent. Ninth graders, included sometimes as top dogs in junior high school and sometimes as underlings in high school, definitely view themselves as teenagers. Their literature choices will often be governed more by interest than by ability; thus, the wealth of high-interest, low readability books that have flooded the market in recent years. Tenth through twelfth graders will still select high-interest books for pleasure reading but are also easily encouraged to stretch their literature muscles by reading more classics.

Because of the rapid social changes, topics that once did not interest young people until they reached their teens - suicide, gangs, homosexuality - are now subjects of books for even younger readers. The plethora of high-interest books reveals how desperately schools have failed to produce on-level readers and how the market has adapted to that need. However, these high-interest books are now readable for younger children whose reading levels are at or above normal. No matter how tastefully written, some contents are inappropriate for younger readers. The problem becomes not so much steering them toward books that they have the reading ability to handle but encouraging them toward books whose content is appropriate to their levels of cognitive and social development. A fifth-grader may be able to read V.C. Andrews book *Flowers in the Attic* but not possess the social/moral development to handle the deviant behavior of the characters. At the same time, because of the complex changes affecting adolescents, the teacher must be well versed in learning theory and child development as well as competent to teach the subject matter of language and literature.

DOMAIN 5. LANGUAGE AND LITERATURE

COMPETENCY 20.0 UNDERSTAND THE HISTORICAL, SOCIAL, CULTURAL, AND TECHNOLOGICAL INFLUENCES SHAPING ENGLISH

Skill 20.1 Demonstrating an understanding that language undergoes constant change.

English is an Indo-European language that evolved through several periods. The origin of English dates to the settlement of the British Isles in the fifth and sixth centuries by Germanic tribes called the Angles, Saxons, and Jutes. The original Britons spoke a Celtic tongue while the Angles spoke a Germanic dialect. Modern English derives from the speech of the Anglo-Saxons who imposed not only their language but also their social customs and laws on their new land. From the fifth to the tenth century, Britain's language was the tongue we now refer to as Old English. During the next four centuries, the many French attempts at English conquest introduced many French words to English. However, the grammar and syntax of the language remained Germanic.

Middle English, most evident in the writings of Geoffrey Chaucer, dates loosely from 1066 to 1509. William Caxton brought the printing press to England in 1474 and increased literacy. Old English words required numerous inflections to indicate noun cases and plurals as well as verb conjugations. Middle English continued the use of many inflections and pronunciations that treated these inflections as separately pronounced syllables. English in 1300 would have been written "Olde Anglishe" with the e's at the ends of the words pronounced as our short a vowel. Even adjectives had plural inflections: "long dai" became "longe daies" pronounced "long-a day-as." Spelling was phonetic, thus every vowel had multiple pronunciations, a fact that continues to affect the language.

Modern English dates from the introduction of The Great Vowels Shift because it created guidelines for spelling and pronunciation. Before the printing press, books were copied laboriously by hand; the language was subject to the individual interpretation of the scribes. Printers and subsequently lexicographers like Samuel Johnson and America's Noah Webster influenced the guidelines. As reading matter was mass produced, the reading public was forced to adopt the speech and writing habits developed by those who wrote and printed books.

Despite many students' insistence to the contrary, Shakespeare's writings are in Modern English. It is important to stress to students that language, like customs, morals, and other social factors, is constantly subject to change. Immigration, inventions, and cataclysmic events change language as much as any other facet of life affected by these changes. The domination of one race or nation over others can change a language significantly. Beginning with the colonization of the New World, English and Spanish became dominant languages in the Western hemisphere.

American English today is somewhat different in pronunciation and sometimes vocabulary from British English. The British call a truck a "lorry;" baby carriages a "pram," short for "perambulator;" and an elevator a "lift." There are very few syntactical differences, and even the tonal qualities that were once so clearly different are converging.

Though Modern English is less complex than Middle English, having lost many unnecessary inflections, it is still considered difficult to learn because of its many exceptions to the rules. It has, however, become the world's dominant language by reason of the great political, military, and social power of England from the fifteenth to the nineteenth century and of America in the twentieth century.

Modern inventions - the telephone, phonograph, radio, television, and motion pictures - have especially affected English pronunciation. Regional dialects, once a hindrance to clear understanding, have fewer distinct characteristics. The speakers from different parts of the United States of America can be identified by their accents, but more and more as educators and media personalities stress uniform pronunciations and proper grammar, the differences are diminishing.

The English language has a more extensive vocabulary than any other language. Ours is a language of synonyms, words borrowed from other languages, and coined words - many of them introduced by the rapid expansion of technology.

It is important for students to understand that language is in constant flux. Emphasis should be placed on learning and using language for specific purposes and audiences. Negative criticism of a student's errors in word choice or sentence structures will inhibit creativity. Positive criticism that suggests ways to enhance communication skills will encourage exploration.

Skill 20.2 Recognizing the significance of historical events that have influenced the development of English (the Norman Conquest, the exchanges between indigenous peoples and Europeans during the European colonization of Africa, Asia, Australia, and North America).

Perhaps the most basic principle about language in understanding its changes and variations is a simple one: language inevitably changes over time. If a community that speaks a homogeneous language and dialect are for some reason separated with no contact between the two resulting communities, over a few generations, they will be speaking different dialects and eventually will have difficulty understanding each other.

Language changes in all its manifestations: At the phonetic level, the sounds of a language will change as will its orthography. The vocabulary level will probably manifest the greatest changes. Changes in syntax are slower and less likely to occur.

For example, English has changed in response to the influences of many other languages and cultures as well as internal cultural changes such as the development of the railroad and the computer; however, its syntax still relies on word order—it has not shifted to an inflected system even though many of the cultures that have impacted it do, in fact, have an inflected language, such as Spanish.

The most significance influence on a language is the blending of cultures. The Norman Conquest that brought the English speakers in the British Isles under the rule of French speakers impacted the language, but it's significant that English speakers did not adopt the language of the ruling class—they did not become speakers of French. Even so, many vocabulary items entered the language in that period. The Great Vowel Shift that occurred between the 14th and 16th centuries is somewhat of a mystery although it's generally attributed to the migration to Southeast England following the plague of the black death. The Great Vowel Shift largely accounts for the discrepancy between orthography and speech—the difficult spelling system in modern English.

Colonization of other countries has also brought new vocabulary items into the language. Indian English not only has its own easily recognizable attributes as does Australian and North American, those cultural interactions have added to items in the usages of each other and in the language at large. The fact that English is the most widely spoken and understood language all over the world in the 21st century implies that it is constantly being changed by the globalized world.

Other influences, of course, impact language. The introduction of television and its domination by the United States has had great influence on the English that is spoken and understood all over the world. The same is true of the computerizing of the world (Tom Friedman called it "flattening" in his *The World is Flat: A Brief History of the Twenty-first Century)*. New terms have been added, old terms have changed meaning ("mouse," for instance), and nouns have been verbalized.

Skill 20.3 Relating English words, derivatives, and borrowings, including slang terms, to their origins in other languages.

Just as countries and families have histories, so do words. Knowing and understanding the origin of a word, where it has been used down through the years, and the history of its meaning as it has changed is an important component of the writing and language teacher's tool kit. Never in the history of the English language or any other language for that matter have the forms and meanings of words changed so rapidly. When America was settled originally, immigration from many countries made it a "melting pot." Immigration accelerated rapidly within the first hundred years, resulting in pockets of language throughout the country.

When trains began to make transportation available and affordable, individuals from those various pockets came in contact with each other, shared vocabularies, and attempted to converse. From that time forward, every generation brought the introduction of a technology that made language interchange not only more possible but more important.

Radio began the trend to standardize dialects. A Bostonian might not be understood by a native of Louisiana, who might not be interested in turning the dial to hear the news or a drama or the advertisements of the vendors that had a vested interest in being heard and understood. Soap and soup producers knew a goldmine when they saw it and created a market for radio announcers and actors who spoke without a pronounced dialect. In return, listeners began to hear the English language in a dialect very different from the one they spoke, and as it settled into their thinking processes, it eventually made its way to their tongues, and spoken English began to lose some of its local peculiarities. It has been a slow process, but most Americans can easily understand other Americans, no matter where they come from. They can even converse with a native of Great Britain with little difficulty. The introduction of television carried the evolution further as did the explosion of electronic communicating devices over the past fifty years.

An excellent example of the changes that have occurred in English is a comparison of Shakespeare's original works with modern translations. Without help, twenty-first-century Americans are unable to read the *Folio*. On the other hand, teachers must constantly be mindful of the vocabularies and etymologies of their students, who are on the receiving end of the escalation brought about by technology and increased global influence and contact.

Skill 20.4 Analyzing regional and social variations in language in the United States.

Dialect differences are basically in pronunciation. Bostoners say "pahty" for "party" and Southerners blend words like "you all" into "y'all." Besides the dialect differences already mentioned, the biggest geographical factors in American English stem from minor word choice variances. Depending on the region where you live, when you order a carbonated, syrupy beverage most generically called a soft drink, you might ask for a "soda" in the South, or a "pop" in the Midwest. If you order a soda in New York, then you will get a scoop of ice cream in your soft drink, while in other areas you would have to ask for a "float."

Skill 20.5 Evaluating the use of jargon in various fields.

See Skill 1.3.

Skill 20.6 Analyzing language associated with print and electronic media.

Conventions for language that appears in print have been developed over several centuries; they change somewhat from generation to generation but compared to the use of language in electronic media, they are fairly static. On the other hand, language use in radio and television has undergone rapid changes. Listening to a radio show from the thirties is a step back in time. The intonation had its own peculiar qualities. Even in its own time, it would not have been recognized as a conversation between two people. Listening to President Franklin Delano Roosevelt's "fireside chats" also takes us back in time, not only because of the content of the speeches but also by the way they were delivered. "Declamation" is a good term for the radio presentation style of that day and even the style of public speeches to some extent. It was notable for rhetorical effect or display. The same is true of television. Listening to early television news shows—Edward R. Murrow, for example—reminds us instantly of an earlier time. It followed in the style of the radio shows. It was declamatory in nature and sounded more like an announcement than a conversation.

Radio and television speech nowadays is much more conversational in tone. In fact, on many of the news shows, there are two or more news people who will carry on a conversation before, after, and between the news stories. This would have seemed peculiar to earlier listeners.

In the early 1940s, the Federal Communications Commission (FCC) established the "Mayflower Doctrine," which prohibited editorializing by stations. However, in 1949, the policy had begun to be relaxed, and the policy that emerged came to be known as the "Fairness Doctrine," which permitted editorializing—that is, presenting a view that might reflect bias—as long as the station was balanced and fair. The FCC took the view that those who were licensed to present news and views were "public trustees" who were obligated to provide reasonable opportunities for discussion and presentation of opposing views and issues important for the public to hear even though they might be controversial. It even went further to insist that those licensees were obligated to aggressively pursue important issues and provide programming that addressed such issues.

Under the Reagan administration in the 1980s, there was pressure to repeal the fairness doctrine, and in 1987 it was, in fact, repealed. Following that repeal, a station could be as partisan as it chose to be without providing free air time for rebuttal. What ensued was talk radio that featured a degree of emotionalism never before encountered on the airwaves. Pew researchers found in 2004 that 17% of the public regularly listens to talk radio, with a much higher ratio of listeners with conservative convictions than those who declare themselves to be liberals.

Rush Limbaugh, a politically conservative commentator established inflammatory, extremely biased radio programming as a genre all its own.

Other, more liberal ones have appeared but none with the success in terms of listeners that Limbaugh has enjoyed. The earliest example of this kind of talk radio commentator was Joe Pyne on a Los Angeles-area station, who would verbally attack listeners, but who was not as political as Limbaugh.

Two rules that were established at the same time as the fairness doctrine and corollary to it, were the personal attack rule and the political editorial rule. These remained in practice even after the repeal of the fairness doctrine. The former, the personal attack rule, applied to a situation where a person or small group was subject to a character attack on a broadcast. The second one, the political editorial rule, had to do with editorials endorsing or opposing candidates for public office. It required that the candidate not endorsed be notified and allowed a reasonable opportunity to respond.

In 2000, the FCC finished the work of the repeal of the fairness doctrine by throwing out these two corollary rules. Many believe that the repeal of the fairness doctrine and the corollary rules has led to a highly-polarized political situation in the country and promotes a blurring of the distinction between news, political advocacy, and political advertising, which has led directly to the proliferation of strident talking heads that clutter the airways in the 21st century. Political and social conservatives suspect that the attempts to revive the fairness doctrine are attempts to silence their voices.

The use of language on the Internet is quite a different thing. In the early days of email, there were unspoken/unwritten rules of conduct that were based on good manners. One was not to use all capital letters or bold letters because that was the same as shouting. Email writers who ignored the rules were severely criticized and shunned. The internet was to be used only for polite conversations. This stage did not last long. Now, just about anything goes. Communications can be blatantly sexual, even to the point of passing along pornographic pictures or highly sexual subject matter. Swear words are used freely. The restraints on shouting and voicing strong emotions have gone by the wayside.

Another aspect of computer language has emerged in recent years as a result of the development of blogs and chat rooms. Bloggers and chatters have a shorthand of their own. It's impossible to understand the messages on most blogs without knowledge of the terminology or a glossary. Unfortunately, the proliferation of opportunities for contact via the Internet has led to many unwanted effects also, the most obvious and most negative its exploitation by sex predators—particularly the opportunity to entice and seduce very young chatters and bloggers. The lawmakers can't keep up with the rapid changes in the social scene brought on by the explosion in personal communications. Parents and teachers must continually be on the alert for signs that unhealthy Internet communications are being engaged in by the young people in their charge.

COMPETENCY 21.0 UNDERSTAND FUNDAMENTAL CONCEPTS RELATING TO THE STRUCTURE, ACQUISITION, USE, AND ANALYSIS OF LANGUAGE

Skill 21.1 Distinguishing structural features of languages (phonological, morphological, syntactic, semantic).

Phonological Awareness

Phonological awareness means the ability of the reader to recognize the sound of spoken language. This recognition includes how these sounds can be blended together, segmented (divided up), and manipulated (switched around). This awareness then leads to phonics, a method for teaching students to read. It helps them "sound out words."

Instructional methods to teach phonological awareness may include any or all of the following: Auditory games and drills during which students recognize and manipulate the sounds of words, separate or segment the sounds of words, take out sounds, blend sounds, add in new sounds, or take apart sound to recombine them in new formations are good way to foster phonological awareness.

Identification of common morphemes, prefixes, and suffixes

This aspect of vocabulary development is to help students look for structural elements within words which they can use independently to help them determine meaning.

The terms listed below are generally recognized as the key structural analysis components.

Root words: A root word is a word from which another word is developed. The second word can be said to have its "root" in the first. This structural component nicely lends itself to a tree with roots illustration which can concretize the meaning for students. Students may also want to literally construct root words using cardboard trees and/or actual roots from plants to create word family models. This is a lovely way to help students own their root words.

Base words: A stand-alone linguistic unit which can not be deconstructed or broken down into smaller words. For example, in the word "re-tell," the base word is "tell."

Contractions: These are shortened forms of two words in which a letter or letters have been deleted. These deleted letter have been replaced by an apostrophe.

Prefixes: These are beginning units of meaning which can be added (the vocabulary word for this type of structural adding is "affixed") to a base word or root word. They can not stand alone. They are also sometimes known as "bound morphemes," meaning that they can not stand alone as a base word.

Suffixes: These are ending units of meaning which can be "affixed" or added on to the ends of root or base words. Suffixes transform the original meanings of base and root words. Like prefixes, they are also known as "bound morphemes," because they can not stand alone as words.

Compound words: Occur when two or more base words are connected to form a new word. The meaning of the new word is in some way connected with that of the base word.

Inflectional endings: Are types are suffixes that impart a new meaning to the base or root word. These endings in particular change the gender, number, tense, or form of the base or root words. Just like other suffixes, these are also termed "bound morphemes."

Syntax

Sentence completeness

Avoid fragments and run-on sentences. Recognition of sentence elements necessary to make a complete thought, proper use of independent and dependent clauses (see *Use correct coordination and subordination*), and proper punctuation will correct such errors.

Sentence structure

Recognize simple, compound, complex, and compound-complex sentences. Use dependent (subordinate) and independent clauses correctly to create these sentence structures.

Simple	Joyce wrote a letter.
Compound	Joyce wrote a letter, and Dot drew a picture.
Complex	While Joyce wrote a letter, Dot drew a picture.
Compound/Complex	When Mother asked the girls to demonstrate their new-found skills, Joyce wrote a letter, and Dot drew a picture.

Note: Do **not** confuse compound sentence elements with compound sentences.

Simple sentence with compound subject
Joyce and Dot wrote letters.
The girl in row three and the boy next to her were passing notes across the aisle.

Simple sentence with compound predicate
> Joyce <u>wrote letters</u> and <u>drew pictures</u>.
> The captain of the high school debate team <u>graduated with honors</u> and <u>studied broadcast journalism in college</u>.

Simple sentence with compound object of preposition
> Coleen graded the students' essays for <u>style</u> and <u>mechanical accuracy</u>.

Skill 21.2 Recognizing typical patterns and individual differences in the language development of children, adolescents, and second-language learners.

Learning approach

Early theories of language development were formulated from learning theory research. The assumption was that language development evolved from learning the rules of language structures and applying them through imitation and reinforcement. This approach also assumed that language, cognitive, and social developments were independent of each other. Thus, children were expected to learn language from patterning after adults who spoke and wrote Standard English. No allowance was made for communication through child jargon, idiomatic expressions, or grammatical and mechanical errors resulting from too strict adherence to the rules of inflection (*childs* instead of *children*) or conjugation (*runned* instead of *ran*). No association was made between physical and operational development and language mastery.

Linguistic approach

Studies spearheaded by Noam Chomsky in the 1950s formulated the theory that language ability is innate and develops through natural human maturation as environmental stimuli trigger acquisition of syntactical structures appropriate to each exposure level. The assumption of a hierarchy of syntax downplayed the significance of semantics. Because of the complexity of syntax and the relative speed with which children acquire language, linguists attributed language development to biological rather than cognitive or social influences.

Cognitive approach

Researchers in the 1970s proposed that language knowledge derives from both syntactic and semantic structures. Drawing on the studies of Piaget and other cognitive learning theorists (see Skill 4.7), supporters of the cognitive approach maintained that children acquire knowledge of linguistic structures after they have acquired the cognitive structures necessary to process language. For example, joining words for specific meaning necessitates sensory motor intelligence.

The child must be able to coordinate movement and recognize objects before she can identify words to name the objects or word groups to describe the actions performed with those objects.

Adolescents must have developed the mental abilities for <u>organizing concepts as well as concrete operations</u>, <u>predicting outcomes</u>, and <u>theorizing</u> before they can assimilate and verbalize complex sentence structures, choose vocabulary for particular nuances of meaning, and examine semantic structures for tone and manipulative effect.

Sociocognitive approach

Other theorists in the 1970s proposed that language development results from sociolinguistic competence. Language, cognitive, and social knowledge are interactive elements of total human development. Emphasis on verbal communication as the medium for language expression resulted in the inclusion of speech activities in most language arts curricula.

Unlike previous approaches, the sociocognitive allowed that determining the appropriateness of language in given situations for specific listeners is as important as understanding semantic and syntactic structures. By engaging in conversation, children at all stages of development have opportunities to test their language skills, receive feedback, and make modifications. As a social activity, conversation is as structured by social order as grammar is structured by the rules of syntax. Conversation satisfies the learner's need to be heard and understood and to influence others. Thus, his choices of vocabulary, tone, and content are dictated by his ability to assess the language knowledge of his listeners. He is constantly applying his cognitive skills to using language in a social interaction. If the capacity to acquire language is inborn, without an environment in which to practice language, a child would not pass beyond grunts and gestures as did primitive man.

Of course, the varying degrees of environmental stimuli to which children are exposed at all age levels creates a slower or faster development of language. Some children are prepared to articulate concepts and recognize symbolism by the time they enter fifth grade because they have been exposed to challenging reading and conversations with well-spoken adults at home or in their social groups. Others are still trying to master the sight recognition skills and are not yet ready to combine words in complex patterns.

Concerns for the teacher

Because teachers must, by virtue of tradition and the dictates of the curriculum, teach grammar, usage, and writing as well as reading and later literature, the problem becomes when to teach what to whom.

The profusion of approaches to teaching grammar alone are mind-boggling. In the universities, we learn about transformational grammar, stratificational grammar, sectoral grammar, etc. But in practice, most teachers, supported by presentations in textbooks and by the methods they learned themselves, keep coming back to the same traditional prescriptive approach - read and imitate - or structural approach - learn the parts of speech, the parts of sentence, punctuation rules, sentence patterns. After enough of the terminology and rules are stored in the brain, then we learn to write and speak. For some educators, the best solution is the worst - don't teach grammar at all.

The same problems occur in teaching usage. How much can we demand students communicate in only Standard English? Different schools of thought suggest that a study of dialect and idiom and recognition of various jargons is a vital part of language development. Social pressures, especially on students in middle and junior high schools, to be accepted within their peer groups and to speak the non-standard language spoken outside the school make adolescents resistant to the corrective, remedial approach. In many communities where the immigrant populations are high, new words are entering English from other languages even as words and expressions that were common when we were children have become rare or obsolete.

Regardless of differences of opinion concerning language development, it is safe to say that a language arts teacher will be most effective using the styles and approaches with which she is most comfortable. And, if she subscribes to a student-centered approach, she may find that the students have a lot to teach her and each other. Moffett and Wagner in the Fourth Edition of *Student-centered Language Arts K-12* stress the three I's: individualization, interaction, and integration. Essentially, they are supporting the socio-cognitive approach to language development. By providing an opportunity for the student to select his own activities and resources, his instruction is individualized. By centering on and teaching each other, students are interactive. Finally, by allowing students to synthesize a variety of knowledge structures, they integrate them. The teacher's role becomes that of a facilitator.

Benefits of the socio-cognitive approach

This approach has tended to guide the whole language movement, currently in fashion. Most basal readers utilize an integrated, cross-curricular approach to successful grammar, language, and usage. Reinforcement becomes an intradepartmental responsibility. Language incorporates diction and terminology across the curriculum. Standard usage is encouraged and supported by both the core classroom textbooks and current software for technology. Teachers need to acquaint themselves with the computer capabilities in their school district and at their individual school sites. Advances in new technologies require the teacher to familiarize herself with programs that would serve her students' needs. Students respond enthusiastically to technology.

Several highly effective programs are available in various formats to assist students with initial instruction or remediation. Grammar texts, such as the Warriner's series, employ various methods to reach individual learning styles. The school library media center should become a focal point for individual exploration.

Second Language Learners

Students who are raised in homes where English is not the first language and/or where standard English is not spoken, may have difficulty with hearing the difference between similar sounding words like "send" and "sent." Any student who is not in an environment where English phonology operates, may have difficulty perceiving and demonstrating the differences between English language phonemes. If students can not hear the difference between words that "sound the same" like "grow" and "glow," they will be confused when these words appear in a print context. This confusion will of course, sadly, impact their comprehension.

Considerations for teaching to English Language Learners include recognition by the teacher that what works for the English language speaking student from an English language speaking family, does not necessarily work in other languages.

Research recommends that ELL students learn to read initially in their first language. It has been found that a priority for ELL should be learning to speak English before being taught to read English. Research supports oral language development, since it lays the foundation for phonological awareness.

Skill 21.3 Applying knowledge of a variety of word identification strategies (analysis of roots, affixes, and cognates).

In the past, the Oxford English Dictionary has been the most reliable source for etymologies. Some of the collegiate dictionaries are also useful. *Merriam-Webster's 3rd Unabridged Dictionary* is useful in tracing the sources of words in American English. *Merriam-Webster's Unabridged Dictionary* may be out of date, so a teacher should also have a *Merriam-Webster's Collegiate Dictionary*, which is updated regularly.

However, there are many up-to-date sources for keeping up and keeping track of the changes that have occurred and are occurring constantly. Google "etymology," for instance, or even the word you're unsure of, and you can find a multitude of sources. Don't trust a single one. The information should be validated by at least three sources. Wikipedia is very useful, but it can be changed by anyone who chooses, so any information on it should be backed up by other sources. If you go to http://www.etymonline.com/sources.php, you will find a long list of resources on etymology.

In order to know when to label a usage "jargon" or "colloquial" nowadays, the teacher must be aware of the possibility that it's a word that is now accepted as standard. In order to be on top of this, the teacher must continually keep up with the etymological aids that are available, particularly online.

Spelling in English is complicated by the fact that it is not phonetic—that is, it is not based on the one-sound/one letter formula used by many other languages. The reason for this is that it is based on the Latin alphabet, which originally had twenty letters, consisting of the present English alphabet minus J, K, V, W, Y, and Z. The Romans added K to be used in abbreviations and Y and Z in words that came from the Greek. This 23-letter alphabet was adopted by the English, who developed W as a ligatured doubling of U and later J and V as consonantal variants of I and U. The result was our alphabet of 26 letters with upper case (capital) and lower case forms.

Spelling is based primarily on 15th century English. The problem is that pronunciation has changed drastically since then, especially long vowels and diphthongs. This Great Vowel Shift affected the seven long vowels. For a long time, spelling was erratic—there were no standards. As long as the meaning was clear, spelling was not considered very important. Samuel Johnson tackled this problem, and his *Dictionary of the English Language* (1755) brought standards to spelling, so important once printing presses were invented. There have been some changes, of course, through the years; but spelling is still not strictly phonetic. There have been many attempts to nudge the spelling into a more phonetic representation of the sounds, but for the most part, all have failed. A good example is Noah Webster's *Spelling Book* (1783), which was a precursor to the first edition (1828) of his *American Dictionary of the English Language.* While there are rules for spelling, and it's important that students learn the rules, there are many exceptions; and memorizing exceptions and giving plenty of opportunities for practicing them seems the only solution for the teacher of English.

Skill 21.4 Recognizing the role of context cues in verifying the correct meaning and pronunciation of words in connected text.

Children who learn to read on schedule and who are avid readers have been seen to have superior vocabularies compared to other children their age. The reason for this is that in order to understand what they read, they often must determine the meaning for a word based on its context. Children who constantly turn to a dictionary for the meaning of a word they don't know will not have this advantage.

This is an important clue for providing students the kinds of exercises and helps they need in order to develop their vocabularies. Learning vocabulary lists is useful, of course, but much less efficient than exercises in determining meaning on the basis of context. It requires an entirely different kind of thinking and learning.

Poetry is also useful for developing vocabulary exercises for children, especially rhymed poetry, where the pronunciation of a term may be deduced by what the poet intended for it to rhyme with. In some poets of earlier periods, the teacher may need to intervene because some of the words that would have rhymed when the poem was written do not rhyme in today's English. Even so, this is a good opportunity to help children understand some of the important principles about their constantly-changing language.

Another good exercise for developing vocabulary is the crossword puzzle. A child's ability to think in terms of analogy is a step upward toward mature language understanding and use. The teacher may construct crossword puzzle using items from the class such as students' names or the terms from their literature or language lessons.

Skill 21.5 Identifying strategies for mastering high-frequency, irregular sight words

Students frequently encounter problems with homonyms—words that are spelled and pronounced the same as another but that have different meanings such as *mean*, a verb, "to intend"; *mean* an adjective, "unkind"; and *mean* a noun or adjective, "average." These words are actually both homonyms and homographs (written the same way).

A similar phenomenon that causes trouble is heteronyms (also sometimes called heterophones), words that are spelled the same but have different pronunciations and meanings (in other words, they are homographs that differ in pronunciation or, technically, homographs that are not homophones). For example, the homographs *desert* (abandon) and *desert* (arid region) are heteronyms (pronounced differently); but *mean* (intend) and *mean* (average) are not. They are pronounced the same, or are homonyms.

Another similar occurrence in English is the capitonym, a word that is spelled the same but has different meanings when it is capitalized and may or may not have different pronunciations. Example: *polish* (to make shiny) and *Polish* (from Poland).

Some of the most troubling homonyms are those that are spelled differently but sound the same. Examples: *its* (3d person singular neuter pronoun) and *it's* ("it is"); *there, their* (3d person plural pronoun) and *they're* ("they are").

Others: *to, too, two;*

Some homonyms/homographs are particularly complicated and troubling. Fluke, for instance is a fish, a flatworm, the end parts of an anchor, the fins on a whale's tail, and a stroke of luck.

Common ones that are troubling to student writers:

accept: tolerate; *except*: everything but.

add: put together with; *ad*: short for advertisement.

allowed: permitted; *aloud*: audibly.

allot: to distribute, allocate; *a lot* (often "*alot*"): much, many (a lot of).

allusion: indirect reference; *illusion*: a distortion of sensory perception.

bare: naked, exposed or very little (bare necessities); *bear*: as a noun, a large mammal and as a verb, to carry.

boy: a male adolescent or child; *buoy*: (noun) a floating marker in the sea.

bridal: pertaining to a bride (bridal gown, bridal suite); *bridle*: (noun) part of a horse's tack.

capital: punishable by death, with an upper-case letter, principal town or city, or wealth and money; *Capitol*: the home of the Congress of the United States and some other legislatures.

chord: group of musical notes; *cord*: rope, long electrical line.

compliment: a praising or flattering remark; *complement*: something that completes.

discreet: tactful or diplomatic; *discrete*: separate or distinct.

dyeing: artificially coloring; *dying*: passing away.

effect: outcome; *affect*: have an effect on.

gorilla: the largest of the great apes; *guerrilla*: a small combat group.

hair: an outgrowth of the epidermis in mammals; *hare*: rabbit.

hoard: to accumulate and store up; *horde*: large group of warriors, mob.

lam: US slang, "on the lam" means "on the run"; *lamb*: a young sheep.

lead: pronounced to rhyme with "seed", to guide or serve as the head of; *lead*: pronounced to rhyme with "head," a heavy metal; *led*: the past tense of "lead."

medal: an award to be strung around the neck; *meddle*: stick one's nose into others' affairs; *metal*: shiny, malleable element or alloy like silver or gold; *mettle*: toughness, guts.

morning: the time between midnight and midday; *mourning*: period of grieving after a death.

past: time before now (past, present and future); *passed*: past tense of "to pass."

piece: portion; *peace*: opposite of war.

peak: tip, height, to reach its highest point; *peek*: to take a brief look; *pique*: fit of anger; to incite (pique one's interest).

Strategies to help students conquer these demons: Practice using them in sentences. Context is useful in understanding the difference. Drill is necessary to overcome the misuses.

COMPETENCY 22.0 UNDERSTAND SIGNIFICANT THEMES, CHARACTERISTICS, TRENDS, WRITERS, AND WORKS IN AMERICAN LITERATURE FROM THE COLONIAL PERIOD TO THE PRESENT, INCLUDING THE LITERARY CONTRIBUTIONS OF WOMEN, MEMBERS OF ETHNIC MINORITIES, AND FIGURES IDENTIFIED WITH PARTICULAR REGIONS

Skill 22.1 Analyzing the significance of major writers (Anne Bradstreet), works (*Walden, Narrative of the Life of Frederick Douglass*), and movements (realism, imagism) to the development of American literature.

The Colonial Period

William Bradford's excerpts from *The Mayflower Compact* relate vividly the hardships of crossing the Atlantic in such a tiny vessel, the misery and suffering of the first winter, the approaches of the American Indians, the decimation of their ranks, and the establishment of the Bay Colony of Massachusetts.

Anne Bradstreet's poetry relates much concerning colonial New England life. From her journals, modern readers learn of the everyday life of the early settlers, the hardships of travel, and the responsibilities of different groups and individuals in the community, Early American literature also reveals the commercial and political adventures of the Cavaliers who came to the New World with King George's blessing.

William Byrd's journal, *A History of the Dividing Line,* concerning his trek into the Dismal Swamp separating the Carolinian territories from Virginia and Maryland makes quite lively reading. A privileged insider to the English Royal Court, Byrd, like other Southern Cavaliers, was given grants to pursue business ventures.

The Revolutionary Period

There were great orations such as Patrick Henry's *Speech to the Virginia House of Burgesses* -- the "Give me liberty or give me death" speech - and George Washington's *Farewell to the Army of the Potomac.* Less memorable and thought rambling by modern readers are Washington's inaugural addresses.

The *Declaration of Independence*, the brainchild predominantly of Thomas Jefferson, with some prudent editing by Ben Franklin, is a prime example of neoclassical writing -- balanced, well crafted, and focused.

Epistles include the exquisitely written, moving correspondence between John Adams and Abigail Adams. The poignancy of their separation - she in Boston, he in Philadelphia - is palpable and real.

The Romantic Period

Nathaniel Hawthorne and Herman Melville are the preeminent early American novelists, writing on subjects definitely regional, specific and American, yet sharing insights about human foibles, fears, loves, doubts, and triumphs. Hawthorne's writings range from children's stories, like the Cricket on the Hearth series, to adult fare of dark, brooding short stories such as "Dr. Heidegger's Experiment," "The Devil and Tom Walker," and "Rapuccini's Daughter." His masterpiece, *The Scarlet Letter*, takes on the society of hypocritical Puritan New Englanders, who ostensibly left England to establish religious freedom, but who have been entrenched in judgmental finger wagging. They ostracize Hester and condemn her child, Pearl, as a child of Satan. Great love, sacrifice, loyalty, suffering, and related epiphanies add universality to this tale. *The House of the Seven Gables* also deals with kept secrets, loneliness, societal pariahs, and love ultimately triumphing over horrible wrong. Herman Melville's great opus, *Moby Dick*, follows a crazed Captain Ahab on his Homeric odyssey to conquer the great white whale that has outwitted him and his whaling crews time and again. The whale has even taken Arab's leg and according to Ahab, wants all of him. Melville recreates in painstaking detail, and with insider knowledge of the harsh life of a whaler out of New Bedford, by way of Nantucket. For those who don't want to learn about every guy rope or all parts of the whaler's rigging, Melville offers up the succinct tale of Billy Budd and his Christ-like sacrifice to the black and white maritime laws on the high seas. An accident results in the death of one of the ship's officers, a slug of a fellow, who had taken a dislike to the young, affable, shy Billy. Captain Vere must hang Billy for the death of Claggert, but knows that this is not right. However, an example must be given to the rest of the crew so that discipline can be maintained.

Edgar Allan Poe creates a distinctly American version of romanticism with his 16 syllable line in "The Raven," the classical "To Helen," and his Gothic "Annabelle Lee." The horror short story can be said to originate from Poe's pen. "The Tell-Tale Heart," "The Cask of Amontillado," "The Fall of the House of Usher," and "The Masque of the Red Death" are exemplary short stories. The new genre of detective story also emerges with Poe's "Murders in the Rue Morgue."

American Romanticism has its own offshoot in the Transcendentalism of Ralph Waldo Emerson and Henry David Thoreau. One wrote about transcending the complexities of life; the other, who wanted to get to the marrow of life, pitted himself against nature at Walden Pond and wrote an inspiring autobiographical account of his sojourn, aptly titled *On Walden Pond*. He also wrote passionately on his objections to the interference of government on the individual in "On the Duty of Civil Disobedience."

Emerson's elegantly crafted essays and war poetry still give validation to several important universal truths. Probably most remembered for his address to Thoreau's Harvard graduating class, "The American Scholar," he defined the qualities of hard work and intellectual spirit required of Americans in their growing nation.

The Transition between Romanticism and Realism

The Civil War period ushers in the poignant poetry of Walt Whitman and his homages to all who suffer from the ripple effects of war and presidential assassination. His "Come up from the Fields, Father" about a Civil War soldier's death and his family's reaction and "When Lilacs Last in the Courtyard Bloom'd" about the effects of Abraham Lincoln's death on the poet and the nation should be required readings in any American literature course. Further, his *Leaves of Grass* gave America its first poetry truly unique in form, structure, and subject matter.

Emily Dickinson, like Walt Whitman, leaves her literary fingerprints on a vast array of poems, all but three of which were never published in her lifetime. Her themes of introspection and attention to nature's details and wonders are, by any measurement, world-class works. Her posthumous recognition reveals the timeliness of her work. American writing had most certainly arrived!

Mark Twain also left giant footprints with his unique blend of tall tale and fable. "The Celebrated Jumping Frog of Calaveras County" and "The Man who Stole Hadleyburg" are epitomes of short story writing. Move to novel creation, and Twain again rises head and shoulders above others by his bold, still disputed, oft-banned *The Adventures of Huckleberry Finn*, which examines such taboo subjects as a white person's love of a slave, the issue of leaving children with abusive parents, and the outcomes of family feuds. Written partly in dialect and southern vernacular, *The Adventures of Huckleberry Finn* is touted by some as the greatest American novel.

Contemporary American Literature

America Drama

The greatest and most prolific of American playwrights include:

Eugene O'Neill -- *Long Day's Journey into Night, Mourning Becomes Electra,* and *Desire Under the Elms*

Arthur Miller -- *The Crucible, All My Sons,* and *Death of a Salesman*

Tennessee Williams -- *Cat on a Hot Tin Roof, The Glass Menagerie,* and *A Street Car Named Desire*

Edward Albee -- *Who's Afraid of Virginia Woolf?, Three Tall Women,* and *A Delicate Balance*

American Fiction

The renowned American novelists of this century include

John Updike -- *Rabbit Run* and *Rabbit Redux*

Sinclair Lewis -- *Babbit* and *Elmer Gantry*

F. Scott Fitzgerald -- *The Great Gatsby* and *Tender is the Night*

Ernest Hemingway -- *A Farewell to Arms* and *For Whom the Bell Tolls*

William Faulkner -- *The Sound and the Fury* and *Absalom, Absalom*

Bernard Malamud -- *The Fixer* and *The Natural*

American Poetry

The poetry of the twentieth century is multifaceted, as represented by Edna St. Vincent Millay, Marianne Moore, Richard Wilbur, Langston Hughes, Maya Angelou, and Rita Lone. Head and shoulders above all others are the many-layered poems of Robert Frost. His New England motifs of snowy evenings, birches, apple picking, stone wall mending, hired hands, and detailed nature studies relate universal truths in exquisite diction, polysyllabic words, and rare allusions to either mythology or the *Bible*.

American Indian Literature

The foundation of American Indian writing is found in story-telling, oratory, autobiographical and historical accounts of tribal village life, reverence for the environment, and the postulation that the earth with all of its beauty was given in trust, to be cared for and passed on to future generations.

Early American Indian writings

Barland, Hal. *When The Legends Die*

Barrett, S.M. Editor: *Geronimo: His Own Story - Apache*

Eastman, C. & Eastman E. *Wigwam Evenings: Sioux Folktales Retold*

Riggs, L. *Cherokee Night* - drama

Twentieth Century Writers

Deloria, V. *Custer Died for your Sins* (Sioux)

Dorris, M. *The Broken Cord: A Family's on-going struggle with fetal alcohol syndrome* (Modoc)

Hogan, L. *Mean Spirited* (Chickasaw)

Taylor, C.F. *Native American Myths and Legends*

Afro-American Literature

The three phases of Afro-American Literature can be broken down as follows:

- Oppression, slavery, and the re-construction of the post-Civil War/rural South

- Inner city strife/single parenting, drug abuse, lack of educational opportunities and work advancement etc. that was controlled by biased and disinterested factions of society.

- Post-Civil Rights and the emergence of the BLACK movement focusing on biographical and autobiographical Black heroes and their contribution to Black and American culture.

Resources:

1. Pre-Civil War

Bethune, Mary McLoed. *Voice of Black Hope*
Fast, Howard. *Freedom Ride*
Haskins, James. *Black Music in America - A History through its People*
Huggins, Nathan Irving. *Black Odyssey*
Lemann, Nicolas. *The Promised Land*
Stowe, Harriet Beecher. *Uncle Tom's Cabin*
Wheatley, Phyllis. *Memoirs and Poems*

2. Post-Civil War and Reconstruction

Armstrong, William. *Sounder*
Bonham, Frank. *Durango Street*
Childress, Alice. *A Hero Ain't Nothin' But a Sandwich*
Gaines, Ernest. *The Autobiography of Miss Jane Pittman*

3. Post Civil War - Present

Angelou, Maya. *I Know Why the Caged Bird Sings*
Baldwin, James. *Go Tell It on the Mountain*
Haley, Alex. *Roots*

Hansberry, Lorraine. *A Raisin in the Sun*
Lee, Harper. *To Kill a Mockingbird*
Hughes, Langston. *I, Too, Sing America*
Wright, Richard. *White Man Listen!* and *Native Son*

Latino/a Literature

In the field of literature, we have two new expanding areas, Latino/a and feminist writers. These authors write to retain cultural heritage, share their people's struggle for recognition, independence, and survival, and express their hopes for the future.

Latino/Latina Writers
De Cervantes, Lora (Chicana). *Starfish*
Cisneros, Sandra (Hispanic). *Red Sweater* and other short story collections
Marquez, Gabriel Garcia (Colombian). *Hundred Years of Solitude*
Nunoz, A. Lopez (Spanish). *Programas Para Dias Especiales*
Neruda, Pablo (Chile). Nobel Prize Winner- Collections of Poetry
Silko, Leslie Marmon (Mexican). *The Time We Climbed Snake Mountain*
Soto, Gary (Mexican). *The Tales of Sunlight*

Feminist / gender concern literature written by women in the United States

Edith Wharton's *Ethan Frome* is a heartbreaking tale of lack of communication, lack of funds, the unrelenting cold of the Massachusetts winter, and a toboggan ride which gnarls Ethan and Mattie just like the old tree which they smash into. The *Age of Innocence*, in contrast to *Ethan Frome*, is set in the upper echelons of fin-de-siècle New York and explores marriage without stifling social protocols.

Willa Cather's work moves the reader to the prairies of Nebraska and the harsh eking out of existence by the immigrant families who choose to stay there and farm. Her most acclaimed works include *My Antonia* and *Death Comes for the Archbishop*.

Kate Chopin's regionalism and local color takes her readers to the upper-crust Creole society of New Orleans and resort isles off the Louisiana coast. "The Story of an Hour" is lauded as one of the greatest of all short stories. Her feminist liberation novel, *The Awakening*, is still hotly debated.

Eudora Welty's regionalism and dialect shine in her short stories of rural Mississippi, especially in "The Worn Path."

Modern black female writers who explore the world of feminist/gender issues as well as class prohibitions are Alice Walker -- (*The Color Purple*), Zora Neale Hurston (*Their Eyes Were Watching God*), and Toni Morrison (*Beloved, Jazz, and Song of Solomon*).

Feminists

Alcott, Louisa May. *Little Women*
Friedan, Betty. *The Feminine Mystique: The Second Stage*
Bronte, Charlotte. *Jane Eyre*
Hurston, Zora Neale. *Their Eyes Were Watching God*
Janeway, Elizabeth. *Woman's World, Woman's Place: A Study in Social
        Mythology*
Chopin, Kate. *The Awakening*
Rich, Adrienne. Arienne Rich's Poetry: *Motherhood As Experience* and *Driving
        into the Wreck*
Woolf, Virginia. *A Room of One's Own*

**Skill 22.2 Analyzing changes in literary form and style in American
literature of the colonial, nineteenth-century, modern, and contemporary
periods.**

American Literature is defined by a number of clearly identifiable periods.

1. Native American works from various tribes

These were originally part of a vast oral tradition that spanned most of
continental America from as far back as before the 15th century.

- Characteristics of native Indian literature include
  - Reverence for and awe of nature.
  - The interconnectedness of the elements in the life cycle.

- Themes of Indian literature often reflect
  - The hardiness of the native body and soul.
  - Remorse for the destruction of their way of life.
  - The genocide of many tribes by the encroaching settlement and
      Manifest Destiny policies of the U. S. government.

2. The Colonial Period in both New England and the South

Stylistically, early colonists' writings were neo-classical, emphasizing order,
balance, clarity, and reason. Schooled in England, their writing and speaking was
still decidedly British even as their thinking became entirely American.

Early American literature reveals the lives and experiences of the New England
expatriates who left England to find religious freedom.

The Revolutionary Period contains non-fiction genres: essay, pamphlet, speech,
famous document, and epistle.

Thomas Paine's pamphlet, *Common Sense*, which, though written by a recently transplanted Englishman, spoke to the American patriots' common sense in dealing with the issues in the cause of freedom.

Other contributions are Benjamin Franklin's essays from *Poor Richard's Almanac* and satires such as "How to Reduce a Great Empire to a Small One" and "A Letter to Madame Gout."

3. The Romantic Period

Early American folktales, and the emergence of a distinctly American writing, not just a stepchild to English forms, constitute the next period.

Washington Irving's characters, Icabod Crane and Rip Van Winkle, create a uniquely American folklore devoid of English influences. The characters are indelibly marked by their environment and the superstitions of the New Englander. The early American writings of James Fenimore Cooper and his Leatherstocking Tales with their stirring accounts of drums along the Mohawk and the French and Indian Wars, the futile British defense of Fort William Henry and the brutalities of this time frame allow readers a window into their uniquely American world. Natty Bumppo, Chingachgook, Uncas, and Magua are unforgettable characters that reflect the American spirit in thought and action.

The poetry of Fireside Poets - James Russell Lowell, Oliver Wendell Holmes, Henry Wadsworth Longfellow, and John Greenleaf Whittier - was recited by American families and read in the long New England winters. In "The Courtin'," Lowell used Yankee dialect to tell a narrative. Spellbinding epics by Longfellow such as *Hiawatha*, *The Courtship of Miles Standish*, and *Evangeline* told of adversity, sorrow, and ultimate happiness in an uniquely American warp. "Snowbound" by Whittier relates the story of a captive family isolated by a blizzard, stressing family closeness. Holmes' "The Chambered Nautilus" and his famous line, "Fired the shot heard round the world," put American poetry on a firm footing with other world writers.

4. The Transition between Romanticism and Realism

During this period such legendary figures as Paul Bunyan and Pecos Bill rose from the oral tradition. Anonymous storytellers around campfires told tales of a huge lumberman and his giant blue ox, Babe, whose adventures were explanations of natural phenomena like those of footprints filled with rainwater becoming the Great Lakes. Or the whirling-dervish speed of Pecos Bill explained the tornadoes of the Southwest. Like ancient peoples, finding reasons for the happenings in their lives, these American pioneer storytellers created a mythology appropriate to the vast reaches of the unsettled frontier.

5. The Realistic Period

The late nineteenth century saw a reaction against the tendency of romantic writers to look at the world through rose-colored glasses. Writers like Frank Norris (*The Pit*) and Upton Sinclair (*The Jungle*) used their novels to decry conditions for workers in slaughterhouses and wheat mills. In *The Red Badge of Courage*, Stephen Crane wrote of the daily sufferings of the common soldier in the Civil War. Realistic writers wrote of common, ordinary people and events using detail that would reveal the harsh realities of life. They broached taboos by creating protagonists whose environments often destroyed them. Romantic writers would have only protagonists whose indomitable wills helped them rise above adversity. Crane's *Maggie: A Girl of the Streets* deals with a young woman forced into prostitution to survive. In "The Occurrence at Owl Creek Bridge," Ambrose Bierce relates the unfortunate hanging of a Confederate soldier.

Upton Sinclair

Short stories, like Bret Harte's "The Outcasts of Poker Flat" and Jack London's "To Build a Fire," deal with unfortunate people whose luck in life has run out. Many writers, sub-classified as naturalists, believed that man was subject to a fate over which he had no control.

6. The Modern Era

The twentieth century American writing can be classified into three basic genres:

- Drama
- Fiction
- Poetry

See Skill 22.1 for highlighted authors and works in these genres.

Skill 22.3 Analyzing passages that illustrate major thematic concerns and stylistic and formal characteristics associated with significant American prose writers (Herman Melville, Willa Cather, Richard Wright, Maxine Hong Kingston) and poets (Walt Whitman, Emily Dickinson, Gwendolyn Brooks, Leslie Marmon Silko).

Herman Melville was born in 1819 and grew up in upper-class New York neighborhoods. His mother was a strict Calvinist Presbyterian and had strong views regarding proper behavior. Herman tended to be a rebellious sort, and to some extent his conflicts regarding his mother's viewpoints were never resolved. When Herman was eleven years old, his father's business failed, and he died shortly afterward. Herman tried working in business for awhile but soon decided he wanted to go to sea.

Working on ships and traveling, he began to write non-fictional pieces about his experiences. In July of 1851, he wrote his most famous work, *Moby Dick*. Before he died, he wrote poems and another well-known novel, *Billy Budd*, which was not published until 1924. Just as he began to write *Moby Dick*, he became friends with Nathaniel Hawthorne, who happened to be his neighbor. Hawthorne's works and friendship became an important influence on his writing.

In *Moby Dick*, the style is indicative of the reportorial writing of the earlier period; however, it is far more than that. It is seen as a great American epic, even though it is not poetry. It was not successful while its author was alive. Its success came much later.

Some Themes:

- Man in conflict with the natural world
- Religion and God's role in the universe
- Good and evil
- Cause and effect
- Duty
- Conscience

Richard Wright was the grandson of slaves and grew up in a time when the lives of African-Americans tended to be very grim. His response to life lived so close to those who had so recently risen from bondage permeates his writing.

His writing went through many changes just as his response to the special reality of life as a black person in a white-dominated world went through many changes. In order to understand his work, the date of the writing—the stage he was undergoing at the time—is very important. He was influenced early by Maxim Gorky, whose own life experience had similarities to Wright's own. Later, he was heavily influenced by Dostoevsky and that writer's themes can be identified in the work from his last period.

Survival for many blacks and black communities required conformity to whatever white people demanded, and Wright rejected that. He felt profoundly alienated and felt that his individuality had been wounded. He became a proletarian revolutionary artist in the earliest years of his career. The American Communist Party nabbed him as their most illustrious recruit to the newly-established literary standards of proletarian realism. He rejected the "conspicuous ornamentation" of institutions imposed by segregation such as the Harlem Renaissance. At the same time, he felt that consciousness must draw its strength from the lore of a great people, his own. He sought, in the early years of the 20th century, to integrate the progressive aspects of the folk culture of the African-Americans into a collective myth that would promote a revolutionary approach to reality.

He left the Communist Party in 1944, largely as a result of his own evolution. *Black Boy*, an autobiographical account of his childhood and young manhood, appeared in 1945. He settled in Paris as a permanent expatriate shortly after its publication. His first stories—*Uncle Tom's Children*—are a re-conception of negro spirituals and black Christianity in which the hero chooses to risk martyrdom in progressively more elevated stages of class consciousness.

Some themes:

- The environment of the South is too small to nourish human beings, especially African-Americans
- Rejection of black militancy
- Violent, battered childhood and victorious adulthood
- Suffocation of instinct and stifling of potential
- Mature reminiscences of a battered childhood
- Black mother's protective nurture and the trauma of an absent or impotent father
- Each is responsible for everyone and everything (later works)

His technique and style are not as important as the impact his ideas and attitudes have had on American life. He set out to portray African-Americans to white readers in such a way that the myth of the uncomplaining, comic, obsequious black man might be replaced.

Willa Cather grew up on the western plains in Nebraska, and much of her best fiction focuses on the pioneering period in that part of the country. She was born in Virginia in 1873 on her family's farm; but in 1884, the family moved to Nebraska where other relatives had settled. Much of the lore that is the basis of her stories came from her visits with immigrant farm women around Red Cloud, where the family eventually made their home.

When she was sixteen, she enrolled at the University of Nebraska in Lincoln where an essay in her English class was favorably accepted and she began to support herself as a journalist.

She moved to Pittsburgh and was working as a writer and editor when she decided that she wanted to teach school. Even so, she continued to develop her writing career. On a trip back to Nebraska, she witnessed a wheat harvest, which triggered her motive for writing about the pioneer period of American history.

Some Themes:

- The American Dream
- Prejudice
- Coming of Age
- Nostalgia

Maxine Hong Kingston's parents were Chinese immigrants who lived in Stockton, California. Her fiction is highly autobiographical, and she weaves Chinese myths and fictionalized history with the aim of exploring the conflicts between cultures faced by Chinese-Americans. Her writing exposes the ordeals of the Chinese immigrants who were so exploited by American companies, particularly railroad and agriculture industries. She also explores relationships within the Chinese families, particularly between parents who were born in China and children who were born in America. In a 1980 *New York Times Book Review* interview, she said "What I am doing in this new book [*China Men*] is churning America."

Some Themes:

- Discovery
- The American Dream
- Male/Female Roles
- Metamorphosis
- Enforced Muteness
- Vocal Expression
- Family

Poets:

Walt Whitman's poetry was more often than not inspired by the Civil War. He is America's greatest romantic poet and many of his poems are related to and come directly from the conflict between the northern and southern states. This is not to say that the war was the only influence; he wrote many poems on topics that are not directly related to it. His major work, *Leaves of Grass,* was revised nine times, the last in 1892 shortly before he died. He used sophisticated linguistic devices much ahead of his time. Even though he dealt with a vast, panoramic vision, his style has a personal and immediate effect on the reader.

When he was born in 1819 on Long Island in New York, it was a time of great patriotism for the new nation; however, he experienced the conflict that presented a serious threat to its survival in the war between the states, and it's no wonder that the conflict became the subject matter for most of his creative output. His father was a carpenter and then a farmer. Walt was the second-born of eight, the first son. He had six years of public education before he went to work for Brooklyn lawyers and began to educate himself in the library. He began his writing career with newspaper articles and eventually wrote short stories that were published in newspapers. His unconventional techniques were his own creation and in *Leaves of Grass* he intended to speak for all Americans.

He worked as a volunteer in hospitals to help care for soldiers, and was deeply affected by the horrors of war that he saw first-hand. His poetry was considered to be indecent by some, and he was both praised and vilified during his lifetime. He died in 1892 of tuberculosis.

Some Themes:
- Imagination vs. Scientific Process
- Individualism

Emily Dickinson has been called the "myth of Amherst" because so little is known of her. She was born in 1830, the second child of Edward and Emily Dickinson. Her family was prominent in Massachusetts and played a major role in the founding of Amherst College. Her father's stern, puritanical control of his family played a pivotal role in the poetry that his daughter eventually wrote. Although he was severe and controlling, he saw that his daughters got a good education. Emily attended Amherst Academy and then Mount Holyoke Female Seminary. She obtained a copy of Emerson's poems in 1850 and began to develop her own beliefs regarding religion and the severe God that her father represented.

Only a few of her poems were published during her lifetime, and she was unknown until after her death. After she withdrew from school, she became more and more reclusive and after the death of her father in 1874, she never again left her home. She died of Bright's disease in 1886. Her sister Lavinia found roughly 2,000 poems on small pieces of paper, which were published in several editions. The first full three-volume edition was released in 1955. She has come to be known for her superb use of concrete language and imagery to express and evoke abstract issues. Most people have a favorite Dickinson poem.

Her themes range widely, but following are a few:

- Sanity/insanity
- Doubt
- Death
- Individuality

- Defiance
- Feminism

Gwendolyn Brooks was the first African American to receive a Pulitzer Prize for Poetry with her acute images of African Americans in the cities of America. Born in 1917 to a schoolteacher and a janitor, she grew up in Chicago. She was named poet laureate of Illinois in 1978 and was the first black woman honorary fellow of the Modern Language Association. Her family was close-knit, and she tended to spend her time reading when she was a child. She began writing poems when she was very young. She has also had a successful teaching career at several universities including City University of New York where she was Distinguished Professor. Gwendolyn was writing about the experience of being black long before it became main-stream. She underwent an evolution in subject matter and thinking about being black as a result of the movement of the sixties toward the validity of African Americans. She died of cancer in 2000. She was eighty-three years old.

Themes:

- Poverty and Racism
- Self-respect
- Heritage
- Community
- Family
- Black Unity
- The Basic Humanness in Everyone
- Black Solidarity
- Pride

Leslie Marmon Silko is a Laguna Indian of mixed ancestry that includes Cherokee, German, English, Mexican, and Pueblo. There were several remarkable women in her life, grandmothers and aunts, who taught her the traditions and stories of the Pueblo. At the same time, her father's role in his tribe also made her aware of the abuses her people had experienced at the hands of the government. The major issue was the land that had been stolen from her people. She believed that she could change things by writing about them.

Some themes:

- Evil
- Reciprocity
- Individual/Community
- Native American Traditions
- Native American Religion
- Mixed Breeds

- Scapegoats
- Racism
- Prejudice

Skill 22.4 Analyzing the literary responses of American writers to social conditions and major historical and religious movements and events (regional subcultures, slavery, civil rights movements, the Vietnam War, immigration), as exemplified in given passages.

Local Color is defined as the presenting of the peculiarities of a particular locality and its inhabitants. This genre began to be seen primarily after the Civil War although there were certainly precursors such as Washington Irving and his depiction of life in the Catskill Mountains of New York. However, the local colorist movement is generally considered to have begun in 1865, when humor began to permeate the writing of those who were focusing on a particular region of the country. Samuel L. Clemens (Mark Twain) is best-known for his humorous works about the southwest such as *The Notorious Jumping Frog of Calaveras County.* The country had just emerged from its "long night of the soul," a time when death, despair, and disaster had preoccupied the nation for almost five years. It's no wonder that the artists sought to relieve the grief and pain and lift spirits nor is it surprising that their efforts brought such a strong response. Mark Twain is generally considered to be not only one of America's funniest writers but one who also wrote great and enduring fiction.

Other examples of local colorists who used many of the same devices are Harriet Beecher Stowe, Bret Harte, George Washington Cable, Joel Chandler Harris, and Sarah Orne Jewett.

Slavery

The best-known of the early writers who used fiction as a political statement about slavery is Harriet Beecher Stowe, author of *Uncle Tom's Cabin.* This was her first novel, and it was published first as a serial in 1851 then as a book in 1852. It brought an angry reaction from people living in the South. This antislavery book infuriated Southerners. However, Stowe, herself, had been angered by the 1850 Fugitive Slave Law that made it legal to indict those who assisted runaway slaves. It also took away rights not only of the runaways but also of the free slaves. She intended to generate a protest of the law and slavery. It was the first effort to present the lives of slaves from their standpoint.

The novel is about three slaves, Tom, Eliza, and George who are together in Kentucky. Eliza and George are married to each other but have different masters. They successfully escape with their little boy, but Tom does not. Although he has a wife and children, he is sold, ending up finally with the monstrous Simon Legree, where he dies at last.

Stowe cleverly used depictions of motherhood and Christianity to stir her readers. When President Lincoln finally met her, he told her it was her book that started the war.

Many writers used the printed word to protest slavery. Some of them include:
- Frederick Douglas
- William Lloyd Garrison
- Benjamin Lay, a Quaker
- Connecticut theologian Jonathan Edward
- Susan B. Anthony

Civil Rights

Many of the abolitionists were also early crusaders for civil rights. However, the 1960s movement focused attention on the plight of the people who had been "freed" by the Civil War in ways that brought about long overdue changes in the opportunities and rights of African Americans. David Halberstam, who had been a reporter in Nashville at the time of the sit-ins by eight young black college students that initiated the revolution, wrote *The Children*, published in 1998 by Random House, for the purpose of reminding Americans of their courage, suffering, and achievements. Congressman John Lewis, Fifth District, Georgia, was one of those eight young men who has gone on to a life of public service. Halberstam records that when older black ministers tried to persuade these young people not to pursue their protest, John Lewis responded: "If not us, then who? If not now, then when?"

Some examples of protest literature:
- James Baldwin, *Blues for Mister Charlie*
- Martin Luther King, *Where Do We Go from Here?*
- Langston Hughes, *Fight for Freedom: The Story of the NAACP*
- Eldridge Cleaver, *Soul on Ice*
- Malcolm X, *The Autobiography of Malcolm X*
- Stokely Carmichael and Charles V. Hamilton, *Black Power*
- Leroi Jones, *Home*

Vietnam

An America that was already divided over the civil rights movement faced even greater divisions over the war in Vietnam. Those who were in favor of the war and who opposed withdrawal saw it as the major front in the war against communism. Those who opposed the war and who favored withdrawal of the troops believed that it would not serve to defeat communism and was a quagmire.

Catch-22 by Joseph Heller was a popular antiwar novel that became a successful movie of the time.

Authors Take Sides on Vietnam, edited by Cecil Woolf and John Bagguley is a collection of essays by 168 well-known authors throughout the world. *Where is Vietnam?* edited by Walter Lowenfels consists of 92 poems about the war.

Many writers were publishing works for and against the war, but the genre that had the most impact was rock music. Bob Dylan was an example of the musicians of the time. His music represented the hippie aesthetic and brilliant, swirling colors and hallucinogenic imagery and created a style that came to be called psychedelic. Some other bands that originated during this time and became well-known for their psychedelic music, primarily about the Vietnam War in the early years, are the Grateful Dead, Jefferson Airplane, Big Brother, Sly and the Family Stone. In England, the movement attracted the Beatles and the Rolling Stones.

Immigration

This has been a popular topic for literature from the time of the Louisiana Purchase in 1804. The recent *Undaunted Courage* by Stephen E. Ambrose is ostensibly the autobiography of Meriwether Lewis but is actually a recounting of the Lewis and Clark expedition. Presented as a scientific expedition by President Jefferson, the expedition was actually intended to provide maps and information for the opening up of the west. A well-known novel of the settling of the west by immigrants from other countries is *Giants in the Earth* by Ole Edvart Rolvaag, himself a descendant of immigrants.

John Steinbeck's *Cannery Row* and *Tortilla Flats* glorifies the lives of Mexican migrants in California. Amy Tan's *The Joy Luck Club* deals with the problems faced by Chinese immigrants.

Leon Uris' *Exodus* deals with the social history that led to the founding of the modern state of Israel. It was published in 1958, only a short time after the Holocaust. It also deals with attempts of concentration camp survivors to get to the land that has become the new Israel. In many ways, it is the quintessential work on immigration—causes and effects.

COMPETENCY 23.0 UNDERSTAND MAJOR THEMES, CHARACTERISTICS, TRENDS, WRITERS, AND WORKS IN BRITISH AND IRISH LITERATURE

Skill 23.1 Analyzing the significance of writers (Chaucer, Shakespeare, Wordsworth, Joyce, Yeats) works (*Paradise Lost, Wuthering Heights, Pygmalion*), and movements (metaphysical poetry, the "kitchen sink" school) to the development of British literature from the Anglo-Saxon period to the present.

There are four major time periods of writings. They are neoclassicism, romanticism, realism, and naturalism. Certain authors, among these Chaucer, Shakespeare, and Donne, though writing during a particular literary period, are considered to have a style all their own.

Neoclassicism: Patterned after the greatest writings of classical Greece and Rome, this type of writing is characterized by balanced, graceful, well-crafted, refined, elevated style. Major proponents of this style are poet laureates, John Dryden and Alexander Pope. The eras in which they wrote are called the Ages of Dryden and Pope. The self is not exalted and focus is on the group, not the individual, in neoclassic writing.

Romanticism: Writings emphasizing the individual. Emotions and feelings are validated. Nature acts as an inspiration for creativity; it is a balm of the spirit. Romantics hearken back to medieval, chivalric themes and ambiance. They also emphasize supernatural, Gothic themes and settings, which are characterized by gloom and darkness. Imagination is stressed. New types of writings include detective and horror stories and autobiographical introspection (Wordsworth). There are two generations in British Literature: First Generation includes William Wordsworth and Samuel Taylor Coleridge whose collaboration, *Lyrical Ballads*, defines romanticism and its exponents. Wordsworth maintained that the scenes and events of everyday life and the speech of ordinary people were the raw material of which poetry could and should be made. Romanticism spread to the United States, where Ralph Waldo Emerson and Henry David Thoreau adopted it in their transcendental romanticism, emphasizing reasoning. Further extensions of this style are found in Edgar Allan Poe's Gothic writings. Second Generation romantics include the ill-fated Englishmen Lord Byron, John Keats, and Percy Bysshe Shelley. Byron and Shelley, who for some most epitomize the romantic poet (in their personal lives as well as in their work), wrote resoundingly in protest against social and political wrongs and in defense of the struggles for liberty in Italy and Greece. The Second Generation romantics stressed personal introspection and the love of beauty and nature as requisites of inspiration.

Realism: Unlike classical and neoclassical writing which, often deal with aristocracies and nobility or the gods, realistic writers deal with the common man and his socio/economic problems in a non-sentimental way. Muckraking, social injustice, domestic abuse, and inner city conflicts are examples of writings by writers of realism. Realistic writers include Thomas Hardy, George Bernard Shaw, and Henrik Ibsen.

Naturalism: This is realism pushed to the maximum, writing which exposes the underbelly of society, usually the lower class struggles. This is the world of penury, injustice, abuse, ghetto survival, hungry children, single parenting, and substance abuse. Émile Zola was inspired by his readings in history and medicine and attempted to apply methods of scientific observation to the depiction of pathological human character, notably in his series of novels devoted to several generations of one French family.

Skill 23.2 Analyzing passages that illustrate significant themes (the ideal of the warrior-hero, the conventions of courtly love) and genres (the morality play, the Elizabethan sonnet) in British literature from the Anglo-Saxon period, the Middle Ages, and the Renaissance.

Anglo-Saxon

The Anglo-Saxon period spans six centuries but produced only a smattering of literature. The first British epic is *Beowulf,* anonymously written by Christian monks many years after the events in the narrative supposedly occurred. This Teutonic saga relates the triumph three times over monsters by the hero, Beowulf. "The Seafarer," a shorter poem, some history, and some riddles are the rest of the Anglo-Saxon canon.

Medieval

The Medieval period introduces Geoffrey Chaucer, the father of English literature, whose *Canterbury Tales* are written in the vernacular, or street language of England, not in Latin. Thus, the tales are said to be the first work of British literature. Next, Thomas Malory's *Le Morte d'Arthur* calls together the extant tales from Europe as well as England concerning the legendary King Arthur, Merlin, Guenevere, and the Knights of the Round Table. This work is the generative work that gave rise to the many Arthurian legends that stir the chivalric imagination.

Renaissance and Elizabethan

The Renaissance, the most important period since it is synonymous with William Shakespeare, begins with importing the idea of the Petrarchan or Italian sonnet into England. Sir Thomas Wyatt and Sir Philip Sydney wrote English versions. Next, Sir Edmund Spenser invented a variation on this Italian sonnet form, aptly called the Spenserian sonnet. His masterpiece is the epic, *The Fairie Queene*, honoring Queen Elizabeth I's reign. He also wrote books on the Red Cross Knight, St. George and the Dragon, and a series of Arthurian adventures. Spencer was dubbed the Poet's Poet. He created a nine-line stanza, eight lines iambic pentameter and an extra-footed ninth line, an alexandrine. Thus, he invented the Spencerian stanza as well.

William Shakespeare, the Bard of Avon, wrote 154 sonnets, 39 plays, and two long narrative poems. The sonnets are justifiably called the greatest sonnet sequence in all literature. Shakespeare dispensed with the octave/sestet format of the Italian sonnet and invented his three quatrains, one heroic couplet format. His plays are divided into comedies, history plays, and tragedies. Great lines from these plays are more often quoted than from any other author. The Big Four tragedies, Hamlet, *Macbeth*, *Othello*, and *King Lear* are acknowledged to be the most brilliant examples of this genre.

Skill 23.3 Analyzing passages that illustrate significant themes and characteristics of major British and Irish literary works of the Enlightenment, the romantic and Victorian periods, and the twentieth century (the satires of Swift, the odes of Keats, the fiction of Woolf, the drama of Beckett).

Seventeenth century

John Milton's devout Puritanism was the wellspring of his creative genius that closes the remarkable productivity of the English Renaissance. His social commentary in such works as *Aereopagitica*, *Samson Agonistes*, and his elegant sonnets would be enough to solidify his stature as a great writer. It is his masterpiece based in part on the Book of Genesis that places Milton very near the top of the rung of a handful of the most renowned of all writers. *Paradise Lost*, written in balanced, elegant Neoclassic form, truly does justify the ways of God to man. The greatest allegory about man's journey to the Celestial City (Heaven) was written at the end of the English Renaissance, as was John Bunyan's *The Pilgrim's Progress*, which describes virtues and vices personified. This work is, or was for a long time, second only to the *Bible* in numbers of copies printed and sold.

The Jacobean Age gave us the marvelously witty and cleverly constructed conceits of John Donne's metaphysical sonnets, as well as his insightful meditations, and his version of sermons or homilies.

"Ask not for whom the bell tolls", and "No man is an island unto himself" are famous epigrams from Donne's *Meditations*. His most famous conceit is that which compares lovers to a footed compass traveling seemingly separate, but always leaning towards one another and conjoined in "A Valediction Forbidding Mourning."

Eighteenth century

Ben Johnson, author of the wickedly droll play, *Volpone,* and the Cavalier *carpe diem* poets Robert Herrick, Sir John Suckling, and Richard Lovelace also wrote during King James I's reign.

The Restoration and Enlightenment reflect the political turmoil of the regicide of Charles I, the Interregnum Puritan government of Oliver Cromwell, and the restoring of the monarchy to England by the coronation of Charles II, who had been given refuge by the French King Louis. Neoclassicism became the preferred writing style, especially for Alexander Pope. New genres, such as *The Diary of Samuel Pepys*, the novels of Daniel Defoe, the periodical essays and editorials of Joseph Addison and Richard Steele, and Alexander Pope's mock epic, *The Rape of the Lock*, demonstrate the diversity of expression during this time.

Writers who followed were contemporaries of Dr. Samuel Johnson, the lexicographer of *The Dictionary of the English Language*. Fittingly, this Age of Johnson, which encompasses James Boswell's biography of Dr. Johnson, Robert Burns' Scottish dialect and regionalism in his evocative poetry and the mystical pre-Romantic poetry of William Blake usher in the Romantic Age and its revolution against Neoclassicism.

Romantic period

The Romantic Age encompasses what is known as the First Generation Romantics, William Wordsworth and Samuel Taylor Coleridge, who collaborated on *Lyrical Ballads,* which defines and exemplifies the tenets of this style of writing. The Second Generation includes George Gordon, Lord Byron, Percy Bysshe Shelley, and John Keats. These poets wrote sonnets, odes, epics, and narrative poems, most dealing with homage to nature. Wordsworth's most famous other works are "Intimations on Immortality" and "The Prelude." Byron's satirical epic, *Don Juan*, and his autobiographical *Childe Harold's Pilgrimage* are irreverent, witty, self-deprecating and, in part, cuttingly critical of other writers and critics. Shelley's odes and sonnets are remarkable for sensory imagery. Keats' sonnets, odes, and longer narrative poem, *The Eve of St. Agnes*, are remarkable for their introspection and the tender age of the poet, who died when he was only twenty-five. In fact, all of the Second Generation died before their times. Wordsworth, who lived to be eighty, outlived them all, as well as his friend and collaborator, Coleridge.

Others who wrote during the Romantic Age are the essayist, Charles Lamb, and the novelist, Jane Austin. The Bronte sisters, Charlotte and Emily, wrote one novel each, which are noted as two of the finest ever written, *Jane Eyre* and *Wuthering Heights*. Marianne Evans, also known as George Eliot, wrote several important novels: her masterpiece, *Middlemarch*, *Silas Marner*, *Adam Bede*, and *Mill on the Floss*.

Nineteenth century

The Victorian Period is remarkable for the diversity and proliferation of work in three major areas. Poets who are typified as Victorians include Alfred, Lord Tennyson, who wrote *Idylls of the King*, twelve narrative poems about the Arthurian legend, and Robert Browning, who wrote chilling, dramatic monologues, such as "My Last Duchess," as well as long poetic narratives such as *The Pied Piper of Hamlin*. His wife Elizabeth wrote two major works, the epic feminist poem, *Aurora Leigh*, and her deeply moving and provocative *Sonnets from the Portuguese*, in which she details her deep love for Robert and his startling, to her, reciprocation. Gerard Manley Hopkins, a Catholic priest, wrote poetry with sprung rhythm. (See Glossary of Literary Terms in 2.2). A. E. Housman, Matthew Arnold, and the Pre-Raphaelites, especially the brother and sister duo, Dante Gabriel Rosetti and Christina Rosetti, contributed much to round out the Victorian Era poetic scene. The Pre-Raphaelites, a group of 19th-century English painters, poets, and critics, reacted against Victorian materialism and the neoclassical conventions of academic art by producing earnest, quasi-religious works. Medieval and early Renaissance painters up to the time of the Italian painter Raphael inspired the group. Robert Louis Stevenson, the great Scottish novelist, wrote his adventure/history lessons for young adults. Victorian prose ranges from the incomparable, keenly woven plot structures of Charles Dickens to the deeply moving Dorset/Wessex novels of Thomas Hardy, in which women are repressed and life is more struggle than euphoria. Rudyard Kipling wrote about Colonialism in India in works like *Kim* and *The Jungle Book,* that create exotic locales and a distinct main point concerning the Raj, the British Colonial government during Queen Victoria's reign. Victorian drama is a product mainly of Oscar Wilde, whose satirical masterpiece, *The Importance of Being Earnest*, farcically details and lampoons Victorian social mores.

Twentieth century

The early twentieth century is represented mainly by the towering achievement of George Bernard Shaw's dramas: *St. Joan, Man and Superman, Major Barbara,* and *Arms and the Man,* to name a few. Novelists are too numerous to list, but Joseph Conrad, E. M. Forster, Virginia Woolf, James Joyce, Nadine Gordimer, Graham Greene, George Orwell, and D. H. Lawrence comprise some of the century's very best.

Twentieth century poets of renown and merit include W. H. Auden, Robert Graves, T. S. Eliot, Edith Sitwell, Stephen Spender, Dylan Thomas, Philip Larkin, Ted Hughes, Sylvia Plath, and Hugh MacDarmid. This list is by no means complete.

Skill 23.4 Recognizing classical archetypes in cross-cultural literary selections.

An archetype is an idealized model of a person, object, or concept from which similar instances are derived, copied, patterned, or emulated. In psychology, an archetype is a model of a person, personality or behavior. Archetypes often appear in literature. William Shakespeare, for example, is known for popularizing many archetypal characters. Although he based many of his characters on existing archetypes from fables and myths, Shakespeare's characters stand out as original by their contrast against a complex, social literary landscape. An image, character, or pattern of circumstances that reoccurs frequently in literature can be considered an archetype.

For example, *Oedipus Rex* has a structure that appears to be repeated in the lives of all men in the sense that all sons are replacements for their fathers. Faulkner, in "Barn Burning" provides an original example that calls forth this archetype.

There are many archetypes, and skillful and creative writers often rely on them to create successful fiction. Some examples of **action archetypes**:

- The search for the killer
- The search for salvation (or the holy grail)
- The search for the hero
- The descent into hell

Some examples of **character archetypes**:
- The double
- The scapegoat
- The prodigal son
- The Madonna and the Magdalene

The family has often been used as a recurring archetypal theme in literature including the Greek play *Oedipus Rex* and other Greek literature such as the *Medea*. Many of Shakespeare's plays also used this archetype: *Hamlet, Romeo and Juliet,* and *King Lear*, for example. Modern writers also use the family archetype, such as *Desire Under the Elms* by Eugene O'Neill and *A Streetcar Named Desire* by Tennessee Williams.

Toni Morrison in her popular novel *Beloved* uses the archetype of family by chronicling the difficulties the protagonist Sethe and her family face before the Civil War as well as during the conflict and afterward. The result is a compelling picture of a family's response to the devastation brought on by slavery.

Skill 23.5 Relating given passages to major historical events and cultural movements that influenced the development of British literature (the reign of Elizabeth I, the Industrial Revolution, World War I, the dissolution of the empire).

The reign of Elizabeth I ushered in a renaissance that led to the end of the medieval age. It was a very fertile literary period. The exploration of the new world expanded the vision of all levels of the social order from royalty to peasant, and the rejection of Catholicism by many in favor of a Christianity of their own opened up whole new vistas to thought and daily life. The manufacture of cloth had increased, driving many people from the countryside into the cities, and the population of London exploded, creating a metropolitan business center. Printing had been brought to England by William Caxton in the 1470s, and literacy increased from 30% in the 15th century to over 60% by 1530. These seem dramatic changes, and they were, but they were occurring gradually.

The Italian renaissance had a great influence on the renaissance in England, and early in the 16th century most written works were in Latin. It was assumed that a learned person must express his thoughts in that language. However, there began to emerge a determination that vernacular English was valuable in writing, and it began to be defended. Elizabeth's tutor, Roger Ascham, for example, wrote in English.

Luther's thesis in 1517, which brought on the Reformation—an attempt to return to pure Christianity—brought on the breakup of western Christendom and eventually the secularization of society and the establishment of the king or queen as the head of this new/old church. This also brought about a new feeling that being religious was also being patriotic; it promoted nationalism.

The ascension of Elizabeth to the throne also followed a very turbulent period regarding succession, and she ruled for 45 peaceful years, which allowed arts and literature to flourish. Although she, herself, was headstrong and difficult, she happened to have very shrewd political instincts and entrusted power to solid, talented men, most particularly Cecil, her Secretary. and Walsingham, whom she put in charge of foreign policy. She identified with her country as no previous ruler had and that, in itself, brought on a period of intense nationalism. She was a symbol of Englishness. The defeat of the Spanish armada in 1588 was the direct result of the strong support she had from her own nation.

Drama was the principal form of literature in this age. Religious plays had been a part of the life of England for a long time, particularly the courtly life.

But in the Elizabethan age, they became more and more secular and were created primarily for courtly entertainment. By the '60s, Latin drama, particularly the tragedies of Seneca and the comedies of Plautus and Terence began to wield an influence in England. Courtyards of inns became favorite places for the presentation of plays; but in 1576, the Earl of Leicester's Men constructed their own building outside the city and called it The Theatre. Other theatres followed. Each had its own repertory company, and performances were for profit but also for the queen and her court. It is said that Shakespeare wrote *The Merry Wives of Windsor* at the specific command of the queen, who liked Falstaff and wanted to see him in love. It was also for the courtly audience that poetry was introduced into drama.

Shakespeare and Marlowe dominated the '80s and '90s; and at the turn of the century, only a few years before Elizabeth's death, Ben Jonson began writing his series of satirical comedies.

Court favor was notoriously precarious and depended on the whims of the queen and others. Much of the satire of the period reflects the disappointment of writers like Edmund Spenser and John Lyly and the superficiality and treachery of the court atmosphere. "A thousand hopes, but all nothing," wrote Lyly, "a hundred promises, but yet nothing."

Not all literature was dictated by the court. The middle classes were developing and had their own style. Thomas Heywood and Thomas Deloney catered to bourgeois tastes.

The two universities were also sources for the production of literature. The primary aim of the colleges was to develop ministers since there was a shortage brought on by the break with the Catholic Church. However, most university men couldn't make livings as ministers or academics, so they wrote as a way of earning income. Nashe, Marlowe, Robert Greene, and George Peele all reveal in their writings how difficult this path was. Remuneration came mostly from patrons. Greene had sixteen different patrons from seventeen books whereas Shakespeare had a satisfactory relationship with the Earl of Southampton and didn't need to seek other support. Publishers would also sometimes pay for a manuscript, which they would then own. Unfortunately, if the manuscript did not pass muster with all who could condemn it—the court, the religious leaders, prominent citizens—it was the author who was on the hot seat. Very few became as comfortable as Shakespeare did. His success was not only in writing, however, but also from his business acumen.

Writing was seen more as a craft than as an art in this period. There was not great conflict between art and nature, little distinction between literature, sports of the field, or the arts of the kitchen.

Balance and control were important in the England of this day, and this is reflected in the writing, the poetry in particular. The sestina, a form in which the last words of each line in the first stanza are repeated in a different order in each of the following stanzas, became very popular. Verse forms range from the extremely simple four-line ballad stanza through the rather complicated form of the sonnet to the elaborate and beautiful eighteen-line stanza of Spenser's *Epithalamion.* Sonnets were called "quatorzains." The term "sonnet" was used loosely for any short poem. "Quatorzains" are fourteen-line poems in iambic pentameter with elaborate rhyme schemes. However, Chaucer's seven-line rhyme royal stanza also survived in the 16th century. Shakespeare used it in *The Rape of Lucrece*, for example. An innovation was Spenser's nine-line stanza, called the Spenserian stanza, as used in *The Faerie Queene.*

As to themes, some of the darkness of the previous period can still be seen in some Elizabethan literature, for example, Shakespeare's Richard II (III.ii152-70). At the same time, a spirit of joy, gaiety, innocence, and lightheartedness can be seen in much of the most popular literature, and pastoral themes became popular. The theme of the burning desire for conquest and achievement was also significant in Elizabethan thought.

Some important writers of the Elizabethan age:
Sir Thomas More (1478-1535)
Sir Thomas Wyatt the Elder (1503-1542)
Sir Philip Sidney (1554-1586)
Edmund Spenser (1552-1599)
Sir Walter Raleigh (1552-1618)
John Lyly (1554-1606)
George Peele (1556-1596)
Christopher Marlowe (1564-1593)
William Shakespeare (1564-1616)

The Industrial Revolution in England began with the development of the steam engine. However, the steam engine was only one component of the major technological, socioeconomic, and cultural innovations of the early 19th century that began in Britain and spread throughout the world. An economy based on manual labor was replaced by one dominated by industry and the manufacture of machinery. The textile industries also underwent very rapid growth and change. Canals were being built, roads were improving, and railways were being constructed.

Steam power (fueled primarily by coal) and powered machinery (primarily in the manufacture of textiles) drove the remarkable amplification of production capacity. All-metal machine tools had entered the picture by 1820 making it possible to produce more machines.

The date of the Industrial Revolution varies according to how it is viewed. Some say that it broke out in the 1780s and wasn't fully perceived until the 1830s or 1840s. Others maintain that the beginning was earlier, about 1760 and began to manifest visible changes by 1830. The effects spread through western Europe and North America throughout the 19th century, eventually affecting all major countries of the world. The impact on society has been compared to the period when agriculture began to develop and the nomadic lifestyle was abandoned.

The first Industrial Revolution was followed immediately by the Second Industrial Revolution around 1850 when the progress in technology and world economy gained momentum with the introduction of steam-powered ships and railways and eventually the internal combustion engine and electrical power generation.

In terms of what was going on socially, the most noticeable effect was the development of a middle class of industrialists and businessmen and a decline in the landed class of nobility and gentry. While working people had more opportunities for employment in the new mills and factories, working conditions were often less than desirable. Exploiting children for labor wasn't new—it had always existed—but it was more apparent and perhaps more egregious as the need for cheap labor increased. In England, laws regarding employment of children began to be developed in 1833. Another effect of industrialization was the enormous shift from hand-produced goods to machine-produced ones and the loss of jobs among weavers and others, which resulted in violence against the factories and machinery beginning in about 1811.

Eventually, the British government took measures to protect industry. Another effect was the organization of labor. Because laborers were now working together in factories, mines, and mills, they were better able to organize to gain advantages they felt they deserved. Conditions were bad enough in these workplaces that the energy to bring about change was significant and eventually trade unions emerged. Laborers learned quickly to use the weapon of the strike to get what they wanted. The strikes were often violent and while the managers usually gave in to most of the demands made by strikers, the animosity between management and labor was endemic.

The mass migration of rural families into urban areas also resulted in poor living conditions, long work hours, extensive use of children for labor, and a polluted atmosphere.

Another effect of industrialization of society was the separation of husband and wife. One person stayed at home and looked after the home and family and the other went off to work, a very different configuration from an agriculture-based economy where the entire family was usually involved in making a living. Eventually, gender roles began to be defined by the new configuration of labor in this new world order.

The application of industrial processes to printing brought about a great expansion in newspaper and popular book publishing. This, in turn, was followed by rapid increases in literacy and eventually in demands for mass political participation.

Romanticism, the literary, intellectual, and artistic movement that occurred along with the Industrial Movement was actually a response to the increasing mechanization of society, an artistic hostility to what was taking over the world. Romanticism stressed the importance of nature in art and language in contrast to the monstrous machines and factories. Blake called them the "dark, satanic mills" in his poem, "And Did Those Feet in Ancient Time."

This movement followed on the heels of the Enlightenment period and was, at least in part, a reaction to the aristocratic and political norms of the previous period. Romanticism is sometimes called the Counter-Enlightenment. It stressed strong emotion, made individual imagination the critical authority, and overturned previous social conventions. Nature was important to the Romanticists and it elevated the achievements of misunderstood heroic individuals and artists who participated in altering society.

Some Romantic Writers:
Johann Wolfgang von Goethe
Walter Scott
Ludwig Tieck
E. T. A. Hoffman
William Wordsworth
Samuel Taylor Coleridge
William Blake
Victor Hugo
Alexander Pushkin
Lord Byron
Washington Irving
James Fenimore Cooper
Henry Wadsworth Longfellow
Edgar Allen Poe
Emily Dickinson
John Keats
Percy Bysshe Shelley

World War I, also known as The First World War, the Great War, and The War to End All Wars raged from July 1914 to the final Armistice on November 11, 1918. It was a world conflict between the Allied Powers led by Great Britain, France, Russia, and the United States (after 1917) and The Central Powers, led by the German Empire, the Austro-Hungarian Empire, and the Ottoman Empire. It brought down four great empires: The Austo-Hungarian, German, Ottoman, and Russian. It reconfigured European and Middle Eastern maps.

More than nine million soldiers died on the various battlefields and nearly that many more in the participating countries' home fronts thanks to food shortages and genocide committed under the cover of various civil wars and internal conflicts. However, more people died of the worldwide influenza outbreak at the end of the war and shortly after than died in the hostilities. The unsanitary conditions engendered by the war, severe overcrowding in barracks, wartime propaganda interfering with public health warnings, and migration of so many soldiers around the world contributed to causing the outbreak to become a pandemic.

The precipitating event of World War I was the June 28, 1914 assassination in Sarajevo of Archduke Franz Ferdinand, heir to the Austrian throne. Gavrilo Princip, a member of a group called Young Bosnia, whose aim included the unification of the South Slavs and independence from Austria, was the assassin. However, the real reasons for the war are still being debated. In the late '20s and early '30s people felt that the war was an accident that precipitated events that simply got out of control. This was used as a major argument for the organization of the League of Nations to prevent such a thing from happening in the future.

At the same time, Germany, France, and Russia were involved in war plans that created an atmosphere where generals and planning staffs were anxious the take the initiatives and make their careers. Once mobilization orders were issued, there was no turning back. Communications problems in 1914 also played a role. Telegraphy and ambassadors were the primary forms of communication, which accounted for disastrous delays from hours to even days.

President Wilson blamed the war on militarism. He felt that aristocrats and military elites had too much control in Germany, Russia, and Austria, and that the war was a consequence of their desire for military power and disdain for democracy. Lenin famously asserted that the worldwide system of imperialism was responsible for the war This argument proved persuasive in the immediate wake of the war and was a precipitating factor in the rise of Marxism and Communism.

A proposal to Mexico to join the war against the Allies was exposed in February, 1917, bringing war closer to America. Further U-boat (German submarines) attacks on American merchant ships led to Wilson's request that Congress declare war on Germany, which it did on April 6, 1917. Following the U.S. declaration of war, countries in the Western Hemisphere, Cuba, Panama, Haiti, Brazil, Guatemala, Nicaragua, Costa Rica, and Honduras declared war on Germany. The Dominican Republic, Peru, Uruguay, and Ecuador contented themselves with the severance of relations. The entry of the United States into the war was the turning point. It's doubtful that the Allies would have won without the infusion of money, supplies, armament, and troops from the Western Hemisphere, primarily from the United States.

The experiences of the war led to a sort of collective national trauma afterwards for all the participating countries. The optimism of the 1900s was entirely gone and those who fought in the war became what is known as "the Lost Generation" because they never fully recovered from their experiences. For the next few years memorials continued to be erected in thousands of European villages and towns.

Certainly a sense of disillusionment and cynicism became pronounced, and nihilism became popular. The world had never before witnessed such devastation, and the depiction in newspapers and on movie screens made the horrors more personal. War has always spawned creative bursts, and this one was no exception. Poetry, stories, and movies proliferated. In fact, it's still a fertile subject for art of all kinds, particularly literature and movies. In 2006, a young director by the name of Paul Gross created, directed, and starred in *Passchendaele* based on the stories told him by his grandfather, who was haunted all his life by his killing of a young German soldier in this War to End All Wars.

Some literature based on World War I:

"The Soldier," poem by Rupert Brooke
Goodbye to All That, autobiography by Robert Graves
"Anthem for Doomed Youth" and "Strange Meeting," poems by Wilfred Owen, published posthumously by Siegfried Sassoon in 1918
"In Flanders Fields," poem by John McCrae
Three Soldiers, novel by John Dos Passos
Journey's End, play by R. C. Sherriff
All Quiet on the Western Front, novel by Erich Maria Remarque
Death of a Hero, novel by Richard Aldington
A Farewell to Arms, novel by Ernest Hemingway
Memoirs of an Infantry Officer, novel by Siegfried Sassoon
Sergeant York, movie directed by Howard Hawks

The dissolution of the British empire, the most extensive empire in world history and for a time the foremost global power, began in 1867 with its transformation into the modern Commonwealth. Dominion status was granted to the self-governing colonies of Canada in 1867, to Australia in 1902, to New Zealand in 1907, to Newfoundland in 1907, and to the newly-created Union of South Africa in 1910. Leaders of the new states joined with British statesmen in periodic Colonial Conferences, the first of which was held in London in 1887.

The foreign relations of the Dominions were conducted through the Foreign Office of the United Kingdom. Although Canada created a Department of External Affairs in 1909, diplomatic relations with other governments continued to be channeled through the Governors-General, Dominion High Commissioners in London, and British legations abroad.

Britain's declaration of war in World War I applied to all of the Dominions, for instance. Even so, the Dominions had substantial freedom in their adoption of foreign policy where this did not explicitly conflict with British interests. The original arrangement of a single imperial military and naval structure became unsustainable as Britain faced new commitments in Europe and the challenge of an emerging German High Seas fleet after 1900, so in 1919 it was decided that the Dominions should have their own navies, reversing a previous agreement that the then Australasian colonies should contribute to the Royal Navy in return for the permanent stationing of a squadron in the region.

The settlement at the end of World War I gave Britain control of Palestine and Iraq after the collapse of the Ottoman Empire in the Middle East. It also ceded control of the former German colonies of Tanganyika, Southwest Africa (now Namibia), and New Guinea. British zones of occupation in Germany after the war were not considered part of the Empire

Although the Allies won the war and Britain's rule expanded into new areas, the heavy costs of the war made it less and less feasible to maintain the vast empire. Economic losses as well as human losses put increasing pressure on the Empire to give up its far-flung imperial posts in Asia and the African colonies. At the same time, nationalist sentiment was growing in both old and new Imperial territories fueled partly by their troops' contributions to the war and the anger of many non-white ex-servicemen at the racial discrimination they had encountered during their service.

Enthusiasm for the Empire coupled with an increase in nationalism in many of the Dominions came together to create resistance to Britain's intention to take military action against Turkey in 1922.

Full Dominion independence was formalized in the 1926 Balfour Declaration and the 1931 State of Westminster. Each Dominion was henceforth to be equal in status to Britain herself, free of British legislative interference, and autonomous in international relations. The Dominions section created with the Colonial Office in 1907 was upgraded in 1925 to a separate Dominions Office and given its own Secretary of State in 1930.

Canada led the way, becoming the first Dominion to conclude an international treaty entirely independently (1923) and obtaining the appointment (1928) of a British High Commissioner in Ottawa, thereby separating the administrative and diplomatic functions of the Governor-General and ending the latter's anomalous role as the representative of the head of state and of the British Government. Canada's first permanent diplomatic mission to a foreign country opened in Washington, D.C. in 1927. Australia followed in 1940.

Egypt, formally independent by 1922 but bound to Britain by treaty until 1936 and under partial occupation until 1956, similarly severed all constitutional links with Britain. Iraq, which became a British Protectorate in 1922, also gained complete independence in 1932.

In 1948, Ireland became a republic, fully independent from the United Kingdom, and withdrew from the Commonwealth. Ireland's constitution claimed the six counties of Northern Ireland as a part of the Republic of Ireland until 1998. The issue over whether Northern Ireland should remain in the United Kingdom or join the Republic of Ireland has divided Northern Ireland's people and led to a long and bloody conflict known as the Troubles. However, the Good Friday Agreement of 1998 brought about a ceasefire between most of the major organizations on both sides, creating hope for a peaceful resolution.

The rise of anti-colonial nationalist movements in the subject territories and the changing economic situation of the world in the first half of the 20th century challenged an imperial power now increasingly preoccupied with issues nearer home. The Empire's end began with the onset of the Second World War when a deal was reached between the British government and the Indian independence movement whereby India would cooperate and remain loyal during the war but after which they would be granted independence. Following India's lead, nearly all of the other colonies would become independent over the next two decades.

In the Caribbean, Africa, Asia, and the Pacific, post-war decolonization was achieved with almost unseemly haste in the face of increasingly powerful nationalist movements, and Britain rarely fought to retain any territory.

Some Representative Literature:

Heart of Darkness, novel by Joseph Conrad
Passage to India novel by E. M. Forster
"Gunga Din," poem by Rudyard Kipling

COMPETENCY 24.0 UNDERSTAND THE LITERATURES OF ASIA, AFRICA, CONTINENTAL EUROPE, LATIN AMERICA, AND THE CARIBBEAN, INCLUDING MAJOR THEMES, CHARACTERISTICS, TRENDS, WRITERS, AND WORKS.

Skill 24.1 Distinguishing major literary forms, works, and writers of ancient civilizations (epic, pastoral ode, the *Upanishads*, Virgil) and their characteristics.

The epic is one of the major forms of narrative literature, which retells chronologically the life of a mythological person or group of persons. This genre has become uncommon since the early 20th century although the term has been used to define certain extraordinarily long prose works and films. Usually a large number of characters, multiple settings, and a long span of time are features that lead to its designation as an epic. This change in the use of this term might indicate that some prose works of the past might be called epics although they were not composed or originally understood as such.

The epic was a natural manifestation of oral poetic tradition in preliterate societies where the poetry was transmitted to the audience and from performer to performer by purely oral means. It was composed of short episodes, each of equal status, interest, and importance, which facilitated memorization. The poet recalls each episode and uses it to recreate the entire epic.

Some Ancient Epics:
The *Iliad* and the *Odyssey*, both ascribed to Homer
Lost Greek epics ascribed to the Cyclic poets:
      Trojan War cycle
      Theban Cycle
      Argonautica by Apollonius of Rhodes
      Mahabharata and *Ramayana*, Hindu mythologies
Aeneid by Virgil
Metamorphoses by Ovid
Argonautica by Gaius Valerius Flaccus

Some Medieval Epics (500-1500)
Beowulf (Anglo-Saxon mythology)
Bhagavata Purana (Sanskrit "Stories of the Lord")
Divina Commedia (*The Divine Comedy*) by Dante Alighieri
The Canterbury Tales by Geoffrey Chaucer
Alliterative Morte Arthure

Some Modern Epics (from 1500)
The Faerie Queene by Edmund Spenser (1596)
Paradise Lost by John Milton (1667)
Paradise Regained by John Milton (1671)
Prince Arthur by Richard Blackmore (1695)

English   190

King Arthur by Richard Blackmore (1697)
The Works of Ossian by James MacPherson (1765)
Hyperion by John Keats (1818)
Don Juan by George Gordon Byron, 6th Baron Byron (1824)

An Ode is generally a long lyric poem and as a form or poetry or song has an extensive history. Though odes vary in topic and occasionally structure, three forms have risen to the foreground in literature. These three forms are identifiable by their different features, and all odes carry characteristics that line up somewhere among the three. They may contain parts from one form and pieces from another, but this is generally true. The two best-known and best-established ode forms are the <u>Pindaric</u> and the <u>Horatian</u> odes of the Greek and Roman traditions respectively.

Named after a 5th century B.C. Greek poet, the Pindaric ode consists of a triadic structure, which emulates the musical movement of the early Greek chorus. Though infrequently attempted in English, some examples do exist. The Horatian ode is also named after a poet. The Roman poet Horace is given credit for this form, which typically has equal-length stanzas with the same rhyme scheme and meter. The Horatian ode, unlike the Pindaric ode, also has a tendency to be personal rather than formal.

Pastoral odes differ from others mostly in subject matter. "Pastoral" designates a literary work that has to do with the lives of shepherds or rural life and usually draws a contrast between the innocence and serenity of the simple life and the discomforts and corruptions of the city and especially court life. The poet's moral, social, and literary views are usually expressed.

In John Keats' short career, his writing shifted from the popular sonnet form to the older form of the ode toward the end of his life. His "Ode on a Grecian Urn," which is about a piece of pottery, is a twist on the pastoral theme. He focuses on the natural scene that is pictured on the urn. Instead of a concern with the disturbing forces of the world as with most pastoral works, he uses the sculptured panel on the urn as a sort of "frozen pastoral" and makes his statement about what is valuable and real.

Some Pastoral Odes:
"Intimations of Immortality" by William Wordsworth
"Ode to a Nightingale" by John Keats
"Ode to Psyche" by John Keats
"Ode to the West Wind" by Percy Bysshe Shelley

The Upanishads are Hindu treatises that deal with broad philosophic problems. The term means "to sit down near" and implies sitting at the feet of a teacher. There are approximately 108 that record views of many teachers over a number of years.

Read chronologically, they exhibit a development toward the concept of a single supreme being and suggest ultimate reunion with it. Of special philosophical concern is the nature of reality.

Their appearance in Europe in the early 19th century captured the interest of philosophers, particularly in Germany. The work of Arthur Schopenhauer is reflective of the Upanishads.

Virgil (Publius Vergilius Maro, later called Virgilius and known in English as Virgil or Vergil, October 15, 70BC/September 21, 19BC) was a Latin poet, author of the *Eclogues,* the *Georgics,* and the *Aeneid.* The Aeneid is a poem of twelve books that became the Roman Empire's national epic.

Virgil has had a strong influence on English literature. Edmund Spenser's *The Faerie Queene* reflects that influence. It was also the model for John Milton's P*aradise Lost*, not only in structure but also in style and diction. The Augustan poets considered Virgil's poetry the ultimate perfection of form and ethical content. He was not so popular during the Romantic period, but Victorians such as Matthew Arnold and Alfred, Lord Tennyson rediscovered Virgil and were influenced by the sensitivity and pathos that had not been so appealing to the Romantics.

Skill 24.2 Recognizing major literary forms, works, writers, and characteristics of world literature written before the modern period in languages other than English (T'ang poetry, romance, *Don Quixote*, Murasaki Shikibu, Tolstoy).

Germany

German poet and playwright, Friedrich von Schiller, is best known for his history plays, *William Tell* and *The Maid of Orleans*. He is a leading literary figure in Germany's Golden Age of Literature. Also from Germany, Rainer Maria Rilke, the great lyric poet, is one of the poets of the unconscious, or stream of consciousness. Germany also has given the world Herman Hesse, (*Siddartha*), Gunter Grass (*The Tin Drum*), and the greatest of all German writers, Goethe.

Scandinavia

Scandinavia has encouraged the work of Hans Christian Andersen in Denmark, who advanced the fairy tale genre with such wistful tales as "The Little Mermaid" and "Thumbelina." The social commentary of Henrik Ibsen in Norway startled the world of drama with such issues as feminism (*The Doll's House* and *Hedda Gabler*) and the effects of sexually transmitted diseases (*The Wild Duck* and *Ghosts)*. Sweden's Selma Lagerlof is the first woman to ever win the Nobel Prize for literature. Her novels include *Gosta Berling's Saga* and the world-renowned *The Wonderful Adventures of Nils*, a children's work.

Russia

Russian literature is vast and monumental. Who has not heard of Fyodor Dostoyevski's *Crime and Punishment*, or *The Brothers Karamazov*, or Count Leo Tolstoy's *War and Peace*? These are examples of psychological realism. Dostoyevski's influence on modern writers cannot be overly stressed. Tolstoy's *War and Peace* is the sweeping account of the invasion of Russia and Napoleon's taking of Moscow, abandoned by the Russians. This novel is called the national novel of Russia. Further advancing Tolstoy's greatness is his ability to create believable, unforgettable female characters, especially Natasha in *War and Peace* and the heroine of *Anna Karenina*. Pushkin is famous for great short stories; Anton Chekhov for drama, (*Uncle Vanya, The Three Sisters, The Cherry Orchard*); Yvteshenko for poetry (*Babi Yar*).

France

France has a multifaceted canon of great literature that is universal in scope, almost always championing some social cause: the poignant short stories of Guy de Maupassant; the fantastic poetry of Charles Baudelaire (*Fleurs du Mal*); and the groundbreaking lyrical poetry of Rimbaud and Verlaine. Drama in France is best represented by Rostand's *Cyrano de Bergerac*, and the neo-classical dramas of Racine and Corneille (*El Cid*). The great French novelists include Andre Gide, Honore de Balzac (*Cousin Bette*), Stendel (*The Red and the Black*), the father/son duo of Alexandre Dumas (*The Three Musketeers* and *The Man in the Iron Mask*. Victor Hugo is the Charles Dickens of French literature, having penned the masterpieces, *The Hunchback of Notre Dame* and the French national novel, *Les Miserables*. The stream of consciousness of Proust's *Remembrance of Things Past*, and the Absurdist theatre of Samuel Beckett and Eugene Ionesco (*The Rhinoceros*) attest to the groundbreaking genius of the French writers.

Spain

Spain's great writers include Miguel de Cervantes (*Don Quixote*) and Juan Ramon Jimenez. The anonymous national epic, *El Cid*, has been translated into many languages.

Italy

Italy's greatest writers include Virgil, who wrote the great epic, *The Aeneid*; Giovanni Boccaccio (*The Decameron*); and Dante Alighieri (*The Divine Comedy*).

Ancient Greece

Greece will always be foremost in literary assessments due to Homer's epics, *The Iliad* and *The Odyssey*. No one, except Shakespeare, is more often cited. Add to these the works of Plato and Aristotle for philosophy; the dramatists Aeschylus, Euripides, and Sophocles for tragedy, and Aristophanes for comedy. Greece is the cradle not only of democracy, but of literature as well.

Far East

The classical Age of Japanese literary achievement includes the father Kiyotsugu Kanami and the son Motokkiyo Zeami who developed the theatrical experience known as No drama to its highest aesthetic degree. The son is said to have authored over 200 plays, of which 100 still are extant.

Katai Tayama (*The Quilt*) is touted as the father of the genre known as the Japanese confessional novel. He also wrote in the "ism" of naturalism. His works are definitely not for the squeamish.

The "slice of life" psychological writings of Ryunosuke Akutagawa gained him acclaim in the western world. His short stories, especially "Rashamon" and "In a Grove," are greatly praised for style as well as content.

China, too, has given to the literary world. Li Po, the T'ang dynasty poet from the Chinese Golden Age, revealed his interest in folklore by preserving the folk songs and mythology of China. Po further allows his reader to enter into the Chinese philosophy of Taoism and to know this feeling against expansionism during the T'ang dynastic rule. Back to the T'ang dynasty, which was one of great diversity in the arts, the Chinese version of a short story was created with the help of Jiang Fang. His themes often express love between a man and a woman.

Skill 24.3 Recognizing major forms, works, writers, and characteristics of modern and contemporary literature written in English outside Great Britain and the United States (the fiction of Stead and of Gordimer, the drama of Soyinka, the poetry of Walcott).

North American Literature

North American literature is divided between the United States, Canada, and Mexico. The American writers have been amply discussed in 22.1. Canadian writers of note include feminist Margaret Atwood, (*The Hand Maiden's Tale*); Alice Munro, a remarkable short story writer; and W. P. Kinsella, another short story writer whose two major subjects are North American Indians and baseball. Mexican writers include 1990 Nobel Prize winning poet, Octavio Paz, (The Labyrinth of Solitude) and feminist Rosarian Castillanos (The Nine Guardians).

Africa

African literary greats include South Africans Nadine Gordimer (Nobel Prize for literature) and Peter Abrahams (*Tell Freedom: Memories of Africa*), an auto-biography of life in Johannesburg. Chinua Achebe (*Things Fall Apart*) and the poet, Wole Soyinka, hail from Nigeria. Mark Mathabane wrote an autobiography *Kaffir Boy* about growing up in South Africa. Egyptian writer, Naguib Mahfouz, and Doris Lessing from Rhodesia, now Zimbabwe, write about race relations in their respective countries. Because of her radical politics, Lessing was banned from her homeland and The Union of South Africa, as was Alan Paton whose seemingly simple story, *Cry, the Beloved Country*, brought the plight of blacks and the whites' fear of blacks under apartheid to the rest of the world.

Skill 24.4 Recognizing major forms, writers, works and characteristics of modern and contemporary world literature in languages other than English (the plays of Brecht, the fiction of Colette and of Garcia Marquez).

Central American/Caribbean Literature

The Caribbean and Central America encompass a vast area and cultures that reflect oppression and colonialism by England, Spain, Portugal, France, and The Netherlands. The Caribbean writers include Samuel Selvon from Trinidad and Armado Valladres of Cuba. Central American authors include dramatist Carlos Solorzano, from Guatemala, whose plays include *Dona Beatriz, The Hapless, The Magician,* and *The Hands of God.*

South American Literature

Chilean Gabriela Mistral was the first Latin American writer to win the Nobel Prize for literature.

She is best known for her collections of poetry, *Desolation and Feeling*. Chile was also home to Pablo Neruda, who, in 1971, also won the Nobel Prize for literature for his poetry. His 29 volumes of poetry have been translated into more than 60 languages, attesting to his universal appeal. *Twenty Love Poems* and *Song of Despair* are justly famous. Isabel Allende is carrying on the Chilean literary standards with her acclaimed novel, *House of Spirits*. Argentine Jorge Luis Borges is considered by many literary critics to be the most important writer of his century from South America. His collections of short stories, *Ficciones*, brought him universal recognition. Also from Argentina, Silvina Ocampo, a collaborator with Borges on a collection of poetry, is famed for her poetry and short story collections, which include *The Fury* and *The Days of the Night*.

Noncontinental European Literature

Horacio Quiroga represents Uruguay, and Brazil has Joao Guimaraes Rosa, whose novel, *The Devil to Pay*, is considered first-rank world literature.

Russian Literature

Boris Pasternak won the Nobel Prize (*Dr. Zhivago*). Aleksandr Solzhenitsyn (*The Gulag Archipelago*) is only recently back in Russia after years of expatriation in Vermont. Ilya Varshavsky, who creates fictional societies that are dystopias, or the opposite of utopias, represents the genre of science fiction.

French Literature

French literature is defined by the existentialism of Jean-Paul Sartre (*No Exit, The Flies, Nausea*), Andre Malraux, (*The Fall*), and Albert Camus (*The Stranger, The Plague*), the recipient of the 1957 Nobel Prize for literature. Feminist writings include those of Sidonie-Gabrielle Colette, known for her short stories and novels, as well as Simone de Beauvoir.

Slavic nations

Austrian writer Franz Kafka (*The Metamorphosis, The Trial,* and *The Castle*) is considered by many to be the literary voice of the first-half of the twentieth century. Representing the Czech Republic is the poet Vaclav Havel. Slovakia has dramatist Karel Capek (*R.U.R.*) Romania is represented by Elie Weisel (*Night*), a Nobel Prize winner.

Far East Literature

Asia has many modern writers who are being translated for the western reading public. India's Krishan Chandar has authored more than 300 stories. Rabindranath

Tagore won the Nobel Prize for literature in 1913 (*Song Offerings*). Narayan, India's most famous writer (*The Guide*), is highly interested in mythology and legends of India. Santha Rama Rau's work, *Gifts of Passage*, is her true story of life in a British school where she tries to preserve her Indian culture and traditional home.

Revered as Japan's most famous female author, Fumiko Hayashi (*Drifting Clouds*) by the time of her death had written more than 270 literary works.

In 1968 the Nobel Prize for literature was awarded to Yasunari Kawabata (*The Sound of the Mountain, The Snow Country*) considered to be his masterpieces. His Palm-of-the-Hand Stories take the essentials of Haiku poetry and transform them into the short story genre.

Modern feminist and political concerns are written eloquently by Ting Ling, who used the pseudonym Chiang Ping-Chih. Her stories reflect her concerns about social injustice and her commitment to the women's movement.

Skill 24.5 Demonstrating awareness of the ways in which world literature reflects cultural characteristics.

World folk-epics are poems (or prose sometimes) that are an integral part of the world view of a people. In many cases, they were original oral texts that were eventually written by a single author or several.

Some examples of world folk-epics:
- *Soundiata,* an African epic
- *Tunkashila,* an American Indian epic
- *Epic of Gilgamesh*, the oldest epic from Mesopotamia and the Mediterranean world
- *Aeneid,* a Roman epic
- *Moby Dick* is considered by some to be an American folk epic.

A **national myth** is an inspiring narrative or anecdote about a nation's past. These often over-dramatize true events, omit important historical details, or add details for which there is no evidence. It can be a fictional story that no one takes to be true, such as *Paul Bunyan,* which was created by French Canadians during the Papineau Rebellion of 1837, when they revolted against the young English Queen. In older nations, national myths may be spiritual and refer to the nation's founding by God or gods or other supernatural beings.

Some national myths:
- The legend of King Arthur in Great Britain
- Sir Francis Drake in England
- The Pilgrims and the Mayflower in the United States

- Pocahontas, who is said to have saved the life of John Smith from her savage father, Powhatan
- The legendary ride of Paul Revere
- The last words of Nathan Hale
- The person of George Washington and apocryphal tales about him such as his cutting down a cherry tree with a hatchet and then facing up to the truth: "I cannot tell a lie."

DOMAIN 6. FUNDAMENTALS OF LITERATURE: CONSTRUCTED-RESPONSE ASSIGNMENT

Content to be addressed by the constructed-response assignment is described in Domain 4.

RESOURCES

1. Abrams, M. H. ed. *The Norton Anthology of English Literature.* 6th ed. 2 vols. New York: Norton, 1979.

    A comprehensive reference for English literature, containing selected works from *Beowulf* through the twentieth century and information about literary criticism.

2. Beach, Richard. "Strategic Teaching in Literature." *Strategic Teaching and Learning: Cognitive Instruction in the Content Areas.* Edited by Beau Fly Jones and others. ASCD Publications, 1987: 135-159.

    A chapter dealing with a definition of and strategic teaching strategies for literature studies.

3. Brown, A. C. and others. *Grammar and Composition 3rd Course.* Boston: Houghton Mifflin, 1984.

    A standard ninth-grade grammar text covering spelling, vocabulary, and reading, listening, and writing skills.

4. Burmeister, L. E. *Reading Strategies for Middle and Secondary School Teachers.* Reading, MA: Addison-Wesley, 1978.

    A resource for developing classrooms strategies for reading and content area classes, using library references, and adapting reading materials to all levels of students.

5. Carrier, W. and B. Neumann, eds. *Literature from the World.* New York: Scribner, 1981.

    A comprehensive world literature text for high school students, with a section on mythology and folklore.

6. Cline, R. K. J. and W. G. McBride. *A Guide to Literature for Young Adults: Background, Selection, and Use.* Glenview, IL: Scott Foresman, 1983.

    A literature reference containing sample readings and an overview of adolescent literature and the developmental changes that affect reading.

7. Coater, Jr. R. B., ed. *Reading Research and Instruction.* Journal of the College Research Association. Pittsburgh, PA 1995.

A reference tool for reading and language arts teachers, covering the latest research and instructional techniques.

8. Corcoran, B. and E. Evans, eds. *Readers, Texts, Teachers.* Upper Montclair, NJ: Boynton/Cook, 1987.

A collection of essays concerning reader response theory, including activities that help students interpret literature and help the teacher integrate literature into the course study.

9. Cutting, Brian. *Moving on in Whole Language: the Complete Guide for Every Teacher.* Bothell, WA: Wright Group, 1992.

A resource of practical knowledge in whole language instruction.

10. Damrosch, L. and others. *Adventures in English Literature.* Orlando, FL: Harcourt, Brace, Jovanovich, 1985.

One of many standard high school English literature textbooks with a solid section on the development of the English language.

11. Davidson, A. *Literacy 2000 Teacher's Resource. Emergent Stages 1&2.* 1990.

12. Devine, T. G. *Teaching Study Skills: A Guide for Teachers.* Boston: Allyn and Bacon, 1981.

13. Duffy, G. G. and others. *Comprehension Instruction: Perspectives and Suggestions.* New York: Longman, 1984.

Written by researchers at the Institute of Research on Teaching and the Center for the Study of Reading, this reference includes a variety of instructional techniques for different levels.

14. Fleming, M. ed. *Teaching the Epic.* Urbana, IL: NCTE, 1974.

Methods, materials, and projects for the teaching of epics with examples of Greek, religious, national, and American epics.

15. Flood, J. ed. *Understanding Reading Comprehension: Cognition, Language, and the Structure of Prose.* Newark, DE: IRA, 1984.

Essays by preeminent scholars dealing with comprehension for learners of all levels and abilities.

16. Fry, E. B. and others. *The Reading Teacher's Book of Lists.* Edgewood Cliffs, NJ: Prentice-Hall, 1984.

A comprehensive list of book lists for students of various reading levels.

17. Garnica, Olga K. and Martha L. King. *Language, Children, and Society.* New York: Pergamon Press, 1981.

18. Gere, A. R. and E. Smith. *Attitude, Language and Change.* Urbana, IL: NCTE, 1979.

A discussion of the relationship between standard English and grammar and the vernacular usage, including various approaches to language instruction.

19. Hayakawa, S. I. *Language in Thought and Action.* 4th ed. Orlando, Fl: Harcourt, Brace, Jovanovich, 1979.

20. Hook, J. N. and others. *What Every English Teacher Should Know.* Champaign, IL: NCTE, 1970.

Research based text that summarizes methodologies and specific application for us with students.

21. Johnson, D. D. and P. D. Pearson. *Teaching Reading Vocabulary.* 2nd ed. New York: Holt, Rinehart, and Winston, 1984.

A student text that stresses using vocabulary study in improving reading comprehension, with chapters on instruction components in the reading and content areas.

22. Kaywell, I. F. ed. *Adolescent Literature as a Complement to the Classics.* Norwood, MA: Christopher-Gordon Pub., 1993.

A correlation of modern adolescent literature to classics of similar themes.

23. Mack, M. ed. *World Masterpieces*. 3rd ed. 2 vols. New York: Norton, 1973.

    A standard world literature survey, with good introductory material on a critical approach to literature study.

24. McLuhan, M. *Understanding Media: The Extensions of Man*. New York: Signet, 1964.

    The most classic work on the effect media has on the public and the power of the media to influence thinking.

25. McMichael, G. ed. *Concise Anthology of American Literature*. New York: Macmillan, 1974.

    A standard survey of American literature text.

26. Moffett, J. *Teaching the Universe of Discourse*. Boston: Houghton Mifflin, 1983.

    A significant reference text that proposes the outline for a total language arts program, emphasizing the reinforcement of each element of the language arts curriculum to the other elements.

27. Moffett, James and Betty Jane Wagner. *Student - Centered Language Arts K-12*. 4th ed. Boston: Houghton Mifflin, 1992.

28. Nelms , B. F. ed. *Literature in the Classroom: Readers, Texts, and Contexts*. Urbana, IL: NCTE, 1988.

    Essays on adolescent and multicultural literature, social aspects of literature, and approaches to literature interpretation.

29. Nilsen, A. P. and K. L. Donelson. *Literature for Today's Young Adults*. 2nd ed. Glenview, IL: Scott, Foresman, and Co., 1985.

    An excellent overview of young adult literature - its history, terminologies, bibliographies, and book reviews.

30. Perrine, L. *Literature: Structure, Sound, and Sense*. 5th ed. Orlando, FL: Harcourt, Brace, Jovanovich, 1988.

    A much revised text for teaching literature elements, genres, and interpretation.

31. Piercey, Dorothy. *Reading Activities in Content Areas: An Ideabook for Middle and Secondary Schools.* 2nd ed. Boston: Allyn and Bacon, 1982.

32. Pooley, R. C. *The Teaching of English Usage.* Urbana, IL: NCTE, 1974.

    A revision of the important 1946 text which discusses the attitudes toward English usage through history and recommends specific techniques for usage instruction.

33. Probst, R. E. *Response and Analysis: Teaching Literature in Junior and Senior High School.* Upper Montclair, NJ: Boynton/Cook, 1988.

    A resource that explores reader response theory and discusses student-centered methods for interpreting literature. Contains a section on the progress of adolescent literature.

34. Pyles, T. and J. Alges. *The Origin and Development of the English Language.* 3rd ed. Orlando, FL: Harcourt, Brace, Jovanovich, 1982.

    A history of the English language; sections social, personal, historical, and geographical influences on language usage.

35. Readence, J. E. and others. *Content Area Reading: an integrated approach.* 2nd ed. Dubuque, IA: Kendall/Hunt, 1985.

    A practical instruction guide for teaching reading in the content areas.

36. Robinson, H. Alan. *Teaching Reading and Study Strategies: The Content Areas.* Boston: Allyn and Bacon, 1978.

37. Roe, B. D. and others. *Secondary School Reading Instruction: The Content Areas.* 3rd ed. Boston: Houghton Mifflin, 1987.

    A resource of strategies for the teaching of reading for language arts teachers with little reading instruction background.

38. Rosenberg, D. *World Mythology: An Anthology of the Great Myths and Epics.* Lincolnwood, IL: National Textbook, 1986.

    Presents selections of main myths from which literary allusions are drawn. Thorough literary analysis of each selection.

39. Rosenblatt, L. M. *The Reader, the Text, the Poem. The Transactional Theory of the Literary work.* Southern Illinois University Press, 1978.

    A discussion of reader response theory and reader-centered methods for analyzing literature.

40. Santeusanio, Richard P. *A Practical Approach to Content Area Reading.* Reading, MA.: Addison-Wesley Publishing Co., 1983.

41. Shepherd, David L. *Comprehensive High School Reading Methods.* 2nd ed. Columbus, OH: Charles F. Merrill Publishing, 1978.

42. Strickland, D. S. and others. *Using Computers in the Teaching of Reading.* New York: Teachers College Press, 1987.

    Resource for strategies for teaching and learning language and reading with computers and recommendations for software for all grades.

43. Sutherland, Zena and others. *Children and Books.* 6th ed. Glenview, IL: Scott, Foresman, and Co., 1981.

    Thorough study of children's literature, with sections on language development theory and chapters on specific genres with synopses of specific classic works for child/adolescent readers.

44. Tchudi, S. and D. Mitchell. *Explorations in the Teaching of English.* 3rd ed. New York: Harper Row, 1989.

    A thorough source of strategies for creating a more student-centered involvement in learning.

45. Tompkins, Gail E. *Teaching Writing: Balancing Process and Product.* 2nd ed. New York: Macmillan, 1994.

    A tool to aid teachers in integrating recent research and theory about the writing process, writing reading connections, collaborative learning, and across the curriculum writing with practices in the fourth through eighth grade classrooms.

46. Warriners, J. E. *English Composition and Grammar.* Benchmark ed. Orlando, FL: Harcourt, Brace, Jovanovich, 1988.

    Standard grammar and composition textbook, with a six book series for seventh through twelfth grades; includes vocabulary study, language history, and diverse approaches to writing process.

Section I: Essay Test

Given are several prompts, reflecting the need to exhibit a variety of writing skills. In most testing situations, 30 minutes would be allowed to respond to each of the prompts. Some tests may allow 60 minutes for the essay to incorporate more than one question or allow for greater preparation and editing time. Read the directions carefully and organize your time wisely.

Section II: Multiple - choice Test

This section contains 125 questions. In most testing situations, you would be expected to answer from 35 - 40 questions within 30 minutes. If you time yourself on the entire battery, take no more than 90 minutes.

Section III: Answer Key

Section I: Essay Prompts

Prompt A

Write an expository essay discussing effective teaching strategies for developing literature appreciation with a heterogeneous class of ninth graders. Select any appropriate piece(s) of world literature to use as examples in the discussion.

Prompt B

After reading the following passage from Aldous Huxley's *Brave New World,* discuss the types of reader responses possible with a group of eight graders.

> "He hated them all - all the men who came to visit Linda. One afternoon, when he had been playing with the other children - it was cold, he remembered, and there was snow on the mountains - he came back to the house and heard angry voices in the bedroom. They were women's voices, and they were words he didn't understand; but he knew they were dreadful words. Then suddenly, crash! something was upset; he heard people moving about quickly, and there was another crash and then a noise like hitting a mule, only not so bony; then Linda screamed. 'Oh, don't, don't, don't!' she said. He ran in. There were three women in dark blankets. Linda was on the bed. One of the women was holding her wrists. Another was lying across her legs, so she couldn't kick. The third was hitting her with a whip. Once, twice, three times; and each time Linda screamed."

Prompt C

Write a persuasive letter to the editor on any contemporary topic of special interest. Employ whatever forms of discourse, style devices, and audience appeal techniques that seem appropriate to the topic.

Section II: Writing and Language Skills

Part A

Directions: In sentences 1 - 15, four words or phrases have been underlined. If you determine that any underlined word or phrase has an error in grammar, usage, or mechanics, circle the letter underneath the underlining. If there are no errors, circle the letter E at the end of the sentence. There is no more than one error in any sentence.

1. The volcanic eruption in Montserrat displaced residents of Plymouth <u>which</u>

                                                                           A

felt that the <u>English government</u> <u>was</u> responsible for <u>their</u> evacuation. **E**

                B   **C**   **D**

2. When the <u>school district</u> privatized the school cafeteria, <u>us</u> students <u>were</u>

               A   **B**   **C**

thrilled to purchase more than soggy <u>French fries</u>. **E**

                                D

3. The homecoming <u>Queen and King</u> <u>were chosen</u> by the <u>student body</u> for

                     A   **B**   **C**

<u>their</u> popularity. **E**

D

4. If the practical joke <u>was</u> <u>Cullen's</u> idea, then he <u>must</u> suffer the

                   A **B**   **C**

<u>consequences</u>. **E**

D

5. She, not her sister, <u>is</u> the one <u>who</u> the librarian <u>has questioned</u> about the

                     A   **B**   **C**

missing books, <u>Butterfly's</u> Ball and the Bears' House. **E**

              D

6. Jack told a <u>credulous</u> story about his trip <u>up the beanstalk</u> because each

               A   **B**

child in the room <u>was convinced</u> <u>by his reasoning</u>. **E**

               C   **D**

7. There <u>are</u> <u>fewer</u> students in school this year despite the <u>principal's</u>

       A   **B**   **C**

prediction of <u>increasing</u> enrollment. **E**

               D

8. My mother is a <u>Methodist</u>. She married a <u>Southern Baptist</u> and took <u>us</u>
                  A   **B**   **C**

    children to the <u>First Baptist church</u> in Stuart. **E**
                  D

9. When we moved from Jacksonville, Florid<u>a,</u> to Little Roc<u>k,</u> Arkansas, my
                                  A   **B**

    <u>Dad</u> <u>was promoted</u> to store manager. **E**
    C   **D**

10. "One of the <u>burglar's</u> had been <u>already</u> <u>apprehended</u> before his colleagues
               A   **B**   **C**

    left the buildin<u>g,"</u> bragged the officer. **E**
              D

11. Walter said <u>that</u> his calculator <u>has been missing</u> <u>since</u> last Monday
              A   **B**   **C**

    <u>responding to my question</u>. **E**
          D

12. Why was the girl <u>that</u> had plenty of money <u>arrested</u> for <u>shoplifting</u> some
                A   **B**   **C**

    trinkets of <u>two dollar's worth</u>? **E**
            D

13. The future <u>will be</u> <u>because of</u> the past; <u>by changing the past</u> <u>would alter</u>
          A   **B**   **C**   **D**

    the future. **E**

14. <u>Mr. Thomas'</u> daughter-in-law encouraged her <u>husband's</u> boss to host a
    A   **B**

    fund-raiser for <u>the United Way</u>, a charity that Mr. Thomas <u>supports</u>. **E**
                B   **D**

15. Miriam decided to remain <u>stationery</u> <u>since</u> <u>to move</u> would startle the horses,
                        A   **B**   **C**

    one of <u>which</u> might bolt. **E**
          D

Part B

Directions: Each underlined portion of sentences 16 - 25 contains one or more errors in grammar, usage, mechanics, or sentence structure. Circle the choice which best corrects the error without changing the meaning of the original sentence. Choice D or E repeats the underlined portion. Select the identical phrase if you find no errors.

16. Joe <u>didn't hardly know his cousin Fred</u>, who'd had a rhinoplasty.

    A. hardly did know his cousin Fred

    B. didn't know his cousin Fred hardly

    C. hardly knew his cousin Fred

    D. didn't know his cousin Fred

    E. didn't hardly know his cousin Fred

17. <u>Mixing the batter for cookies</u>, the cat licked the Crisco from the cookie sheet.

    A. While mixing the batter for cookies

    B. While the batter for cookies was mixing

    C. While I mixed the batter for cookies

    D. While I mixed the cookies

    E. Mixing the batter for cookies

18. Mr. Brown is a school volunteer <u>with a reputation and twenty years service</u>.

    A. with a reputation for twenty years' service

    B. with a reputation for twenty year's service

    C. who has served twenty years

    D. with a service reputation of twenty years

    E. with a reputation and twenty years service

19. Walt Whitman was famous for <u>his composition, *Leaves of Grass*, serving as a nurse during the Civil War, and a devoted son.</u>

    A. *Leaves of Grass*, his service as a nurse during the Civil War, and a devoted son

    B. composing *Leaves of Grass*, serving as a nurse during the Civil War, and being a \ devoted son

    C. his composition, *Leaves of Grass*, his nursing during the Civil War, and his devotion as a son

    D. having authored *Leaves of Grass*, served as a nurse during the Civil War, and as a devoted son

    E. his composition, *Leaves of Grass*, serving as a nurse during the Civil War, and a devoted son.

20. A teacher <u>must know not only her subject matter but also the strategies of</u> <u>content teaching</u>.

   A. must not only know her subject matter but also the strategies of content teaching

   B. not only must know her subject matter but also the strategies of content teaching

   C. must not know only her subject matter but also the strategies of content teaching

   D. must know not only her subject matter but also the strategies of content teaching

21. My English teacher, Mrs. Hunt, <u>is nicer than any teacher at school and is</u> the most helpful.

   A. is as nice as any teacher at school and is

   B. is nicer than any other teacher at school and is

   C. is as nice as any other teacher at school and is

   D. is nicer than any teacher at school and is

22. The teacher <u>implied</u> from our angry words that there was conflict <u>between you and me</u>.

   A. implied ... between you and I

   B. inferred... between you and I

   C. inferred...between you and me

   D. implied ... between you and me

23. There were <u>fewer pieces</u> of evidence presented during the second trial.

   A. fewer peaces

   B. less peaces

   C. less pieces

   D. fewer pieces

24. Mr. Smith <u>respectfully submitted his resignation and had</u> a new job.

   A. respectively submitted his resignation and has

   B. respectively submitted his resignation before accepting

   C. respectfully submitted his resignation because of

   D. respectfully submitted his resignation and had

25. **Wally <u>groaned, "Why</u> do I have to do an oral interpretation <u>of "The Raven."</u>**

   A. groaned, "Why ... of 'The Raven' ?"

   B. groaned "Why ... of "The Raven" ?

   C. groaned ",Why ... of "The Raven?"

   D. groaned, "Why ... of "The Raven."

Part C

Directions: Select the best answer in each group of multiple choices.

26. The synonyms "gyro," "hero," and "submarine" reflect which influence on language usage?

A. social

B. geographical

C. historical

D. personal

27. The following passage is written from which point of view?

As she mused the pitiful vision of her mother's life laid its spell on the very quick of her being - that life of commonplace sacrifices closing in final craziness. She trembled as she heard again her mother's voice saying constantly with foolish insistence: Derevaun Seraun! Derevaun Seraun !*
* "The end of pleasure is pain!" (Gaelic)

A. First person, narrator

B. Second person, direct address

C. Third person, omniscient

D. First person, omniscient

28. The literary device of personification is used in which example below?

A. "Beg me no beggary by soul or parents, whining dog!"

B. "Happiness sped through the halls cajoling as it went."

C. "O wind thy horn, thou proud fellow."

D. "And that one talent which is death to hide."

29. Which of the writers below is a renowned Black poet?

A. Maya Angelou

B. Sandra Cisneros

C. Richard Wilbur

D. Richard Wright

30. Which of the following is not one of the four forms of discourse?

A. exposition

B. description

C. rhetoric

D. persuasion

31. Among junior-high school students of low-to-average readability levels which work would most likely stir reading interest?

    A. *Elmer Gantry*, Sinclair Lewis

    B. *Smiley's People*, John LeCarre

    C. *The Outsiders*, S. E. Hinton

    D. *And Then There Were None*, Agatha Christie

32. "Every one must pass through Vanity Fair to get to the celestial city" is an allusion from a

    A. Chinese folk tale.

    B. Norse saga.

    C. British allegory.

    D. German fairy tale.

33. Which teaching method would be most effective for interesting underachievers in the required senior English class?

    A. Assign use of glossary work and extensively footnoted excerpts of great works.

    B. Have students take turns reading aloud the anthology selection.

    C. Let students choose which readings they'll study and write about.

    D. Use a chronologically arranged, traditional text, but assigning group work, panel presentations, and portfolio management.

34. Which poem is typified as a villanelle?

    A. "Do not Go Gentle into That Good Night"

    B. "Dover Beach"

    C. *Sir Gawain and the Green Knight*

    D. *Pilgrim's Progress*

35. **Which term best describes the form of the following poetic excerpts?**

And more to lulle him in his slumber soft,
A trickling streame from high rock tumbling downe,
And ever-drizzling raine upon the loft.
Mixt with a murmuring winde, much like a swowne
No other noyse, nor peoples troubles cryes.
As still we wont t'annoy the walle'd towne,
Might there be heard: but careless Quiet lyes,
Wrapt in eternall silence farre from enemyes.

A. Ballad

B. Elegy

C. Spenserian stanza

D. Octava rima

36. **Which poet was a major figure in the Harlem Renaissance?**

A. e. e. cummings

B. Rita Dove

C. Margaret Atwood

D. Langston Hughes

37. **To understand the origins of a word, one must study the**

A. synonyms.

B. inflections.

C. phonetics.

D. etymology.

38. **Which sonnet form describes the following?**

My galley charg'ed with
   forgetfulness
      Through sharp seas, in
      winter night doth pass
      'Tween rock and rock; and
      eke mine enemy, alas,
That is my lord steereth with
   cruelness.
And every oar a thought in
   readiness,
      As though that death were
      light in such a case.
      An endless wind doth tear
      the sail apace
      Or forc'ed sighs and trusty
      fearfulness.
A rain of tears, a cloud of dark
   disdain,
      Hath done the wearied
      cords great hinderance,
      Wreathed with error and eke
      with ignorance.
      The stars be hid that led me
      to this pain
      Drowned is reason that
      should me consort,
      And I remain despairing of
      the poet.

A. Petrarchan or Italian sonnet

B. Shakespearean or
   Elizabethan sonnet

C. Romantic sonnet

D. Spenserian sonnet

39. **What is the salient literary feature of this excerpt from an epic?**

Hither the heroes and the
nymphs resort,
To taste awhile the pleasures of
a court;
In various talk th'instructive
hours they passed,
Who gave the ball, or paid the
visit last;
One speaks the glory of the
English Queen,
And another describes a
charming Indian screen;
A third interprets motion, looks
and eyes;
At every word a reputation dies.

A. Sprung rhythm

B. Onomatopoeia

C. Heroic couplets

D. Motif

40. **What were two major characteristics of the first American literature?**

A. Vengefulness and
   arrogance

B. Bellicosity and derision

C. Oral delivery and reverence
   for the land

D. Maudlin and self-pitying
   egocentricism

41. Arthur Miller wrote *The Crucible* as a parallel to what twentieth century event?

   A. Sen. McCarthy's House un-American Activities Committee Hearing

   B. The Cold War

   C. The fall of the Berlin Wall

   D. The Persian Gulf War

42. Latin words that entered the English language during the Elizabethan Age include

   A. allusion, education, and esteem.

   B. vogue and mustache.

   C. canoe and cannibal.

   D. alligator, cocoa, and armadillo.

43. Which of the following is not a characteristic of a fable?

   A. animals that feel and talk like humans.

   B. happy solutions to human dilemmas.

   C. teaches a moral or standard for behavior.

   D. illustrates specific people or groups without directly naming them.

44. Which of the following is not an example of the subject of a tall-tale?

   A. John Henry.

   B. Paul Bunyan.

   C. George Washington.

   D. Rip Van Winkle.

45. If a student has a poor vocabulary the teacher should recommend that

   A. the student read newspapers, magazines and books on a regular basis.

   B. the student enroll in a Latin class.

   C. the student write the words repetitively after looking them up in the dictionary.

   D. the student use a thesaurus to locate synonyms and incorporate them into his/her vocabulary.

46. Which author did not write satire?

   A. Joseph Addison

   B. Richard Steele

   C. Alexander Pope

   D. John Bunyan

47. **Which of the following was not written by Jonathan Swift?**

    A. "A Voyage to Lilliput"

    B. "A Modest Proposal"

    C. "Samson Agonistes"

    D. "A Tale of a Tub"

48. **Which is not a Biblical allusion?**

    A. The patience of Job

    B. Thirty pieces of silver

    C. "Man proposes; God disposes"

    D. "Suffer not yourself to be betrayed by a kiss"

49. **Which definition below is the best for defining diction?**

    A. The specific word choices of an author to create a particular mood or feeling in the reader.

    B. Writing which explains something thoroughly.

    C. The background, or exposition, for a short story or drama.

    D. Word choices which help teach a truth or moral.

50. **Which is the best definition of free verse, or *vers libre*?**

    A. Poetry which consists of an unaccented syllable followed by an unaccented sound.

    B. Short lyrical poetry written to entertain but with an instructive purpose.

    C. Poetry which does not have a uniform pattern of rhythm.

    D. A poem which tells a story and has a plot.

51. **Which is not an accepted point of view in literary works?**

    A. First person, omniscient

    B. Third person, narrative

    C. First person, limited

    D. Third person, internal

52. **Which is an untrue statement about a theme in literature?**

    A. The theme is always stated directly somewhere in the text.

    B. The theme is the central idea in a literary work.

    C. All parts of the work (plot, setting, mood) should contribute to the theme in some way.

    D. By analyzing the various elements of the work, the reader should be able to arrive at an indirectly stated theme.

53. **Which is not a true statement concerning an author's literary tone?**

    A. Tone is partly revealed through the selection of details.

    B. Tone is the expression of the author's attitude toward his/her subject.

    C. Tone in literature is usually satiric or angry.

    D. Tone in literature corresponds to the tone of voice a speaker uses.

54. **In the teaching of poetry, the teacher should include all of the following but one. Select the answer which is not appropriate for all poetry instruction.**

    A. Setting and audience

    B. Theme and tone

    C. Pattern and diction

    D. Diction and rhyme scheme

55. **Which of the following definitions best describes a parable?**

    A. A short entertaining account of some happening, usually using talking animals as characters.

    B. A slow, sad song or poem, or prose work expressing lamentation.

    C. An extended narrative work expressing universal truths concerning domestic life.

    D. A short, simple story of an occurrence of a familiar kind, from which a moral or religious lesson may be drawn.

56. **Which of the following is the best definition of existentialism?**

   A. The philosophical doctrine that matter is the only reality and that everything in the world, including thought, will and feeling, can be explained only in terms of matter.

   B. Philosophy which views things as they should be or as one would wish them to be.

   C. A philosophical and literary movement, variously religious and atheistic, stemming from Kierkegaard and represented by Sartre.

   D. The belief that all events are determined by fate and are hence inevitable.

57. **Which of the following is the best definition of imagism?**

   A. A doctrine which teaches that comfort is the only goal of value in life.

   B. A movement in modern poetry (c 1910-1918) characterized by precise, concrete images, free verse, and suggestion rather than complete statement.

   C. The belief that people are motivated in all their only by self-centeredness.

   D. The doctrine that the human mind cannot know where there is a God or an ultimate cause, or anything beyond material phenomenon.

58. **Which definition below best fits that of naturalism?**

    A. Belief that the writer or artist should apply scientific objectivity in his/her observation and treatment of life without imposing value of judgments.

    B. The doctrine that teaches that the existing world is the best to be hoped for.

    C. The doctrine which teaches that God is not a personality, but that all laws, forces and manifestations of the universe are God-related.

    D. A philosophical doctrine which professes that the truth of all knowledge must always be in question.

59. **The tendency to emphasize and value the qualities and peculiarities of life in a particular area of geographic site is a definition of**

    A. pragmatism.

    B. regionalism.

    C. pantheism.

    D. abstractionism.

60. **A traditional, anonymous story ostensibly with a historical basis, serving usually to explain some phenomenon of nature or the creation of earth and mankind, for example, is a definition of a**

    A. proverb.

    B. idyll.

    C. myth.

    D. epic.

61. **The arrangement and relationship of words in sentences or sentence structure best describes**

    A. style.

    B. discourse.

    C. thesis.

    D. syntax.

62. **A form of discourse which explains or informs is**

    A. exposition

    B. narration.

    C. persuasion.

    D. description.

63. The substitution of "went to his rest" for "died" is an example of a/an

    A. bowdlerism.

    B. jargon.

    C. euphemism.

    D. malapropism

64. A conversation between two or more people is called a

    A. parody.

    B. dialogue.

    C. monologue.

    D. analogy.

65. "Clean as a whistle" or "Easy as falling off a log" are examples of

    A. semantics.

    B. parody.

    C. irony.

    D. clichés.

66. Which of the following is most true of expository writing?

    A. It is mutually exclusive of other forms of discourse.

    B. It can incorporate other forms of discourse in the process of providing supporting details.

    C. It should never employ informal expression.

    D. It should be scored only with a summative evaluation.

67. The appearance of a Yankee from Connecticut in the Court of King Arthur is an example of a/an

    A. rhetoric.

    B. parody.

    C. paradox.

    D. anachronism

68. The quality in a work of literature which evokes feelings of pity or compassion is called

    A. colloquy.

    B. irony.

    C. pathos.

    D. paradox.

69. "I'll die if I don't pass this course" is an example of

    A. barbarism.

    B. oxymoron.

    C. hyperbole.

    D. antithesis.

70. An extended metaphor which compares two very dissimilar things - one lofty, one lowly, is a definition of a/an

    A. antithesis.

    B. aphorism.

    C. apostrophe.

    D. conceit.

71. A figure of speech in which someone absent or something inhuman is addressed as though present and able to respond describes

    A. personification.

    B. synecdoche.

    C. metonymy.

    D. apostrophe.

72. Certain slang or jargon expressions peculiar to a certain ethnicity, age, economic, or professional group are called

    A. aphorisms.

    B. allusions.

    C. idioms.

    D. euphemisms.

73. Which of the following is a complex sentence?

    A. Anna and Margaret read a total of fifty-four books during summer vacation.

    B. The youngest boy on the team had the best earned run average, which mystifies the coaching staff.

    C. Earl decided to attend Princeton; his twin brother Roy, who aced the ASVAB test, will be going to Annapolis.

    D. "Easy come, easy go," Marcia moaned.

74. **Followers of Piaget's learning theory believe that adolescents in the formal operations period**

   A. behave properly from fear of punishment rather than from a conscious decision to take a certain action.

   B. see the past more realistically and can relate to people from the past more than preadolescents.

   C. are less self-conscious and thus more willing to project their own identities into those of fictional characters.

   D. have not yet developed a symbolic imagination.

75. **Which of the following is a formal reading level assessment?**

   A. a standardized reading test

   B. a teacher-made reading test

   C. an interview

   D. a reading diary.

76. **Middle and high school students are more receptive to studying grammar and syntax**

   A. through worksheets and end -of-lesson practices in textbooks.

   B. through independent, homework assignments.

   C. through analytical examination of the writings of famous authors.

   D. though application to their own writing.

77. **Which statement below best describes an author and his/her work?**

   A. Zora Neale Hurston's *Their Eyes Were Watching God* dealt autobiographically with the strong faith that helped her through the years of her poor upbringing in rural Florida.

   B. Willa Cather's works, such as *My Antonia*, depict the regionalism of the Deep South.

   C. Emily Dickinson gained national recognition during her lifetime for the publication of over 300 poems.

   D. Upton Sinclair's writings, such as *The Jungle*, represent the optimism and trust of the American citizenry for its government.

78. **Which of the following is the least preferable strategy for teaching literature?**

   A. teacher-guided total class discussion

   B. small group discussion

   C. teacher lecture

   D. dramatization of literature selections

79. **Which event triggered the beginning of Modern English?**

   A. Conquest of England by the Normans in 1066

   B. Introduction of the printing press to the British Isles

   C. Publication of Samuel Johnson's lexicon

   D. American Revolution

80. **Which of the following is not true about the English language?**

   A. English is the easiest language to learn.

   B. English is the least inflected language.

   C. English has the most extensive vocabulary of any language.

   D. English originated as a Germanic tongue.

81. **Which of the following is not a technique of prewriting?**

   A. Clustering

   B. Listing

   C. Brainstorming

   D. Proofreading

82. **Which of the following is not an approach to keep students ever conscious of the need to write for audience appeal?**

    A. Pairing students during the writing process

    B. Reading all rough drafts before the students write the final copies

    C. Having students compose stories or articles for publication in school literary magazines or newspapers

    D. Writing letters to friends or relatives

83. **The Elizabethans wrote in**

    A. Celtic.

    B. Old English.

    C. Middle English.

    D. Modern English.

84. **Which of the following writers never won the Nobel Prize for literature?**

    A. Gabriel Garcia-Marquez of Colombia

    B. Nadine Gordimer of South Africa

    C. Pablo Neruda of Chile

    D. Alice Walker of the United States

85. **The children's literature genre came into its own in the**

    A. seventeenth century.

    B. eighteenth century.

    C. nineteenth century.

    D. twentieth century.

86. **Recognizing the quality of empathy in literature is a/an**

    A. emotional response.

    B. interpretive response.

    C. critical response.

    D. evaluative response.

87. **Which of the following should not be included in the opening paragraph of an informative essay?**

    A. Thesis sentence

    B. Details and examples supporting the main idea

    C. A broad general introduction to the topic

    D. A style and tone that grabs the reader's attention

88. **What is the figure of speech present in line one below in which the dead body of Caesar is addressed as though he were still a living being?**

"O, pardon me, thou bleeding piece of earth
That I am meek and gentle with these butchers."
Marc Antony from Julius *Caesar*

A. Apostrophe

B. Allusion

C. Antithesis

D. Anachronism

89. **What is the prevailing form of discourse in this passage?**

"It would have been hard to find a passer-by more wretched in appearance.
He was a man of middle height, stout and hardy, in the strength of maturity; he might have been forty-six or seven. A slouched leather cap hid half his face, bronzed by the sun and wind, and dripping with sweat."

A. Description

B. Narration

C. Exposition

D. Persuasion

90. **In most phases of writing, the most serious drawback of using a computer is**

A. the copy looks so good that students tend to overlook major mistakes.

B. the spell check and grammar programs discourage students from learning proper spelling and mechanics.

C. the speed with which corrections can be made detracts from the exploration and contemplation of composing.

D. the writer loses focus by concentrating on the final product rather than the details.

91. **A youngster, watching a movie in which a train derailed, exclaims, "Wow, look how many cars fell off the tracks. There's junk everywhere. The engineer must have really been asleep." Based on Piaget's beliefs about child moral judgments, the fact that the child is impressed by the wreckage and assigns blame to the engineer indicates that he is approximately**

A. ten years old.

B. twelve years old.

C. fourteen years old.

D. sixteen years old.

92. **Oral debate is most closely associated with which form of discourse?**

    A. Description

    B. Exposition

    C. Narration

    D. Persuasion

93. **Most of S. E. Hinton's novels - *The Outsiders* - are written on the sixth grade reading level. They have the greatest reader appeal to**

    A. sixth graders.

    B. ninth graders.

    C. twelfth graders.

    D. adults.

94. **Which aspect of language is innate?**

    A. Biological capability to articulate sounds understood by other humans

    B. Cognitive ability to create syntactical structures

    C. Capacity for using semantics to convey meaning in a social environment

    D. Ability to vary inflections and accents

95. **Which of the following titles is known for its scathingly condemning tone?**

    A. Boris Pasternak's *Dr. Zhivago*

    B. Albert Camus' *The Stranger*

    C. Henry David Thoreau's "On the Duty of Civil Disobedience"

    D. Benjamin Franklin's "Rules by Which A Great Empire May be Reduced to a Small One"

96. **Which of the following is not a theme of Native American writing?**

    A. Emphasis on the hardiness of the human body and soul

    B. The strength of multi-cultural assimilation

    C. Contrition for the genocide of native peoples

    D. Remorse for the loss of the Indian way of life

97. If a student uses inappropriate language that includes slang and expletives, what is the best course of action to take in order to influence the student's formal communication skills?

A. ask the student to paraphrase their writing, that is, translate it into language appropriate for the school principal to read.

B. refuse to read the student's papers until he conforms to a more literate style.

C. ask the student to read his work aloud to the class for peer evaluation.

D. rewrite the flagrant passages to show the student the right form of expression.

98. Which of the following contains an error in possessive inflection?

A. Doris's shawl

B. mother's-in-law frown

C. children's lunches

D. ambassador's briefcase

99. Homer's *Iliad* and *Odyssey* are taught in different grade levels from state to state and district to district. Which of the following would be the most significant factor in approaching the teaching of these classic works wherever they appear in the curriculum ?

A. Identifying a translation on the appropriate reading level

B. Determining the students' interest level

C. Selecting an appropriate evaluative technique

D. Determining the scope and delivery methods of background study

100. A punctuation mark indicating omission, interrupted thought, or an incomplete statement is a/an

A. ellipsis.

B. anachronism

C. colloquy.

D. idiom.

101. In the phrase "the Cabinet conferred with the president," Cabinet is an example of a/an

A. metonym

B. synecdoche

C. metaphor

D. allusion

102. The technique of starting a narrative at a significant point in the action and then developing the story through flashbacks is called

A. in medias res

B. octava rima

C. irony

D. suspension of willing disbelief

103. The inverted triangle introduction to an essay requires that the thesis sentence occur

A. at the beginning of the paragraph.

B. in the middle of the paragraph.

C. at the end of the paragraph.

D. in the second paragraph.

104. A student composition intended for providing information should contain a minimum of how many paragraphs?

A. three

B. four

C. five

D. six

105. In a timed essay test of an hour's duration, no more than ____ minutes should be devoted to prewriting.

A. five

B. ten

C. fifteen

D. twenty

106. Which of the following sentences is properly punctuated?

A. The more you eat; the more you want.

B. The authors - John Steinbeck, Ernest Hemingway, and William Faulkner - are staples of modern writing in American literature textbooks.

C. Handling a wild horse, takes a great deal of skill and patience.

D. The man, who replaced our teacher, is a comedian.

107. **The students in Mrs. Cline's seventh grade language arts class were invited to attend a performance of *Romeo and Juliet* presented by the drama class at the high school. In preparation for the performance, they should**

    A. read the play as a homework exercise.

    B. read a synopsis of the plot and a biographical sketch of the author.

    C. examine a few main selections from the play to become familiar with the language and style of the author.

    D. read a condensed version of the story and practice attentive listening skills.

108. **"The *U.S.S. Constitution* is the old man of the sea" is an example of**

    A. hyperbole.

    B. simile.

    C. allegory.

    D. metaphor.

109. **Which of the following sentences contains a capitalization error?**

    A. The commander of the English navy was Admiral Nelson.

    B. Napoleon was the president of the French First Republic.

    C. Queen Elizabeth II is the Monarch of the entire British Empire.

    D. William the Conqueror led the Normans to victory over the British.

110. **Which of the following sentences contains a subject-verb agreement error?**

    A. Both mother and her two sisters were married in a triple ceremony.

    B. Neither the hens nor the rooster is likely to be served for dinner.

    C. My boss, as well as the company's two personnel directors, have earned their ten-year pins.

    D. Amanda and the twins are late again.

111. A technique used to allow students to present written ideas without interruption of the flow of thoughts is called

A. brainstorming.

B. mapping.

C. listing.

D. free writing.

112. A formative evaluation of student writing

A. requires a thorough marking of mechanical errors with a pencil or pen.

B. making comments on the appropriateness of the student's interpretation of the prompt and the degree to which the objective was met.

C. should require that the student hand in all the materials produced during the process of writing.

D. several careful readings of the text for content, mechanics, spelling, and usage.

113. The practice of reading a piece of student writing to assess the overall impression of the product is

A. holistic evaluation.

B. portfolio assessment.

C. analytical evaluation.

D. using a performance system.

114. Modeling is a practice that allows students to

A. create a style unique to their own language capabilities.

B. emulate the writing of professionals.

C. paraphrase passages from good literature.

D. peer evaluate the writings of other students.

115. The writing of Russian naturalists is

A. optimistic

B. pessimistic.

C. satirical.

D. whimsical.

116. Most children's literature prior to the development of popular literature was intended to be didactic. Which of the following would not be considered didactic?

A. "A Visit from St. Nicholas" by Clement Moore

B. *McGuffey's Reader*

C. any version of *Cinderella*

D. parables from the *Bible*

117. Words prevalent in Poe's "The Bells" like *twanging* and *tintinnabulation* are examples of

A. onomatopoeia.

B. consonance.

C. figurative language.

D. free verse.

118. Which of the following is a characteristic of blank verse?

A. Meter in iambic pentameter

B. Clearly specified rhyme scheme

C. Lack of figurative language

D. Unspecified rhythm

119. American colonial writers were primarily

A. Romanticists.

B. Naturalists.

C. Realists.

D. Neo-classicists.

120. Charles Dickens, Robert Browning, and Robert Louis Stevenson were

A. Victorians.

B. Medievalists.

C. Elizabethans.

D. Absurdists.

121. The most significant drawback to applying learning theory research to classroom practice is that

A. today's students do not acquire reading skills with the same alacrity as when greater emphasis was placed on reading classical literature.

B. development rates are complicated by geographical and cultural differences that are difficult to overcome.

C. homogeneous grouping has contributed to faster development of some age groups.

D. social and environmental conditions have contributed to an escalated maturity level than research done twenty or more years ago would seem to indicate.

122. Overcrowded classes prevent the individual attention needed to facilitate language development. This drawback can be best overcome by

A. dividing the class into independent study groups.

B. assigning more study time at home.

C. using more drill practice in class.

D. team teaching.

123. Which of the following responses to literature are middle school students not yet prepared to assimilate?

A. Interpretive

B. Evaluative

C. Critical

D. Emotional

124. Which of the following is exhibited most in the hierarchy of needs for adolescents who are becoming more team-oriented in their approach to learning?

A. Need for competence

B. Need for love/acceptance

C. Need to know

D. Need to belong

125. **What is the best course of action when a child refuses to complete a reading/literature assignment on the grounds that is morally objectionable?**

A. Speak with the parents and explain the necessity of studying this work.

B. Encourage the child to sample some of the text before making a judgment.

C. Place the child in another teacher's class where students are studying an acceptable work.

D. Provide the student with alternative selections that cover the same performance standards as the assignment that the student views as morally objectionable.

ANSWER KEY

1.	A	27.	C	53.	C	79.	B	105.	B
2.	B	28.	B	54.	A	80.	A	106.	B
3.	A	29.	A	55.	D	81.	D	107.	D
4.	A	30.	C	56.	C	82.	B	108.	D
5.	B	31.	C	57.	B	83.	D	109.	C
6.	A	32.	C	58.	A	84.	D	110.	C
7.	E	33.	C	59.	B	85.	C	111.	D
8.	D	34.	A	60.	C	86.	D	112.	B
9.	C	35.	D	61.	D	87.	B	113.	A
10.	A	36.	D	62.	A	88.	A	114.	B
11.	D	37.	D	63.	C	89.	A	115.	B
12.	D	38.	A	64.	B	90.	C	116.	A
13.	C	39.	C	65.	D	91.	A	117.	A
14.	E	40.	C	66.	B	92.	D	118.	A
15.	A	41.	A	67.	D	93.	B	119.	D
16.	C	42.	A	68.	C	94.	A	120.	A
17.	C	43.	B	69.	C	95.	D	121.	D
18.	A	44.	C	70.	D	96.	B	122.	A
19.	B	45.	A	71.	D	97.	A	123.	B
20.	D	46.	D	72.	C	98.	B	124.	D
21.	B	47.	C	73.	B	99.	A	125.	D
22.	C	48.	C	74.	B	100.	A		
23.	D	49.	A	75.	A	101.	A		
24.	C	50.	C	76.	D	102.	A		
25.	A	51.	A	77.	A	103.	C		
26.	B	52.	A	78.	C	104.	C		

Section II: Writing and Language Skills

Directions: In sentences 1-15, four words or phrases have been underlined. If you determine that any underlined word or phrase has an error in grammar, usage, or mechanics, circle the letter underneath the underlining. If there are no errors, circle the letter E at the end of the sentence. There is no more than one error in any sentence.

1. The volcanic eruption in Montserrat displaced residents of Plymouth <u>which</u>
A

   felt that the <u>English government</u> <u>was</u> responsible for <u>their</u> evacuation   E
   B   C   D

   The error is A. "Which" is a relative pronoun whose antecedent is "residents of Plymouth". This antecedent represents persons, not things. If the antecedent were a thing or things, then "which" would be correct. The correct pronoun would be "who".

2. When the <u>school district</u> privatized the school cafeteria, <u>us</u> students <u>were</u>
A   B   C

   thrilled to purchase more than soggy <u>French fries</u>   E
   D

   The error is B. "Us" is not a subject pronoun, and this is what is needed here: "We" is the right pronoun.

3. The homecoming <u>Queen and King</u> <u>were chosen</u> by the <u>student body</u> for <u>their</u>
A   B   C   D

   popularity   E

   The error is A. "Queen and King" are used as nouns here, and not as names, or as the title of a real sovereign: for example, Queen Elizabeth. Since the words "king and queen" are nouns, they are not capitalized.

4. If the practical joke <u>was</u> <u>Cullen's</u> idea, then he <u>must</u> suffer the <u>consequences</u>
E

                   A   B   C   D

The error is A. In a sentence beginning with "If" and expressing a condition, it is necessary to use the correct subjunctive forms: "If I were, if you were, if he/she/it were, if we were, if you were, if they were". The sentence here should read: "If the practical joke were Cullen's idea..."

5. She, not her sister, <u>is</u> the one <u>who</u> the librarian <u>has questioned</u> about the
                    A   B   C
missing books, <u>Butterfly's</u> Ball and the Bear's House   E
              D

The error is B. The relative pronoun "who" is not correct here: "who" is the subject of a verb, not the object. In this sentence, the subject is "the librarian". The correct relative pronoun here is "whom", which is the object of the verb "has questioned".

6. Jack told a <u>credulous</u> story about his trip <u>up the beanstalk</u> because each
              A   B
child in the room <u>was convinced</u> <u>by his reasoning</u>   E
                       C   D

The error is A: Only a person can be credulous, not a thing. It should read: "Jack told an incredible story about his trip..."

7. There <u>are</u> <u>fewer</u> students in school this year despite the <u>principal's</u> prediction

              A B   C
of <u>increasing</u> enrollment   E

The answer is E: There are no grammatical or syntactical errors in this sentence.

8. My mother is a <u>Methodist</u>. She married a <u>Southern Baptist</u> and took <u>us</u>
                  A   B   C
children to the <u>First Baptist church</u> in Stuart   E
                   D
The error is D: The name of the church should be completely capitalized. It should read: "... the First Baptist Church."

9. When we moved from Jacksonville, Florida, to Little Rock, Arkansas, my
                                      A   B

    Dad was promoted to store manager. E
     C   D

    The error is C: "dad" is a noun, which is indicated by the possessive "my".
    Only name gets capitalized.

10. "One of the burglar's was already apprehended before his colleagues left
                    A   B   C

    the building," bragged the officer. E
        D

    The error is A: "burglar" should be in the plural: "burglars". In this sentence, it
    is Written as a possessive, which is incorrect here. If we had the possessive,
    we should have a sentence such as: "the burglar's mistake caused him to be
    arrested".

11. Walter said that his calculator has been missing since last Monday
               A   B   C

    responding to my question. E
        D

    The error is D: the gerund and its object ("responding to my question"), are
    not where they should be. The sentence should read: "Walter, responding to
    my question, said that his calculator has been missing since last Monday."

12. Why was the girl that had plenty of money arrested for shoplifting some
                     A   B   C

    trinkets of two dollar's worth? E
           D

    The error is D. The sentence should read: "… trinkets of two dollars'
    worth". As it is, "two dollar's worth" is in the singular possessive, which is
    wrong here.

13. The future will be because of the past: by changing the past would alter the
               A   B   C   D

    future. E

    The answer is C: "by" is not necessary here. The sentence should read:
    "… because of the past: changing the past would alter the future."

14. <u>Mr Thomas</u>' daughter-in-law encouraged her <u>husband's</u> boss to host a
      A   B

    fund-raiser for <u>the United Way</u>, a charity that Mr Thomas <u>supports</u>.   E
                   C   D

The answer is E. There are no errors in this sentence.

15. Miriam decided to remain <u>stationary since</u> <u>to move</u> would startle the
                       A   B C

   horses, one of <u>which</u> might bolt.   E
           D

The error is A: "stationary" is not an adjective used for persons.

Part B

Each underlined portion of sentences 16-25 contains one or more errors in grammar, usage, mechanics, or sentence structure. Circle the choice which best corrects the error without changing the meaning of the original sentence. Choice D or E repeats the underlined portion. Select the identical phrase if you find no error.

16. Joe <u>didn't hardly know his cousin Fred</u> who'd had a rhinoplasty.

    A. hardly did know his cousin Fred

    B. didn't know his cousin Fred hardly

    C. hardly knew his cousin Fred

    D. didn't know his cousin Fred

    E. didn't hardly know his   cousin Fred

    The answer is C: when using the adverb "hardly" to modify the verb, one should not use the verb in the negative, since "hardly" already restricts the sense so much that it is almost a negative.   .

17. <u>Mixing the batter for cookies</u>, the cat licked the Crisco from the cookie sheet.

    A. While mixing the batter for cookies

    B. While the batter for cookies was Mixing

    C. While I mixed the batter for cookies

    D. While I mixed the cookies

    E. Mixing the batter for cookies

    The answer is C. A and E give the impression that the cat was mixing the batter (it is a "dangling modifier"), B that the batter was mixing itself, and D lacks precision: it is the batter that was being mixed, not the cookies themselves.

18. Mr Brown is a school volunteer with a reputation and twenty years service

    A. with a reputation for twenty years' service

    B. with a reputation for twenty year's service

    C. who has served twenty years

    D. with a reputation and twenty years service

    E. with a reputation and twenty years service

The answer is A. B is a singular genitive ('s), C lacks the reputation part, and D and E lack   the genitive plural (s') that is necessary here.

19. Walt Whitman was famous for <u>his composition, _Leaves of Grass,_ serving as a nurse during the Civil War, and a devoted son</u>

    A. _Leaves of Grass,_ his service as a a nurse during the Civil War, and a devoted son

    B. composing _Leaves of Grass,_ serving as a nurse during the Civil War, and being a devoted son

    C. his composition, _Leaves of Grass,_ his nursing during the Civil War, and his devotion as a son

    D. his composition, _Leaves of Grass,_ serving as a nurse during the Civil War, and a devoted son

    E. his composition, _Leaves of Grass,_ serving as a nurse during the Civil War, and a devoted son

The answer is B: in order to be parallel, the sentence needs three gerunds. The other sentences use both gerunds and nouns, which is a lack of parallelism.

20. A teacher <u>must know not only her subject matter but also the strategies of content teaching</u>

    A.   must not only know her subject matter but also the strategies of content teaching

    B.   not only must know her subject matter but also the strategies of content teaching

    C.   must not know only her subject matter but also the strategies of content teaching

    D.   must know not only her subject matter but also the strategies of content teaching

The answer is D: "not only" must come directly before the verb it modifies.

21. My English teacher, Mrs. Hunt, <u>is nicer than any teacher at school and is</u> the most helpful

    A. is as nice as any teacher at school and is

    B. is nicer than any other teacher at school and is

    C. is as nice as any other teacher at school and is

    D. is nicer than any teacher at school and is

The answer is C. When comparing one thing to others in a group, you need to exclude the thing under comparison from the rest of the group. Thus, you need the word "other" in the sentence.

22. The teacher <u>implied</u> from our angry words that there was conflict <u>between</u> <u>you and me</u>

    A.   Implied... between you and I

    B.   Inferred... between you and I

    C.   Inferred... between you and me

    D.   Implied... between you and me

The answer is C: the difference between the verb "to imply" and the verb "to infer" is that implying is directing an interpretation toward other people; to infer is to deduce an interpretation from someone else's discourse. Moreover, "between you and I" is grammatically incorrect: after a preposition here "and"), a disjunctive pronoun (me, you, him, her, us, you, them) is needed.

23. There were <u>fewer pieces</u> of evidence presented during the second trial

    A. fewer peaces

    B. less peaces

    C. less pieces

    D. fewer pieces

The answer is D. "less" is impossible in the plural, and "peace" is the opposite of war, not a "piece" of evidence.

24. Mr Smith <u>respectfully submitted his resignation and had</u> a new job.

    A. respectfully submitted his resignation and has

    B. respectfully submitted his resignation before accepting

    C. respectfully submitted his resignation because of

    D. respectfully submitted his resignation and had

The answer is C. A eliminates any relationship of causality between submitting the resignation and having the new job. B just changes the sentence and does not indicate the fact that Mr Smith had a new job before submitting his resignation. D means that Mr Smith first submitted his resignation, then got a new job.

25. Wally <u>groaned, "Why</u> do I have to do an oral interpretation of "The Raven."

    A. groaned, "Why... of 'The Raven'?"

    B. groaned "Why... of "The Raven"?

    C. groaned ", Why... of "The Raven?"

    D. groaned, "Why... of "The Raven."

The answer is A. The question mark in a quotation that is an interrogation should be within the quotation marks. Also, when quoting a work of literature within another quotation, one should use single quotation marks ('...') for the title of this work, and they should close before the final quotation mark.

26. The synonyms "gyro," "hero," and "submarine" reflect which influence on language usage?

A. social

B. geographical

C. historical

D. personal

The answer is B. They are interchangeable but their use depends on the region of the United States, not on the social class of the speaker. Nor is there any historical context around any of them. The usage can be personal, but will most often vary with the region.

27. The following passage is written from which point of view?

As she mused the pitiful vision of her mother's life laid its spell on the very quick of her being –that life of commonplace sacrifices closing in final craziness. She trembled as she heard again her mother's voice saying constantly with foolish insistence: Dearevaun Seraun! Dearevaun Seraun!*

* "The end of pleasure is pain!"

(Gaelic)

A. First person, narrator

B. Second person, direct address

C. Third person, omniscient

D. First person, omniscient

The answer is C. The passage is clearly in the third person (the subject is "she"), and it is omniscient since it gives the characters' inner thoughts.

28. The literary device of personification is used in which example below?

    A. "Beg me no beggary by soul or
        parents, whining dog!"

    B. "Happiness sped through the halls cajoling as it went."

    C. "O wind thy horn, thou proud
        fellow."

    D. "And that one talent which is death to hide."

The answer is C. It gives human characteristics to an inanimate object.

**29. Which of the writers below is
a renowned Black poet?**

    A. Maya Angelou

    B. Sandra Cisneros

    C. Richard Wilbur

    D. Richard Wright

The answer is A. Among her most famous work are *I Know Why the Caged Bird Sings* (1970), *And Still I Rise* (1978), and *All God's Children Need Traveling Shoes* (1986). Richard Wilbur is a poet and a translator of French dramatists Racine et Moliere, but he is not African American. Richard Wright is a very important African American author of novels such as *Native Son* and *Black Boy* or *The Outsider*. However, he was not a poet. Sandra Cisneros is a Latina author who is very important in developing Latina Women's literature,

30. Which of the following is not one of the four forms of discourse?

    A. exposition

    B. description

    C. rhetoric

    D. persuasion

The answer is C. Exposition, description and persuasion are styles of writing and ways of influencing a reader or a listener. Rhetoric, on the other hand, is theoretical. It is the theory of expressive and effective speech. Rhetorical figures are ornaments of speech such as anaphora, antithesis, metaphor, etc.

31. Among junior-high school students of low-to-average readability levels which work would most likely stir reading interest?

    A. *Elmer Gantry*, Sinclair Lewis

    B. *Smiley's People*, John Le Carre

    C. *The Outsiders*, S.E. Hinton

    D. *And Then There Were None*, Agatha Christie.

The answer is C. The students can easily identify with the characters and the gangs in the book. S.E. Hinton has actually said about this book: "*The Outsiders* is definitely my best-selling book; but what I like most about it is how it has taught a lot of kids to enjoy reading."

32. **"Every one must pass through Vanity Fair to get to the celestial city" is an allusion from a**

    A. Chinese folk tale.

    B. Norse saga.

    C. British allegory.

    D. German fairy tale.

    The answer is C. This is a reference to John Bunyan's *Pilgrim's Progress from this World to That Which Is to Come* (Part I, 1678; Part II, 1684), in which the hero Christian flees the City of Destruction and must undergo different trials tests to get the The Celestial City.

33. **Which teaching method would be most effective for interesting underachievers in the required senior English class?**

    A. Assign use of glossary work and extensively footnoted excerpts of great works.

    B. Have students take turns reading aloud the anthology selection

    C. Let students choose which readings they'll study and write about.

    D. Use a chronologically arranged, traditional text, but assigning group work, panel presentations, and portfolio management

    The answer is C. It will encourage students to react honestly to literature. Students should take notes on what they're reading so they will be able to discuss the material. They should not only react to literature, but also experience it. Small-group work is a good way to encourage them. The other answers are not fit for junior-high or high school students. They should be encouraged, however, to read critics of works in order to understand criteria work.

34. Which poem is typified as a villanelle?

   A. "Do not go gentle into that Good Night"

   B. "Dover Beach"

   C. *Sir Gawain and the Green Knight*

   D. *Pilgrim's Progress*

The answer is A. This poem by Dylan Thomas typifies the villanelle because it was written as such. A villanelle is a form which was invented in France in the XVIth century, and used mostly for pastoral songs. It has an uneven number (usually five) of tercets rhyming *aba*, with a final quatrain rhyming *abaa*. This poem is the most famous villanelle written in English. "Dover Beach" by Matthew Arnold is not a villanelle, while *Sir Gawain and The Green Knight* was written in alliterative verse by an unknown author usually referred to as The Pearl Poet around 1370. The *Pilgrim's Progress* is a prose allegory by John Bunyan.

Which term best describes the form of the following poetic excerpt?

And more to lulle him in his
 slumber soft,
A trickling streake from high rock
 tumbling downe,
And ever-drizzling raine upon
 the loft.
Mixt with a murmuring winde,
 much like a swowne
No other noyse, nor peoples
 troubles cryes.
As still we wont t'annoy the
 walle'd towne,
Might there be heard: but
 careless Quiet lyes,
Wrapt in eternall silence farre
 from enemyes.

A. Ballad

B. Elegy

C. Spenserian stanza

D. Octava rima

The answer is D. The Octava Rima is a specific eight-line stanza whose rhyme scheme is abababcc.

35. Which poet was a major figure in the Harlem Renaissance?

    A. E.E. Cummings

    B. Rita Dove

    C. Margaret Atwood

    D. Langston Hughes

The answer is D. Hughes' collection of verse includes *The Weary Blues* (1926), *Shakespeare in Harlem* (1942), and *The Panther and the Lash* (1967). e. e. cummings referred the lower case in the spelling of his name until the 1930's. He is also a celebrated poet, but is not a part of the Harlem Renaissance. Rita Dove is a very famous African American poet, but she was born in 1952 and therefore is not a part of the Harlem Renaissance. Margaret Atwood is a Canadian novelist.

36. To understand the origins of a word, one must study the

    A. synonyms

    B. inflections

    C. phonetics

    D. etymology

The answer is D. A synonym is an equivalent of another word and can substitute for it in certain contexts. Inflection is a modification of words according to their grammatical functions, usually by employing variant word-endings to indicate such qualities as tense, gender, case, and number. Phonetics are the science devoted to the physical analysis of the sounds of human speech, including their production, transmission, and perception.

37. Which sonnet form describes the following?

My galley charg'd with
    forgetfulness,
Through sharp seas, in
    winter night doth pass
'Tween rock and rock; and
    eke mine enemy, alas,
That is my lord steereth with
    cruelness.
And every oar a thought with
    readiness,
As though that death were
    light in such a case.
An endless wind doth tear
    the sail apace
Or forc'ed sighs and trusty
    fearfulness.
A rain of tears, a cloud of dark
    disdain,
Hath done the wearied
    cords great hinderance,
Wreathed with error and eke
    with ignorance.
The stars be hid that led me
    to this pain
Drowned is reason that
    should me consort,
And I remain despairing
    of the poet

A.   Petrarchan or Italian sonnet

B.   Shakespearian or
     Elizabethan sonnet

C. Romantic sonnet

E. Spenserian sonnet

The answer is A. The Petrarchan Sonnet, also known as Italian sonnet, is named after the Italian poet Petrarch (1304-74). It is divided into an octave rhyming *abbaabba* and a sestet normally rhyming *cdecde*.

39. What is the salient literary feature of this excerpt from an epic?

Hither the heroes and the nymphs resorts,

To taste awhile the pleasures of a court;

In various talk th'instructive hours they passed,

Who gave the ball, or paid the visit last;

One speaks the glory of the English Queen,

And another describes a charming Indian screen;

A third interprets motion, looks and eyes;

At every word a reputation dies.

A. Sprung rhythm

B. Onomatopoeia

C. Heroic couplets

D. Motif

The answer is C. A couplet is a pair of rhyming verse lines, usually of the same length. It is one of the most widely used verse-forms in European poetry. Chaucer established the use of couplets in English, notably in the *Canterbury Tales*, using rhymed iambic pentameters (a metrical unit of verse having one unstressed syllable followed by one stressed syllable) later known as heroic couplets. Other authors who used heroic couplets include Ben Jonson, Dryden, and especially Alexander Pope, who became the master of them.

40. What were two major characteristics of the first American literature?

A. Vengefulness and arrogance

B. Bellicosity and derision

C. Oral delivery and reverence
   for the land

D. Maudlin and self-pitying
   egocentricism

The answer is D. This characteristic can be seen in Captain John Smith's work, as well as William Bradford's, and Michael Wigglesworth's works.

41. Arthur Miller wrote *The Crucible* as a parallel to what twentieth century event?

A. Sen. McCarthy's House un-American Activities Committee Hearing?

B. The Cold War

C. The fall of the Berlin wall

D. The Persian Gulf War

The answer is A. The episode of the seventeenth century witch hunt in Salem, Mass., gave Miller a storyline that was very comparable to what was happening to persons suspected of communist beliefs in the 1950's.

42. Latin words that entered the English language during the Elizabethan age include

A. allusion, education, and esteem

B. vogue and mustache

C. canoe and cannibal

D. alligator, cocoa, and armadillo

The answer is A. (Self explainatory.)

43. Which of the following is not a characteristic of a fable?

A. animals that feel and talk like humans.

B. happy solutions to human dilemmas.

C. teaches a moral or standard for behavior.

D. illustrates specific people or groups without directly naming them.

The answer is D. A fable is a short tale with animals, humans, gods, or even inanimate objects as characters. Fables often conclude with a moral, delivered in the form of an epigram (a short, witty, and ingenious statement in verse). Fables are among the oldest forms of writing in human history: it appears in Egyptian papyri of c1,500 BC. The most famous fables are those of Aesop, a Greek slave living in about 600 BC. In India, the Pantchatantra appeared in the third century. The most famous modern fables are those of seventeenth century French poet Jean de La Fontaine.

44. Which of the following is not an example of the subject of a tall tale?

    A. John Henry

    B. Paul Bunyan

    C. George Washington

    D. Rip Van Winkle

The answer is C. A tall tale is a Folklore genre, originating on the American frontier, in which the physical attributes, capabilities, and exploits of characters are wildly exaggerated. This is the case of giant logger Paul Bunyan of the American Northwestern forests. James Stevens traced Paul Bunyan to a French Canadian logger named Paul Bunyon. He won a reputation as a great fighter in the Papineau Rebellion against England in 1837 and later became famous as the boss of a logging camp. Paul Bunyan's first appearance in print seems to be in an advertising pamphlet, *Paul Bunyan and His Big Blue Ox*, published by the Red River Company. It immediately became very popular and was reissued many times. George Washington is not a fictional character; he was the first president of the United States.

45. If a student has a poor vocabulary the teacher should recommend that

    A. the student read newspapers, magazines and books on a regular basis.

    B. the student enroll in a Latin class.

    C. the student write the words repetitively after looking them up in the dictionary.

    D. the student use a thesaurus to locate synonyms and incorporate them into his/her vocabulary

The answer is A. It is up to the teacher to help the student choose reading material, but the student must be able to choose where s/he will search for the reading pleasure indispensable for enriching vocabulary.

46. Which author did not write satire?

A. Joseph Addison

B. Richard Steele

C. Alexander Pope

D. John Bunyan

The answer is D. John Bunyan was a religious writer, known for his autobiography, *Grace Abounding To The Chief of Sinners*, as well as other books, all religious in their inspiration, such as *The Holy City, or the New Jerusalem* (1665), *A Confession of my Faith, and a Reason of my Practice* (1672), or *The Holy War* (1682).

47. Which of the following was not written by Jonathan Swift?

A. "A Voyage to Lilliput"

B. "A Modest Proposal"

C. Samson Agonistes"

D. "A Tale of a Tub"

The answer is C. *Samson Agonistes* is a poem by John Milton. It was published in 1671 in the same volume as *Paradise regain'd*.

48. Which is not a Biblical allusion?

    A. The patience of Job

    B. Thirty pieces of silver

    C. "Man proposes; God disposes"

    D. "Suffer not yourself to be betrayed by a kiss"

C is the answer. This saying is attributed to Thomas à Kempis (1379-1471) in his *Imitation of Christ,* Book 1, chapter 19.

49. Which definition is the best for defining diction?

    A. The specific word choices of an author to create a particular mood or feeling in the reader.

    B. Writing which explains something thoroughly.

    C. The background, or exposition, for a short story or drama.

    D. Word choices which help teach a truth or moral.

The answer is A. Diction refers to an author's choice of words, expressions and style to convey his/her meaning.

50. Which is the best definition of free verse, or *vers libre*?

    A. Poetry which consists of an unaccented syllable followed by an unaccented sound.

    B. Short lyrical poetry written to entertain but with an instructive purpose.

    C. Poetry which does not have a uniform pattern of rhythm.

    D. A poem which tells the story and has a plot

C is the answer. Free verse has lines of irregular length (but it does not run on like prose). In addition there is often no rhyme scheme or only a few rhymes.

51. Which is not an accepted point of view in literary works?

    A. First person, omniscient.

    B. Third person, narrative.

    C. First person, limited.

    D. Third person, internal.

The answer is A. If a story is narrated in the first person, the point of view cannot be omniscient; it is limited to the view of the first person narrator.

52. Which is an untrue statement about a theme in literature?

    A. The theme is always stated directly somewhere in the text.

    B. The theme is the central idea in a literary work.

    C. All parts of the work (plot, setting, mood) should contribute to the theme in some way.

    D. By analyzing the various elements of the work, the reader should be able to arrive at an indirectly stated theme.

The answer is A. The theme may be stated directly, but it can also be implicit in various aspects of the work, such as the interaction between characters, symbolism, or description.

53. Which is not a true statement concerning an author's literary tone?

    A. Tone is partly revealed through the selection of details.

    B. Tone is the expression of the author's attitude towards his/her subject.

    C. Tone in literature is usually satiric or angry.

    D. Tone in literature corresponds to the tone of voice a speaker uses.

The answer is C. Tone in literature conveys a mood and can be as varied as the tone of voice of a speaker (see D), e.g. sad, nostalgic, whimsical, angry, formal, intimate, satirical, sentimental, etc.

54. In the teaching of poetry, the teacher should include all of the following but one. Select the answer which is not appropriate for all poetry instruction.

   A. Setting and audience

   B. Theme and tone

   C. Pattern and diction

   D. Diction and rhyme scheme

The answer is A. Setting and audience are important elements of narrative but there are many poems where the setting and audience are unimportant.

55. Which of the following definitions best describes a parable?

   A. A short entertaining account of some happening, usually using talking animals as characters.

   B. A slow, sad song or poem, or prose work expressing lamentation.

   C. An extensive narrative work expressing universal truths concerning domestic life.

   D. A short, simple story of an occurrence of a familiar kind, from which a moral or religious lesson may be drawn.

The answer is D. A parable is usually brief, and should be interpreted as an allegory teaching a moral lesson. Jesus's forty parables are the model of the genre, but modern, secular examples exist: such as Wilfred Owen's *The Parable of The Young Man and The Young* (1920), or John Steinbeck's prose work *The Pearl* (1948).

56. Which of the following is the best definition of existentialism?

A. The philosophical doctrine that matter is the only reality and that everything in the world, including thought, will and feeling, can be explained only in terms of matter.

B. Philosophy which views things as they should be or as one would wish them to be.

C. A philosophical and literary movement, variously religious and atheistic, stemming from Kierkegaard and represented by Sartre.

D. The belief that all events are determined by fate and are hence inevitable.

The answer is C. Even though there are other very important thinkers in the movement known as Existentialism, such as Camus and Merleau-Ponty, Sartre remains the main figure in this movement.

57. Which is the best definition of Imagism?

A. A doctrine which teaches that comfort is the only goal of value in life.

B. A movement in modern poetry (c. 1910-1918) characterized by precise, concrete images, free verse, and suggestion rather than complete statement.

C. The belief that people are motivated in all their [sic] only by self-centeredness.

D. The doctrine that the human mind cannot know where there is a God or an ultimate cause, or anything beyond material phenomenon.

The answer is B. The group was led by Ezra Pound at first, but he left for Vorticism and was replaced by Amy Lowell. They rejected 19th century poetry and were looking for clarity and exactness. Their poems were usually short and built around a single image. Other writers representative of the movement are Richard Addington, "H.D." (Hilda Doolittle), F.S. Flint, D.H. Lawrence, Ford Madox Ford, and William Carlos Williams.

58. Which definition below best fits that of naturalism?

A. A belief that the writer or artist should apply scientific objectivity in his/her observation and treatment of life without imposing value judgments.

B. The doctrine that teaches that the existing world is the best to be hoped for.

C. The doctrine which teaches that God is not a personality, but that all laws, forces and manifestations of the universe are God-related.

D. A philosophical doctrine which professes that the truth of all knowledge must always be in question.

The answer is A. Naturalism is a movement that was started by French writers Jules and Edmond de Goncourt with their novel *Germinie Lacerteux* (1865), but its real leader is Emile Zola, who wanted to bring "a slice of life" to his readers. His saga, *Les Rougon Macquart*, consists in twenty-two novels depicting various aspects of social life. English writing authors representative of this movement include George Moore and George Gissing in England, but the most important naturalist novel in English is Theodore Dreiser's *Sister Carrie*.

59. The tendency to emphasize and value the qualities and peculiarities of life in a particular area of geographic site is a definition of

A. pragmatism.

B. regionalism.

C. pantheism.

D. abstractionism.

The answer is B. Pragmatism is a philosophical doctrine according to which there is no absolute truth. All truths change their trueness as their practical utility increases or decreases. The main representative of this movement is William James who in 1907 published *Pragmatism: A New Way for Some Old Ways of Thinking*. Pantheism is a philosophy according to which God is omnipresent in the world, everything is God and God is everything. The great representative of this sensibility is Spinoza. Also, the works of writers such as Wordsworth, Shelly and Emerson illustrate this doctrine.

Abstract Expressionism is one of the most important movements in American art. It began in the 1940's with artists such as Willem de Kooning, Mark Rothko and Arshile Gorky. The paintings are usually large and non representational.

60. A traditional, anonymous story ostensibly with a historical basis, serving usually to explain some phenomenon of nature or the creation of earth and mankind, for example, is a definition of a

A. proverb.

B. idyll.

C. myth.

D. epic.

The answer is C. A myth is usually traditional and anonymous and explains natural and supernatural phenomena. Myths are usually about creation, divinity, the significance of life and death, and natural phenomena.

61. The arrangement and relationship of words in sentences or sentence structure best describes

    A. style.

    B. discourse.

    C. thesis.

    D. Syntax.

The answer is D. Syntax is the grammatical structure of sentences.

62. A form or discourse which explains or informs is

    A.   exposition.

    B.   narration.

    C.   .persuasion.

    D.   description.

The answer is A. Exposition sets forth a systematic explanation of any subject. It can also introduce the characters of a literary work, and their situations in the story.

63. The substitution of "went to his rest" for "died" is an example of a/an

    A. bowdlerism.

    B. jargon.

    C. euphemism.

    D. malapropism.

The answer is C. A euphemism replaces an unpleasant or offensive word or expression by a more agreeable one. It also alludes to distasteful things in a pleasant manner, and it can even paraphrase offensive texts.

64. A conversation between two or more people is called a

    A. parody.

    B. dialogue.

    C. monologue.

    D. analogy.

The answer is B. Dialogues are indispensable to dramatic work, and they often appear in narrative and poetry. A parody is a work that adopts the subject and structure of another work in order to ridicule it. A monologue is a work or part of a work written in the first person. An analogy illustrates an idea by means of a more familiar one that is similar or parallel to it.

65. "Clean as a whistle or "Easy as falling of a log" are examples of

   A. semantics.

   B. parody.

   C. irony.

   D. clichés.

The answer is D. A cliché is a phrase or expression that has become dull due to overuse.

66. Which of the following is more true of expository writing?

   A. It is mutually exclusive of other forms of discourse.

   B. It can incorporate other forms of discourse in the process of providing supporting details.

   C. It should never employ informal expression.

   D. It should only be scored with a summative evaluation.

The answer is B. Expository writing sets forth an explanation or an argument about any subject.

67. The appearance of a Yankee from Connecticut in the Court of King Arthur is an example of a/an

    A. rhetoric.

    B. parody.

    C. paradox.

    D. anachronism.

The answer is D. Anachronism is the placing of characters, persons, events or things out of their time. Very famous examples of anachronism are Shakespeare's clock in *Julius Caesar*, and billiards in Antony and Cleopatra.

68. The quality in a work of literature which evokes feelings of pity or compassion is called

    A. colloquy.

    B. irony.

    C. pathos.

    D. paradox

The answer is C. A very well known example of pathos is Desdemona's death in Othello, but there are many other examples of pathos.

69. "I'll die if I don't pass this course" is an example of

A. barbarism.

B. oxymoron.

C. hyperbole.

D. antithesis.

The answer is C. A hyperbole is an exaggeration for the sake of emphasis. It is a figure of speech that should not be understood literally. Hyperboles appear in everyday vernacular as well as in literature.

70. An extended metaphor which compares two very dissimilar things – one lofty, one lowly, is a definition of a/an

A. antithesis.

B. aphorism.

C. apostrophe.

D. Conceit.

The answer is D. A conceit is an unusually far-fetched metaphor in which an object, person or situation is presented in a parallel and simpler analogue between two apparently very different things or feelings, one very sophisticated and one very ordinary, usually taken either from nature or a well known every day concept.familiar to both reader and author alike. The conceit was first developed by Petrarch and spread to England in the sixteenth century.

71. A figure of speech in which someone absent or something inhuman is addressed as though as though present and able to respond describes

    A. personification.

    B. synechdoche.

    C. metonymy

    D. apostrophe.

The answer is A. Personification gives human reactions and thoughts to animals, things and abstract ideas alike. This figure of speech is often present in allegory: for instance, the Giant Despair in John Bunyon's *Pilgrim's Progress.* Also, fables use personification to make animals able to speak.

72. Certain slang or jargon expressions peculiar to a certain ethnicity, age, economic, or professional group are called

    A. aphorisms.

    B. allusions.

    C. idioms.

    D. euphemisms.

The answer is C. An idiom is a word or expression that cannot be translated word for word in another language, such as "I am running low on gas". By extension, it is used for a way of speaking and writing typical of a group of people.

73. Which of the following is a complex sentence?

A. Anna and Margaret read a total of fifty-four books during summer vacation.

B. The youngest boy on the team had the best earned run average which mystifies the coaching staff.

C. Earl decided to attend Princeton; his twin brother Roy, who aced the ASVAB test, will be going to Annapolis.

D. "Easy come, easy go," Marcia moaned.

The answer is B. Here, the use of the relative pronoun "which", whose antecedent is "the best run average, introduces a clause that is dependent on the independent clause "The youngest boy on the team had the best run average". The idea expressed in the subordinate clause is subordinate to the one expressed in the independent clause.

74. Followers of Piaget's learning theory believe that adolescents in the formal operations period

A. behave properly from fear of punishment rather than from a conscious decision to take a certain action.

B. see the past more realistically and can relate to people from the past more than preadolescents.

C. are less self-conscious and thus more willing to project their own identities into those of fictional characters.

D. have not yet developed a symbolic imagination.

The answer is B, since according to Piaget, adolescents 12-15 years old begin thinking beyond the immediate and obvious, and theorize. Their assessment of events shifts from considering an action as "right" or "wrong" to considering the intent and behavior in which the action was performed. Fairy tale or other kinds of unreal characters have ceased to satisfy them and they are able to recognize the difference between pure history and historical fiction.

75. Which of the following is a formal reading assessment?

A. a standardized reading test

B. a teacher-made reading test

C. an interview

D. a reading diary

The answer is A. If assessment is standardized, it has to be objective, whereas B, C and D are all subjective assessments.

76. Middle and high school students are more receptive to studying grammar and syntax

A. through worksheets and end of lessons practices in textbooks.

B. through independent, homework assignment.

C. through analytical examination of the writings of famous authors.

D. through application to their own writing.

The answer is D. At this age, students learn grammatical concepts best through practical application in their own writing.

77. Which statement below best describes an author and his/her work?

A. Zora Neale Hurston's *Their Eyes Were Watching God* dealt autobiographically with the strong faith that helped her through the years of her poor upbringing in rural Florida.

B. Willa Cather's works, such as *My Antonia,* depict the regionalism of the Deep South.

C. Emily Dickinson gained national recognition for the publication of over 300 poems.

D. Upton Sinclair's writings, such as *The Jungle*, represent the optimism and trust of the American citizenry for its government.

The answer is A. Zora Neal Hurston's autobiographical novel tells of her experience with poverty and racism in the South. She was also very influential in gender studies.

78. Which of the following is the least preferable strategy for teaching literature?

A. teacher-guided total class discussion

B. small group discussion

C. teacher lecture

D. dramatization of literature selections

The answer is C. In order to engage students' interest, it is necessary that they be involved whether through discussion or dramatization. A lecture is a much too passive technique to involve students of this age.

79. Which event triggered the beginning of Modern English?

    A. Conquest of England by the Normans in 1066

    B. Introduction of the printing press to the British Isles

    C. Publication of Samuel Johnson's lexicon.

    D. American Revolution

The answer is B. With the arrival of the written word, reading matter became mass produced, so the public tended to adopt the speech and writing habits printed in books and the language became more stable.

80. Which of the following is not true about the English language?

    A. English is the easiest language to learn.

    B. English is the least inflected language.

    C. English has the most extensive vocabulary of any language.

    D. English originated as a Germanic tongue.

The answer is A. Just like any other language, English has inherent difficulties which make it difficult to learn, even though English has no declensions such as those found in Latin, Greek, or contemporary Russian, or a tonal system such as the one Chinese has.

81. Which of the following is not a technique of prewriting?

A. Clustering

B. Listing

C. Brainstorming

D. Proofreading

The answer is D. Proofreading cannot be a method of prewriting, since it is done on already written texts only.

82. Which of the following is not an approach to keep students ever conscious of the need to write for audience appeal?

A. Pairing students during the writing process

B. Reading all rough drafts before the Students write the final copies

C. Having students compose stories or articles for publication in school literary magazines or newspapers

D. Writing letters to friends or relatives

The answer is D. Reading all rough drafts will not encourage the students to take control of their text and might even inhibit their creativity. On the contrary, pairing students will foster their sense of responsibility, and having them compose stories for literary magazines will boost their self esteem as well as their organization skills. As far as writing letters is concerned, the work of authors such as Madame de Sevigne in the seventeenth century is a good example of epistolary literary work.

83. The Elizabethans wrote in

A. Celtic

B. Old English

C. Middle English

D. Modern English

The answer is D. There is no document written in Celtic in England, and a work such as *Beowulf* is representative of Old English in the eighth century. It is also the earliest Teutonic written document. Before the fourteenth century, little literature is known to have appeared in Middle English, which had absorbed many words from the Norman French spoken by the ruling class, but at the and of the fourteenth century there appeared the works of Chaucer, John Gower, and the novel *Sir Gawain and The Green King.* The Elizabethans wrote in modern English and their legacy is very important: they imported the Petrarchan, or Italian, sonnet, which Sir Thomas Wyatt and Sir Philip Sydney illustrated in their works. Sir Edmund Spencer invented his own version of the Italian sonnet and wrote *The Faerie Queene.*

Other literature of the time include the hugely important works of Shakespeare and Marlowe.

84. Which of the following writers never won the Nobel Prize for Literature?

A. Gabriel Garcia-Marquez of Colombia

B. Nadine Gordimer of South Africa

C. Pablo Neruda of Chile

D. Alice Walker of the United States

The answer is D. Even though Alice Walker received the Pulitzer Price and the American Book Award for her best known novel, *The Color Purple*, and is the author of six novels and three collections of short stories that have received wide critical acclaim, she has not yet received the Nobel Prize. In addition to her novels and short stories, she has also written three books of essays and five volumes of poetry.

85. The children's literature genre came into its own in the

A. seventeenth century

B. eighteenth century

C. nineteenth century

D. twentieth century

The answer is A. In the seventeenth Century, authors such as Jean de La Fontaine and his *Fables*, Pierre Perreault's *Tales*, Mme d'Aulnoye's Novels based on old folktales and Mme de Beaumont's *Beauty and the Beast* all created a children's literature genre. In England, Perreault was translated and a work allegedly written by Oliver Smith, *The renowned History of Little Goody Two Shoes*, also helped to establish children's literature in England.

86. Recognizing the quality of empathy in literature is an/a

A. emotional response.

B. interpretive response.

C. critical response.

D. evaluative response.

The answer is C. In critical responses students make value judgments about the quality and atmosphere of a text. Through class discussion and written assignments, students react to and assimilate a writer's style and language.

87. Which of the following should not be included in the opening paragraph of an informative essay?

A. Thesis sentence

B. Details and examples supporting the main idea

C. broad general introduction to the topic

D. A style and tone that grabs the reader's attention

The answer is B. The introductory paragraph should introduce the topic, capture the reader's interest, state the thesis and prepare the reader for the main points in the essay. Details and examples, however, should be given in the second part of the essay, so as to help develop the thesis presented at the end of the introductory paragraph, following the inverted triangle method consisting of a broad general statement followed by some information, and then the thesis at the end of the paragraph.

88. What is the figure of speech present in line one below in which the dead body of Caesar is addressed as though he were still a living being?

O, pardon me, though Bleeding piece of earth

That I am meek and gentle with

These butchers.

Marc Antony from *Julius Caesar*

A. Apostrophe

B. Allusion

C. Antithesis

D. Anachronism

The answer is A. This rhetorical figure addresses personified things, absent people or gods. An allusion, on the other hand, is a quick reference to a character or event known to the public. An antithesis is a contrast between two opposing viewpoints, ideas, or presentation of characters. An anachronism is the placing of an object or person out of its time with the time of the text. The best known example is the clock in Shakespeare's *Julius Caesar*.

89. What is the prevailing form of discourse in this passage?

"It would have been hard to find a passer-by more wretched in appearance. He was a man of middle height, stout and hardy, in the strength of maturity; he might have been forty-six or seven. A slouched leather cap hid half his face, bronzed by the sun and wind, and dripping with sweat.

    A.   Description

    B.   Narration

    C. Exposition

    D. Persuasion

The answer is A. A description presents a thing or a person in detail, and tells the reader about the appearance of whatever it is presenting. Narration relates a sequence of events (the story) told through a process of narration (discourse), in which events are recounted in a certain order (the plot). Narration implies a narratee, who can be the reader, another character, or the public in a theater. Exposition is an explanation or an argument within the narration. It can also be the introduction to a play or a story. Persuasion strives to convince either a character in the story or the reader.

90. In most phases of writing, the most serious drawback of using a computer is

    A. the copy looks so good that students tend to overlook major mistakes.

    B. the spell check and grammar programs discourage students from learning proper spelling and mechanics.

    C. the speed with which corrections can be made detracts from the exploration and contemplation of composing.

    D. the writer loses focus by concentrating on the final product rather than the details.

The answer is C. Because the process of revising is very quick with the computer, it can discourage contemplation, exploring, and examination, which are very important in the process of writing.

91. A youngster, watching a movie in which a train derailed, exclaims, "Wow, look at how many cars fell off the tracks. There's junk everywhere. The engineer must have really been asleep." Based on Piaget's beliefs about child moral judgments, the fact that the child is impressed by the wreckage and assigns blame to the engineer indicates that he is approximately

    A. ten years old.

    B. twelve years old.

    C. fourteen years old.

    D. sixteen years old.

The answer is A. According to Piaget's theory, children seven to eleven years old begin to apply logic to concrete things and experiences. They can combine performance and reasoning to solve problems. They have internalized moral values and are willing to confront rules and adult authority.

92. Oral debate is most closely associated with which for of discourse?

    A. Description

    B. Exposition

    C. Narration

    D. Persuasion

The answer is D. It is extremely important to be convincing while having an oral debate. This is why persuasion is so important, because this is the way that you can influence your audience.

93. Most of S.E. Hinton's novels – *The Outsiders*- are written on the sixth grade reading level. They have the greatest reader appeal to

    A. sixth graders.

    B. ninth graders.

    C. twelfth graders.

    D. adults.

The answer is B. Adolescents are concerned with their hanging bodies, their relationships with each other and adults, and their place in society. Reading *The Outsiders* makes them confront different problems that they are only now beginning to experience as teenagers, such as gangs and social identity. The book is universal in its appeal to adolescents.

94. Which aspect of language is innate?

    A. Biological capability to articulate sounds understood by other humans

    B. Cognitive ability to create syntactical structures

    C. Capacity for using semantics to convey meaning in a social environment

    D. Ability to vary inflections and accents

A is the answer. Language ability is innate and the biological capability to produce sounds lets children learn semantics and syntactical   structures through trial and error. Linguists agree that language is first a vocal system of word symbols that enable a human to communicate his/her feelings, thoughts, and desires to other human beings.

95. Which of the following titles is known for its scathingly condemning tone?

    A. Boris Pasternak's *Dr Zhivago*

    B. Albert Camus' *The Stranger*

    C. Henry David Thoreau's "On the Duty of Civil Disobedience"

    D. Benjamin Franklin's "Rules by Which a Great Empire May Be Reduced to a Small One"

The answer is D. In this work, Benjamin Franklin adopts a scathingly ironic tone to warn the British about the probable outcome in their colonies if they persist with their policies. These are discussed one by one in the text, and the absurdity of each is condemned.

96. Which of the following is not a theme of Native American writing?

    A. Emphasis on the hardiness of the human body and soul

    B. The strength of multi-cultural assimilation

    C. Contrition for the genocide of native peoples

    D. Remorse for the love of the Indian way of life

The answer is B. Native American literature was first a vast body of oral traditions from as early as before the fifteenth century. The characteristics include reverence for and awe of nature and the interconnectedness of the elements in the life cycle. The themes often reflect the hardiness of body and soul, remorse for the destruction of the Native American way of life, and the genocide of many tribes by the encroaching settlements of European Americans. These themes are still present in today's contemporary Native American literature, such as in the works of Duane Niatum, Gunn Allen, Louise Erdrich and N. Scott Momaday.

97. **If a student uses inappropriate language that includes slang and expletives, what is the best course of action to take in order to influence the student's formal communication skills?**

A.   ask the student to paraphrase their writing, that is, translate it into language appropriate for the school principal to read.

B.   refuse to read the student's papers until he conforms to a more literate style.

C.   ask the student to read his work aloud to the class for peer evaluation.

D.   rewrite the flagrant passages to show the student the right form of expression.

The answer is A. Asking the student to write for a specific audience will help him become more involved in his writing. If he continues writing to the same audience—the teacher—he will continue seeing writing as just another assignment and he will not apply grammar, vocabulary and syntax the way they should be. By paraphrasing his own writing, the student will learn to write for a different public.

98. **Which of the following contains an error in possessive inflection?**

   A. Doris's shawl

   B. mother's-in-law frown

   C. children's lunches

   D. ambassador's briefcase

The answer is B. Mother-in-Law is a compound common noun and the inflection should be at the end of the word, according to the rule.

99. Homer's *Iliad* and *Odyssey* are taught at different grade levels from state to state and district to district. Which of the following would be the most significant factor in approaching the teaching of these classic works wherever they appear in the curriculum?

A. Identifying a translation on the appropriate reading level

B. Determining the students' interest level

C. Selecting an appropriate evaluative technique

D. Determining the scope and delivery methods of background study

The answer is A. Students will learn the importance of these two works if the translation reflects both the vocabulary that they know and their reading level. Greece will always be foremost in literary assessments due to Homer's works. Homer is the most often cited author, next to Shakespeare. Greece is the cradle of both democracy and literature. This is why it is so crucial that Homer be included in the works assigned.

100. A punctuation mark indicating omission, interrupted thought, or an incomplete statement is a/an

A. ellipsis.

B. anachronism.

C. colloquy.

D. idiom.

The answer is A. In an ellipsis, word or words that would clarify the sentence's message are missing, yet it is still possible to understand them from the context.

101. In the phrase "The Cabinet conferred with the President", Cabinet is an example of a/an

A. metonym

B. synecdoche

C. metaphor

D. allusion

The answer is B. In a synecdoche, a whole is referred to by naming a part of it. Also, a synecdochy can name something by a more general entity of which it is a part: for example, the Cabinet for the Government.

102. The technique of starting a narrative at a significant point in the action and then developing the story through flashbacks is called

A. in medias res

B. octava rima

C. irony

D. suspension of willing disbelief

The answer is A, as its Latin translation suggests: in the middle of things. An octava rima is a specific eight-line stanza of poetry whose rhyme scheme is abababcc. Lord Byron's *Don Juan* is written in octava rima. Irony is an unexpected disparity between what is stated and what is really implied by the author. Benjamin Franklin's "Rules by Which A Great Empire May be Reduduced to a Small One", and Voltaire's tales, are texts which are written using irony. Drama is what Coleridge calls "the willing suspension of disbelief for the moment, which constitutes poetic faith."

103. **The inverted triangle introduction to an essay requires that the thesis sentence occur**

A. at the beginning of the paragraph.

B. in the middle of the paragraph.

C. at the end of the paragraph.

D. in the second paragraph.

The answer is C. The introduction to an essay should begin with a broad general statement, followed by one or more sentences adding interest and information to the topic. The thesis should be written at the end of the introduction.

104. A student composition intended for providing information should contain a minimum of how many paragraphs?

A. three

B. four

C. five

D. six

The answer is C. The student should write an introduction, then three body paragraphs making three points with at least two supporting details each with a final sentence each time, followed by a conclusion.

105. In a timed essay test of an hour's duration, no more than _____ minutes should be devoted to prewriting

A. five

B. ten

C. fifteen

D. twenty

The answer is B. In the hour the student has to write the essay, s/he should not take more than ten minutes prewriting. As the student pre-writes, s/he should remember to have at least three main points and at least two to three details to support the main ideas.

106. Which of the following sentences is properly punctuated?

A. The more you eat; the more you want.

B. The authors – John Steinbeck, Ernest Hemingway, and William Faulkner- are staples of modern writing in American literature textbooks.

C. Handling a wild horse, takes a great deal of skill and patience.

D. The man, who replaced our teacher, is a comedian.

The answer is B. Dashes should be used instead of commas when commas are used elsewhere in the sentence for amplification or explanation –here within the dashes.

107. The students in Mrs. Cline's seventh grade language art class were invited to attend a performance of *Romeo and Juliet* being presented by the drama class at the high school. In preparation for the performance, they should

A. read the play as a homework exercise.

B. read a synopsis of the plot and a biographical sketch of the author.

C. examine a few main selections from the play to become familiar with the language and style of the author.

D. read a condensed version of the story and practice attentive listening skills.

The answer is D. By reading a condensed version of the story, students will know the plot and therefore be able to follow the play on stage. It is also important for them to practice listening techniques such as one one-to-one tutoring and peer-assisted reading.

108. "The *U.S.S.* Constitution is the old man of the sea" is an example of

    A. allusion.

    B. simile.

    C. allegory.

    D. metaphor.

The answer is D. The metaphor is the most common rhetorical figure. It refers to something through the use of another word or expression, and by this introduces a comparison between what is being compared and what it is compared to: the metaphor pretends that the two things compared are identical. An allusion is a reference to someone, something, or a work of art, and it relies on the reader's familiarity with what is mentioned. A simile is different from a metaphor because the comparison it makes between two unlike things is introduced by "as" or "like". An allegory is a representation of something abstract through mostly personification, such as Liberty through the Statue of Liberty. John Bunyan's *Pilgrim's Progress* is also an example of allegories, through its human qualities being personified into characters.

109. Which of the following sentences contains a capitalization error?

    A. The commander of the English navy was Admiral Nelson

    B. Napoleon was the president of the French First Republic

    C. Queen Elizabeth II is the Monarch of the British Empire

    D. William the Conqueror led the Normans to victory over the British

The answer is C. Words that represent titles and offices are not capitalized unless used with a proper name. This is not the case here.

110. Which of the following sentences contains a subject-verb agreement error?

    A. Both mother and her two sisters were married in a triple ceremony.

    B. Neither the hen nor the rooster is likely to be served for dinner.

    C. My boss, as well as the company's two personnel directors, have earned their ten-year pins.

    D. Amanda and the twins are late again.

The answer is C. The reason for this is because the true subject of the verb is "My boss", not "two personnel directors".

111. A technique used to allow students to present written ideas without interruption of the flow of thoughts is called

    A. brainstorming.

    B. mapping.

    C. listing.

    D. Free writing.

The answer is D. Free writing fourteen or fifteen minutes allows the student to write out his/her thoughts about a subject. This technique allows the student to develop ideas s/he is conscious of, but it also helps him/her develop ideas that belong to the subconscious. It is important to let the flow of ideas run through the hand. If the student gets stuck, s/he can write the last sentence over again until inspiration comes back.

112. A formative evaluation of student writing

A. requires thorough markings of mechanical errors with a pencil or pen.

B. making comments on the appropriateness of the student's interpretation of the prompt and the degree to which the objective was met.

C. should require that the student hand in all the materials produced during the process of writing.

D. several careful readings of the text for content, mechanics, spelling, and usage.

The answer is B. It is important to give students numerous experiences with formative evaluation (evaluation as the student writes the piece). Formative evaluation will assign points to every step of the writing process, even though it is not graded. The criteria for the writing task should be very clear, and the teacher should read each step twice. Responses should be non critical and supportive, and the teacher should involve students in the process of defining criteria, and make it clear that formative and summative evaluations are two distinct processes.

113. The practice of reading a piece of student writing to assess the overall impression of the product is

A. holistic evaluation.

B. portfolio assessment.

C. analytical evaluation.

D. using a performance system.

The answer is A. Holistic Scoring assesses a piece of writing as a whole. Usually a paper is read quickly through once to get a general impression. The writing is graded according to the impression of the whole work rather than the sum of its parts. Often holistic scoring uses a rubric that establishes the overall criteria for a certain score to evaluate each paper.

114. Modeling is a practice that allows students to

A. create a style unique to their own language capabilities.

B. emulate the writing of professionals.

C. paraphrase passages from good literature.

D. peer evaluate the writings of other students.

The answer is B. Modeling has students analyze the writing of a professional writer, and try to reach the same level of syntactical, grammatical and stylistic mastery as the author whom they are studying.

115. The writing of Russian naturalists is

A. optimistic.

B. pessimistic.

C. satirical.

D. whimsical.

The answer is B. Although the movement, which originated with the critic Vissarion Belinsky, was particularly strong in the 1840's, it can be said that the works of Dostoievsky, Tolstoy, Tchekov, Turgeniev and Pushkin owe much to it. These authors' works are among the best in international literature, yet are shrouded in stark pessimism. Tolstoy's *Anna Karenina* or Dostoievsky's *Crime and Punishment* are good examples of this dark outlook.

116. Most children's literature prior to the development of popular literature was intended to be didactic. Which of the following would not be considered didactic?

A. "A Visit from St. Nicholas" by Clement Moore

B. *McGuffy's Reader*

C. any version of *Cinderella*

D. parables from the *Bible*

The answer is A. "A Visit from St. Nicholas" is a cheery, non-threatening child's view of the "night before Christmas."

117. Words prevalent in Poe's "The Bells" like *tolling, knelling* and *tintinnabulation* are examples of

A. onomatopoeia.

B. consonance.

C. figurative language.

D. free verse.

The answer is A. An onomatopoeia is a word, or a group of words, which evoke a sound in their meanings or in the way they sound. In this example, these three words evoke the different sounds made by the bells.

118. Which of the following is a characteristic of blank verse?

A. Meter in iambic pentameter

B. Clearly specified rhyme scheme

C. Lack of figurative language

D. Unspecified rhythm

The answer is A. An iamb is a metrical unit of verse having one unstressed syllable followed by one stressed syllable. This is the most commonly used metrical verse in English and American poetry. An iambic pentameter is a ten-syllable verse made of five of these metrical units, either rhymed as in sonnets, or unrhymed as in free –or blank-verse.

119. American colonial writers were primarily

A. Romanticists.

B. Naturalists.

C. Realists.

D. Neo-classicists.

The answer is D. The early colonists had been schooled in England, and even though their writing became quite American in content, their emphasis on clarity and balance in their language remains British. This literature reflects the lives of the early colonists, such as William Bradford's excerpts from *The Mayflower Compact*, Anne Bradstreet's poetry and William Byrd's journal, *A History of the Dividing Line*.

120. Charles Dickens, Robert Browning, and Robert Louis Stevenson were

A. Victorians.

B. Medievalists.

C. Elizabethans.

D. Absurdists.

The answer is A. The Victorian Period is remarkable for the diversity and quality of its literature. Robert Browning wrote chilling monologues such as "My Last Duchess", and long poetic narratives such as *The Pied Piper of Hamlin*. Robert Louis Stevenson wrote his works partly for young adults, whose imaginations were quite taken by his *Treasure Island* and *The Case of Dr Jekyll and Mr Hyde*. Charles Dickens tells of the misery of the time and the complexities of Victorian society in novels such as *Oliver Twist* or *Great Expectations*.

121. The most significant drawback to applying learning theory research to classroom practice is that

A. today's students do not acquire reading skills with the same alacrity as when greater emphasis was placed on reading classical literature.

B. development rates are complicated by geographical and cultural differences that are difficult to overcome.

C. homogeneous grouping has contributed to faster development of some age groups.

D. social and environmental conditions have contributed to an escalated maturity level than research done twenty of more years ago would seem to indicate.

The answer is D. Because of the rapid social changes, topics which did not use to interest younger readers are now subjects of books for even younger readers. There are many books dealing with difficult topics and it is difficult for the teacher to steer students toward books which they are ready for and to try to keep them away from books whose content, although well written, is not yet appropriate for their level of cognitive and social development. There is a fine line between this and censorship.

122. Overcrowded classes prevent the individual attention needed to facilitate language development. This drawback can be best overcome by

A. dividing the class into independent study groups.

B. assigning more study time at home.

C. using more drill practice in class.

D. Team teaching.

The answer is A. Dividing a class into small groups fosters peer enthusiasm and evaluation, and sets an atmosphere of warmth and enthusiasm. It is much preferable to divide up the class into smaller study groups than to engage into lecturing, which will bore students and therefore may fail to deliver the message of the lesson and of the work being studied or the prewriting being performed. Also, it is preferable to do this than to involving the whole class in a general teacher-led discussion, because this favors the loquacious and inhibits the shy.

123. Which of the following responses to literature are middle school students not yet prepared to assimilate?

A. Interpretive

B. Evaluative

C. Critical

D. Emotional

The answer is B. Middle school readers will exhibit both emotional and interpretive responses. In Middle/Junior High School, organized study models make it possible for the student to identify main ideas and supporting details, to recognize sequential order, to distinguish fact from opinion, and to determine cause/effect relationships. Also, a child's being able to say why a particular book was boring or why a particular poem made him/her sad evidences critical reactions on a fundamental level. It is a bit early for evaluative responses, however. These depend on the reader's consideration of how the piece represents its genre, how well it reflects the social/ethical mores of a given society, and how well the author has approached the subject for freshness and slant. Evaluative responses are only made by a few advanced high school students.

124. Which of the following is exhibited most in the hierarchy of needs for adolescents who are becoming more team-oriented in their approach to learning?

A. Need for competence

B. Need for love/acceptance

C. Need to know

D. Need to belong

The answer is B. In Abraham's Maslow's theory of Humanistic Development, there is a hierarchy of needs, from basic physiological needs to the need for self-actualization. The need for love presupposes that every human being needs to love and be loved. With young children this reciprocal need is directed at and received from family members, pets and friends. In older children and adolescents this need does not disappear but on the contrary extends to new recipients such as peers and the subjects of romance.

125. What is the best course of action when a child refuses to complete a reading/ literature assignment on the grounds that it is morally objectionable?

A. Speak with the parents and explain the necessity of studying this work

B. Encourage the child to sample some of the text before making a judgment

C. Place the child in another teacher's class where they are studying an acceptable work

D. Provide the student with alternative selections that cover the same performance standards that the rest of the class is learning.

The answer is D. In the case of a student finding a reading offensive, it is the responsibility of the teacher to assign him/her with another title. As a general rule, it is always advisable to notify parents if a particularly sensitive piece is to be studied.

XAMonline, INC. 21 Orient Ave. Melrose, MA 02176

Toll Free number 800-301-4647

TO ORDER Fax 781-662-9268 OR www.XAMonline.com

NEW YORK STATE TEACHER CERTIFICATION
EXAMINATION   - NYSTCE - 2007

PO#   Store/School:

Address 1:

Address 2 (Ship to other):

City, State Zip

 Credit card number_____-_____-_____-_____   expiration_____

EMAIL _____

PHONE   FAX

13# ISBN 2007	TITLE	Qty	Retail	Total
978-158197-866-7	NYSTCE ATS-W ASSESSMENT OF TEACHING SKILLS 90, 91		$34.95	
978-1-58197-867-4	NYSTCE ATAS ASSESSMENT OF TEACHING ASSISTANT SKILLS 095		$29.95	
978-1-58197-854-4	CST BIOLOGY 006		$59.95	
978-1-58197-855-1	CST CHEMISTRY 007		$73.50	
978-1-58197-865-0	CQST COMMUNICATION AND QUANTITATIVE SKILLS TEST 080		$29.95	
1-58197-144-3	CST EARTH SCIENCE 008		$34.95	
978-1-58197-851-3	CST ENGLISH 003		$34.95	
978-1-58197-862-9	CST FAMILY AND CONSUMER SCIENCES 072		$34.95	
978-1-58197-858-2	CST FRENCH SAMPLE TEST 012		$15.00	
978-1-58197-868-1	LAST LIBERAL ARTS AND SCIENCE TEST 001		$34.95	
978-1-58197-863-6	CST LIBRARY MEDIA SPECIALIST 074		$34.95	
1-58197-627-5	CST LITERACY 065		$34.95	
978-1-58197-852-0	CST MATH 004		$59.95	
978-1-58197-872-8	CST MULTIPLE SUBJECTS 002 SAMPLE TEST		$34.95	
978-1-58197-850-6	CST MUTIPLE SUBJECTS 002		$59.95	
1-58197-133-8	CST PHYSICAL EDUCATION 076		$34.95	
978-1-58197-857-5	CST PHYSICS 009		$15.00	
978-1-58197-853-7	CST SOCIAL STUDIES 005		$59.95	
978-1-58197-859-9	CST SPANISH 020		$34.95	
978-1-58197-860-5	CST STUDENTS WITH DISABILITIES VOL.1 060		$59.95	
			SUBTOTAL	
			Ship	$8.25
			TOTAL	

Printed in the United States
66232LVS00011B